SPECTRUM

NEW YORK
Test Prep

Grade 5

Published by Spectrum
an imprint of Carson-Dellosa Publishing LLC
Greensboro, NC

Spectrum
An imprint of Carson-Dellosa Publishing LLC
P.O. Box 35665
Greensboro, NC 27425 USA

© 2005 Carson-Dellosa Publishing LLC. The purchase of this material entitles the buyer to reproduce worksheets and activities for classroom use only—not for commercial resale. Reproduction of these materials for an entire school or district is prohibited. No part of this book may be reproduced (except as noted above), stored in a retrieval system, or transmitted in any form or by any means (mechanically, electronically, recording, etc.) without the prior written consent of Carson-Dellosa Publishing LLC. Spectrum is an imprint of Carson-Dellosa Publishing LLC.

Printed in the USA • All rights reserved.   ISBN 978-0-7696-3495-1

04-334118091

Table of Contents

What's Inside? 5

Language Arts

Reading
Standards and What They Mean 7
  Practice Pages
    Reading Similar Books 8
    Reading Informational Texts 9
    Finding Information in Texts 10
    Reading for Understanding 12
    Skimming Texts 14
    Comparing Different Texts 15
    Using Technology to Support Reading 17
    Recording the Year's Reading 19
  Mini-Test 1 20

Grammar and Usage of the English Language
Standards and What They Mean 21
  Practice Pages
    Grammar 22
    Paragraph Structure 24
    Punctuation 26
    Sentence Construction 27
    Spelling 28
    Making Writing Easier to Understand 29
    Rearranging Text 30
    Adding and Deleting Text 31
    Using Reference Materials 32
  Mini-Test 2 34

Literature
Standards and What They Mean 35
  Practice Pages
    Identifying Similarities and Differences
      in Theme 36
    Author's Influence on Meaning 38
    Different Forms of Literature 40
    Analyzing Characters 42
    Developing Ideas About Character and
      Setting 44
    Making Inferences 46
    Drawing Conclusions 48
    Finding Favorites 50
    Creating a Written Work 51
  Mini-Test 3 52

How Am I Doing? 53

Final Language Arts Test 54
  Answer Sheet 58

Mathematics

Arithmetic and Number Concepts
Standards and What They Mean 60
  Practice Pages
    Using Place Value and Expanded Notation 62
    Using Powers of Ten 64
    Rounding Numbers 65
    Estimating 66
    Prime and Composite Numbers 67
    Using Arithmetic Facts 68
    Adding and Subtracting Large Numbers 69
    Multiplying by 3-Digit Numbers 70
    Dividing by 2-Digit Numbers 71
    Proper and Improper Fractions 72
    Greatest Common Factors and Least
      Common Multiples 73
    Prime Factorizations 74
    Adding Fractions 75
    Subtracting Fractions 76
    Multiplying and Dividing Fractions 77
    Finding Equivalent Fractions 78
    Adding and Subtracting Decimal Numbers 79
    Multiplying and Dividing Decimal Numbers 80
    Decimals and Money 81
    Fractions, Decimals, and Percents 82
    Comparing Decimals and Fractions 83
    Representing Changes in Quantity 84
    Number Lines 85
    Adding Integers Using the Number Line 86
  Mini-Test 1 87

Geometry and Measurement
Standards and What They Mean 89
  Practice Pages
    Estimating and Measuring Length, Distance,
      Mass, Volume, and Capacity 90
    Identifying Equivalent Units of Measure 91
    Estimating Weights 92
    Identifying Relationships Among
      Time Elements 93
    Finding the Perimeter and Area of
      Rectangles and Squares 94
    Measuring Area and Perimeter Using
      Square Tiles 95
    Circles and Planes 96
    Constructing a Circle 97
    Relationship Between Diameter, Radius,
      and Circumference 98
    Reading and Naming Coordinates 99
    Plotting Coordinates 100
    Finding Volume 101
    Two-Dimensional and Three-Dimensional
      Views 102
    Scale Drawings and Ratio 103
  Mini-Test 2 104

Function and Algebra Concepts
Standards and What They Mean 105
  Practice Pages
    Recognizing and Describing Patterns
      and Functions 106
    Identifying Patterns and Relationships 107
    Using Patterns and Functions to
      Solve Problems 108
    Using Variables 109

Functional Relationships 110
Understanding the Relationship
  Between Two Quantities 111
Writing and Solving Open Sentences 112
Order of Operations 113
Writing and Solving Addition and
  Multiplication Inequities 114
Mini-Test 3 115

Statistics and Probability Concepts
Standards and What They Mean 116
Practice Pages
  Displaying Data 117
  Interpreting Graphs 118
  Interpreting Double Bar Graphs 119
  Interpreting Circle Graphs 120
  Using Appropriate Graphs 121
  Range, Mean, Median, and Mode 122
  Predicting 123
  Probability 124
  Using Models 125
  Using Samples 127
Mini-Test 4 128

Mathematical Process
Standards and What They Mean 129
Practice Pages
  Analyzing Word Problems 130
  Solving Problems 131
  Explaining How to Solve Problems 132
  Exact and Approximate Answers 133
  Using Math in Other Subjects 134
  Mathematical Tools 135
Mini-Test 5 136

How Am I Doing? 137
Final Mathematics Test 139
Answer Sheet 143

Social Studies

Themes
Standards and What They Mean 144
Practice Pages
  Cultural Diversity in the United States,
    Canada, and Latin America 146
  Key Turning Points in United States,
    Canadian, and Latin American History 147
  Important Figures and Groups in
    United States, Canadian, and Latin
    American History 148
  Using Maps 149
  Physical Characteristics of the United
    States, Canada, and Latin America 150
  Cultural Characteristics of the United
    States, Canada, and Latin America 151
  How Human Actions Modify the
    Environment 153
  The Economies of the United States,
    Canada, and Latin America 155
  Governments of the United States,
    Canada, and Latin America 157
  Patriotic Celebrations 158
  International Organizations 159
Mini-Test 1 160

Skills and Strategies
Standards and What They Mean 161
Practice Pages
  Locating Primary and Secondary Sources . . . 163
  Identifying Primary and Secondary Sources . . 164
  Skimming a Text 165
  Organizing Information 166
  Using Print and Nonprint Sources 168
  Differentiating Relevant From Irrelevant
    Information 169
  Interpreting Information From Primary and
    Secondary Sources 170
  Evaluating Information 172
  Making and Questioning Hypotheses 173
  Drawing Conclusions and Making
    Predictions 174
  Writing a Document-Based Essay 175
  Writing a Research Report 178
  Expressing and Supporting Opinions 180
  Delivering an Oral Report 181
  Collecting Social Studies Written Work 182
  Identifying and Solving Problems 183
Mini-Test 2 184

How Am I Doing? 186
Final Social Studies Test 187
Answer Sheet 191

ANSWER KEY **192**

What's Inside?

This workbook is designed to help you and your fifth grader understand what he or she will be expected to know on the New York fifth-grade tests.

Practice Pages
The workbook is divided into a language arts, mathematics, and social studies section. Each section has practice activities that have questions similar to those that will appear on the tests. Students should use a pencil to fill in the correct answers and to complete any writing on these activities.

New York City Standards
Before each practice section is a list of the standards covered by that section. The shaded *What it means* sections will help to explain any information in the standards that might be unfamiliar.

New York Standards
This book is set up using the most up-to-date New York City standards, as they are more current and broken into individual grade levels (unlike New York State standards). The New York State standards and how they compare to the New York City standards are outlined in the back of this book.

Mini-Tests and Final Tests
Practice activities are grouped by standard. When each group is completed the student can move on to a mini-test that covers the material presented on those practice activities. After an entire set of standards and accompanying activities are completed, the student should take the final test, which incorporates material from all the practice activities in that section.

Final Test Answer Sheet
The final tests have a separate answer sheet that mimics the style of the answer sheet the students will use on the tests. The answer sheet appears at the end of each final test.

How Am I Doing?
The *How Am I Doing?* pages are designed to help students identify areas where they are proficient and areas where they still need more practice. Students can keep track of each of their mini-test scores on these pages.

Answer Key
Answers to all the practice activities, mini-tests, and final tests are listed by page number and appear at the end of the book.

Frequently Asked Questions

What kinds of information does my child have to know to pass the test?

The New York State and City Boards of Education provide a list of the knowledge and skills that students are expected to master at each grade level. The practice activities in this workbook provide students with practice in each of these areas.

Are there special strategies or tips that will help my child do well?

The workbook provides sample questions that have content similar to that on the state tests. Test-taking tips are offered throughout the book.

How do I know what areas my child needs help in?

A special *How Am I Doing?* section will help you and your fifth grader evaluate progress. It will pinpoint areas where more work is needed as well as areas where your student excels.

© Carson-Dellosa Publishing

New York Language Arts
Content Standards

The language arts section of the New York City Standards measures knowledge in three different areas:

1. Reading
2. Grammar and Usage of the English Language
3. Literature

The language arts section of the New York State Standards measures knowledge of language in four areas:

1.0 Language for Information and Understanding
    1.1: Listening and Reading
    1.2: Speaking and Writing

2.0 Language for Literacy Response and Expression
    2.1: Listening and Reading
    2.2: Speaking and Writing

3.0 Language for Critical Analysis and Evaluation
    3.1: Listening and Reading
    3.2: Speaking and Writing

4.0 Language for Social Interaction
    4.1: Listening and Speaking
    4.2: Reading and Writing

New York Language Arts
Table of Contents

Reading
    Standards and What They Mean 7
    Practice Pages 8
    Mini-Test 1 20

Grammar and Usage of the English Language
    Standards and What They Mean 21
    Practice Pages 22
    Mini-Test 2 34

Literature
    Standards and What They Mean 35
    Practice Pages 36
    Mini-Test 3 52

How Am I Doing? 53

Final Language Arts Test 54

Answer Sheet 58

Language Arts Standards

1.0 Reading
By the end of the school year, students should:
1.A Read and understand:
    1.A.1 At least twenty-five books.
    1.A.2 At least four books about one subject, or by the same writer, or in one genre of literature. *(See page 8.)*

What it means:
- **Genre** is a type, or category, of writing. Some examples of genre include fiction, biographies, poetry, and fables. Each genre is characterized by various differences in form. For example, a fable differs from the broader category of fiction in that it has a moral or character lesson.

    1.A.3 Informational texts (such as reference materials, newspapers and magazines, and textbooks) related to all school subjects. *(See pages 9–11.)*
1.B Show evidence of understanding their reading in both writing and classroom discussion. *(See pages 12–13.)*
1.C Skim texts to get an overview of content or locate specific information. *(See page 14.)*
1.D Put together ideas and information from different books, making decisions about what is most important. *(See pages 15–16.)*
1.E Read familiar books aloud:
    1.E.1 With accuracy and expression.
    1.E.2 Using strategies for self-correction.
    1.E.3 Using strategies to figure out unfamiliar words.
1.F Read silently and independently.
1.G Use technology to support reading. *(See pages 17–18.)*
1.H Keep a record of the year's reading to show goals and accomplishments. *(See page 19.)*

Name _____ Date _____

Language Arts   **Reading**

| 1.A.2 |

Reading Similar Books

DIRECTIONS: From the library, borrow at least four books about one subject, or by the same writer, or in the same genre (for example, mystery, comedy, or science fiction). Read them and write a brief summary of each. Then, answer the questions.

1. Title _____
   Author _____
   Summary _____
   _____
   _____
   _____
   _____
   _____

2. Title _____
   Author _____
   Summary _____
   _____
   _____
   _____
   _____
   _____

3. Title _____
   Author _____
   Summary _____
   _____
   _____
   _____
   _____
   _____

4. Title _____
   Author _____
   Summary _____
   _____
   _____
   _____
   _____

5. What are the main differences in the books you chose?
   _____
   _____
   _____
   _____
   _____
   _____
   _____
   _____

6. In what ways are the books you chose the same?
   _____
   _____
   _____
   _____
   _____
   _____
   _____
   _____

7. Which book did you like the most? Why?
   _____
   _____
   _____
   _____
   _____
   _____
   _____

Name _____ Date _____

Language Arts
Reading

1.A.3 Reading Informational Texts

DIRECTIONS: The passages below are from a newspaper, instruction manual, textbook, or biography. Read the passages. Then, identify the source of each. Each source is used only once.

1. The best way to understand the food web is to study a model of it. Refer to Figure 2.3 to see a model of a food web in a deciduous forest. In Chapter 1, we identified animals as either herbivores, carnivores, or omnivores. Which animals in Figure 2.3 could best be described as herbivores?

   _____

2. LONDON, England—Buckingham Palace announced today that Queen Elizabeth will make a short visit to the United States early next week. She will be attending the annual Westhampton Flower Show in Westhampton, Connecticut. The Queen has made several trips to the flower show, often accompanied by other members of the royal family. Last year the prize-winning rose at the show was named in honor of the Queen.

   _____

3. Wolfgang Amadeus Mozart was born on January 27, 1756, in Austria. When he was just three years old, he learned to play the harpsichord. He was composing music by the time he was five years old. At the age of six, he was invited to perform for the Empress of Austria. Mozart astonished people with his musical ability. He was called a child genius.

   _____

4. Step 1: Find Pieces A, B, and C and Main Frame 1.
   Step 2: Insert Piece A into the square slot on Piece B.
   Step 3: Insert Piece C into the round slot on Piece B.
   Step 4: Snap the assembled ABC assembly into Main Frame 1.

   _____

DIRECTIONS: Read each of the titles below and identify the type of informational text.

5. *Sports Weekly*
   - (A) magazine
   - (B) textbook
   - (C) essay
   - (D) reference book

6. *Dinner in Under an Hour*
   - (F) newspaper
   - (G) cookbook
   - (H) science journal
   - (J) computer manual

7. *Roget's Thesaurus*
   - (A) magazine
   - (B) textbook
   - (C) essay
   - (D) reference book

8. *The New York Times*
   - (F) newspaper
   - (G) cookbook
   - (H) science journal
   - (J) computer manual

Name _____ Date _____

Language Arts
1.A.3

Finding Information in Texts

Reading

DIRECTIONS: Use the table of contents and index below to answer the questions on the next page.

Table of Contents	
Chapter	**Page**
Questions	
1 The Natural World	3
2 The Human Body	33
3 The Home Planet	59
4 Numbers and Formulas	71
Answers	
5 The Natural World	105
6 The Human Body	155
7 The Home Planet	203
8 Numbers and Formulas	227

Index

antibodies, 50, 188

ants, 3, 105

aspirin, 41, 170

bats, 30, 151

Big Dipper, 143

brain, 171

calcium, 53, 193

centipedes, 21, 136

color, 92, 189

digestion, 130–131, 166

dolphins, 14, 124

doves, mourning, 12, 120

eardrums, 179

evergreens, 8

fever, 170, 182

food allergies, 39, 167

hay fever, 163

hurricanes, 60, 205, 206

insect bites, 48, 183

jet engine, 239–240

kerosene, 222

leap years, 255

lips, 179

10

© Carson-Dellosa Publishing

Name _____ Date _____

1. In which chapter would you probably find a question about the liver's function?
   - (A) Chapter 1
   - (B) Chapter 2
   - (C) Chapter 4
   - (D) Chapter 6

2. From looking at the table of contents and index, which of the topics below would most likely be covered in Chapter 1?
   - (F) mumps and measles
   - (G) plants and animals
   - (H) earthquakes
   - (J) helicopters

3. On which page might you find an answer about why your face turns red when you perspire?
   - (A) page 7
   - (B) page 38
   - (C) page 65
   - (D) page 157

4. Which of these topics is found in Chapter 3?
   - (F) jet engine
   - (G) hay fever
   - (H) hurricanes
   - (J) lips

5. From looking at the index and table of contents, who would most likely be interested in this book?
   - (A) someone who loves to read novels
   - (B) someone who enjoys science trivia
   - (C) someone who wants to know how to build a tree house
   - (D) someone who wants to plant a garden

6. On which page would you find information about why some people cannot eat nuts?
   - (F) page 48
   - (G) page 171
   - (H) page 163
   - (J) page 39

7. What vocabulary word might you expect to find in Chapter 3?
   - (A) bone marrow
   - (B) metamorphic rocks
   - (C) dominant gene
   - (D) brain stem

8. In which chapter might you find the question, "Why does February have 29 days in some years and not in others?"
   - (F) Chapter 1
   - (G) Chapter 2
   - (H) Chapter 3
   - (J) Chapter 4

9. What might the title of this book be?
   - (A) *Weather in Our World*
   - (B) *The Amazing Human Machine*
   - (C) *Science Questions and Answers*
   - (D) *How to Study*

10. In the space below, create a table of contents for a book you'd like to write on your favorite subject.

    _____
    _____
    _____
    _____

Language Arts

Reading for Understanding

DIRECTIONS: Read the story and answer the questions on the next page.

Bonkers for Baseball

I remember a special Mother's Day back in 1939. My mom was a big baseball fan so my father treated us to tickets for the Brainford Bisons game. We sat in box seats owned by my father's company. It was an exciting day.

Before the game began, we started talking to a woman sitting in a nearby box seat. We learned that she was the mother of the Beulah Blaze's pitcher. Her son, Brian Falls, had been pitching in the minor leagues for three years. This was the first time she had ever seen him pitch in a professional game.

For the special event, Brian Falls had treated his mother to a box seat. He had the box decorated in flowers. Mrs. Falls was so excited. She told us that she had always encouraged Brian to become a baseball player. Her dream for her son had come true.

My team wasn't doing very well in the early innings. With Brian Falls pitching, the Brainford Bisons' batters kept striking out. Then, Falls threw a fastball to the plate. The batter swung at it. He caught a piece of it and fouled it off. The foul ball flew into the crowd. It came straight toward us! My dad and I reached into the air to catch it, but the ball veered left and hit Mrs. Falls in the head. She was knocked unconscious. We couldn't believe it—out of all the people in the stands, the ball hit the pitcher's mother! Mrs. Falls was rushed to the hospital. For the rest of the game we wondered what had happened to her. Later we learned the rest of the story.

Brian Falls left the game to accompany his mom to the hospital. He was so upset that he told her he would quit the game. His mother, who was recovering nicely, convinced him to stay in baseball. It's a good thing, because three years later he joined the major leagues.

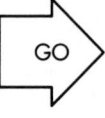

Name _____   Date _____

1. What would be another good title for this story?
   - (A) *Mother's Day at the Ballpark*
   - (B) *Making It in the Majors*
   - (C) *Brian Falls: His Career in Baseball*
   - (D) *The Brainsford Bisons Steal Home*

2. Here is a time line of what happens in the story. Which of these events should go in the empty box?

   | The family goes to the baseball game for Mother's Day. |

   | |

   | A foul ball is hit into the stands. |

   | Brian Falls joins the major leagues. |

   - (F) Mrs. Falls convinces Brian not to quit baseball.
   - (G) Mrs. Falls is taken to the hospital.
   - (H) The family discovers that the woman they've been talking with is the mother of the Beulah Blaze's pitcher.
   - (J) The ball is almost caught by the narrator.

3. Why do you suppose Brian Falls had his mother's box seat decorated with flowers?
   - (A) because he wanted to impress his friends
   - (B) because it was the first time she had seen him pitch professionally
   - (C) because he was in the major leagues
   - (D) because she told him not to quit

4. Why was Mrs. Falls taken to the hospital?
   - (F) because she needed to tell Brian to stay in the game
   - (G) because she was a nurse
   - (H) because she was sick
   - (J) because she was hit by a foul ball

5. Mrs. Falls probably taught Brian to _____.
   - (A) follow his dreams
   - (B) give up when things got too hard
   - (C) play baseball
   - (D) fight against his opponents

6. From reading the passage, how do you suppose the narrator feels about baseball?
   - (F) He thinks it's a silly game.
   - (G) He despises it.
   - (H) He is bored with it.
   - (J) He enjoys it.

STOP

Name _____   Date _____

Language Arts
1.C

Skimming Texts

Reading

DIRECTIONS: Skim the passage. Then, read the questions. Refer back to the passage to find the answers. You do not have to read the story over again for each question.

Swimming Star

Every day, thousands of people cross the channel of water between France and England in planes, ferries, and even trains. An American athlete, Gertrude Caroline Ederle, however, used a different method. She was the first woman to swim across the English Channel.

Gertrude Ederle was born in New York City in 1906. She dedicated herself to the sport of swimming at an early age and enjoyed great success. Before long, she was on her way to becoming one of the most famous American swimmers of her time. When she was sixteen, Ederle broke seven records in one day at a swimming competition in New York. Two years later, in 1924, she represented the United States at the Olympic Games, winning a gold medal in the 400-meter freestyle relay.

After her Olympic victory, she looked for an even greater challenge. One of the most difficult swims is to cross the 21-mile wide English Channel. The seas in the channel can be rough, and the water is cold. In the past, the feat had been accomplished only by male swimmers. Most people believed that the swim was too difficult for a woman, but Ederle wanted to prove them wrong. She didn't make it on her first attempt, but in 1926 she tried again. Leaving from the coast of France, Ederle had to swim even longer than planned because of heavy seas. She went an extra fourteen miles and still managed to beat the world record by almost two hours. This accomplishment made her an instant heroine at the age of twenty.

1. What is the main idea of the passage?
   - (A) Swimming is a fun sport.
   - (B) Winning an Olympic medal will make you wealthy.
   - (C) If you want to be very successful at something, you have to start at a young age.
   - (D) Hard work and dedication can lead to great success.

2. Which event happened first in the passage about Ederle's life?
   - (F) She swam across the English Channel.
   - (G) She broke seven swimming records in a single day of competition.
   - (H) She won an Olympic gold medal.
   - (J) She looked for more challenges.

3. Based on the information in the passage, what word probably describes Ederle's personality?
   - (A) imaginative
   - (B) passive
   - (C) lazy
   - (D) determined

4. According to the passage, why was Ederle considered a heroine?
   - (F) because she was a generous person
   - (G) because she had done something that no other woman had ever done
   - (H) because she was a great swimmer
   - (J) because she rescued someone

© Carson-Dellosa Publishing

Name _____ Date _____

Language Arts   **Reading**

1.D   Comparing Different Texts

DIRECTIONS: Read both stories. Then, answer the questions.

One Afternoon in March

One afternoon in March, I went for a walk. After being cooped up all winter, it felt good to wander around outside. It was still cold, but some of the snow was beginning to melt.

I was walking down the street when something caught my eye. I leaned down and found two silver dollars shining in a half-melted snow bank. *Buried treasure!* was my first thought. So, I dug through the snow looking for more. Of course, I just ended up with really cold hands. I slipped the two coins into my pocket and went home colder but richer.

I began to think about how to spend the money. I could add it to my skateboard fund. Or I could use it to buy a soda and hot pretzel, my favorite snack. The possibilities were exciting.

Two days later, Mary Ann and her little sister were searching the snow banks. *Finders keepers,* was my first thought. I didn't need to get to the losers weepers part since Suzy was already crying for real.

"I dropped them right here," she said between tears. Her hands were cold and red from digging in the snow.

"Maybe they got shoved down the street with the snow plow. Let's dig over here." Mary Ann's voice sounded optimistic.

They'll never know, was my second thought, and I walked past them toward Wisser's house.

"Phil, have you seen two silver dollars?" asked Mary Ann. Suzy looked up from digging. Her eyes were hopeful.

"Coins?" *Look innocent,* was my third thought.

"Yeah, Suzy dropped two silver dollars along here last week."

"Silver dollars?"

"Yeah," said Suzy. "They're thick and big." She brushed the snow off her red hands and wiped the tears from her face. Her eyes were as red as her hands.

Lie, was my fourth thought. "As a matter of fact," I hesitated, "I dug two coins out of that snow bank just a few days ago. I wondered who might have lost them."

Suzy leaped on me, hugging me. "Oh, thank you, thank you."

© Carson-Dellosa Publishing   **15**

It's Not My Fault

Almost every day at school, I eat lunch with Heather. Tracy is my friend, too, but she usually eats with Melody and Jordan. Every now and then, I eat lunch at their table, but not this time. Tracy was angry at me. I needed Heather's advice.

"You be the judge. I need an objective opinion. Tracy says I'm a liar," I said as I took a bite of my ham sandwich.

"About what?" Heather asked.

"It doesn't matter. I'm honest, right?"

"Honest about what?" Heather took a sip of milk.

"Honest. You know, trustworthy, direct, truthful," I smiled.

Heather hesitated and then nodded. "Yeah, you're pretty honest. Except the time you lied to your folks about your math grade. And then the time you . . ."

"Math grades don't count, and the time I went shopping with Tracy doesn't count either."

"Shopping? What about the time you went shopping with Tracy?" Heather looked confused.

"It's not my fault that Tracy didn't want you to come. I didn't want to hurt your feelings. So, she told me to tell you I was sick."

"So you lied to me," Heather accused, raising her voice. I could tell she was really upset. She was usually very quiet.

"I didn't lie. Tracy made up the lie."

"Don't blame Tracy because you lied to me," Heather said as she ripped the cellophane covering off her brownie.

"It's not my fault. Plus, you're way too sensitive," I said. Then, I gulped my milk.

"Cheryl, the point is simple. You lie to your friends and then blame them for your mistakes," Heather said. "So, no, you're not really honest."

"Forget it," I said. I could see that Heather was still hurt about Tracy. She wouldn't understand my problem. "I gotta go. I'll see you tomorrow."

1. Explain in a few words what theme both of these stories have in common.

2. Who is probably the better friend, Phil or Cheryl? Why?

3. The moral of *It's Not My Fault* should be

4. The moral of *One Afternoon in March* should be

Language Arts

1.G

Using Technology to Support Reading

Reading

DIRECTIONS: Read the passage. Then, answer the questions on the next page.

Niagara Falls

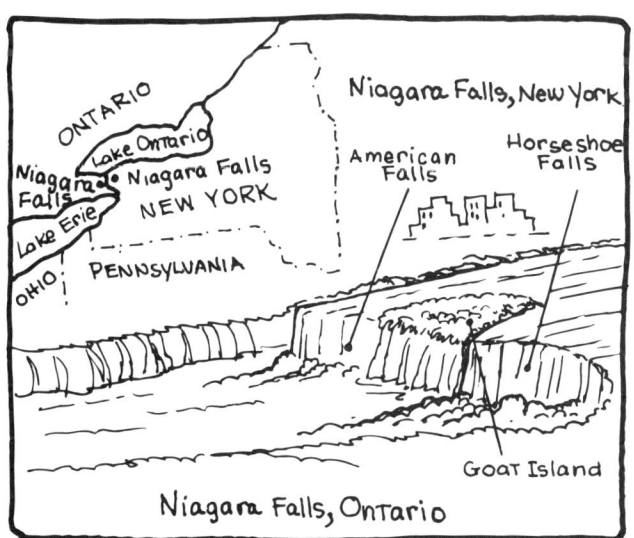

Niagara Falls is one of the most spectacular natural wonders of the world. Part of the Falls is in Ontario, Canada, and part is in New York State.

The Falls are supplied by the Niagara River, which connects Lake Ontario and Lake Erie. The Niagara Falls are located midway in the river. They pour 500,000 tons of water a minute into a deep gorge.

Scientists believe that Niagara Falls was formed after the last ice sheet from the Ice Age withdrew from the area. The surface of the land was changed by the ice. This caused waterways and streams to develop new paths. The result was an overflow of Lake Erie, which produced Niagara Falls. Scientists believe that the Falls are approximately 20,000 years old.

The Falls are formed over an outer layer of hard dolomitic limestone. This covers a softer layer of shale. The shale is more easily worn away, which causes the harder limestone to form an overhanging edge. This allows the Falls to drop straight down at a sharp angle, which produces a spectacular sight.

Over the years, the outer layer has broken off at times. This is causing the Falls to gradually move back up the river. This erosion is happening to the American Falls at the rate of three to seven inches a year. But the edge of the Horseshoe Falls is being worn back at the rate of approximately three feet a year.

Over the years, Niagara Falls has been a spectacular attraction for sightseers. Observation towers and a special area, Cave of the Winds, behind the Falls, have allowed remarkable views. At night, the Falls are flooded with lights. A steamer, called the *Maid of the Mist,* takes visitors for a ride around the base of the Falls.

Niagara Falls has also irresistibly drawn daredevils who have wanted to test their courage. One such man, Charles Blondin, crossed the Falls on a tightrope in 1859. Four days later, he crossed again, only this time with a blindfold. A month later, he crossed for the third time carrying a man on his shoulders. And as if that weren't daring enough, he returned to cross the Falls once again—on stilts!

© Carson-Dellosa Publishing

Name _____ Date _____

 If you do not have access to the Internet, use library resources to answer the questions.

1. Use an online dictionary to find definitions to at least three terms in the passage. Write each word and its definition in the space below. (*Hint:* Both *www.dictionary.com* or *www.m-w.com/home.htm* are good online dictionaries.)

   Term: _____

   Definition: _____
   _____
   _____

   Term: _____

   Definition: _____
   _____
   _____

   Term: _____

   Definition: _____
   _____
   _____

2. Use an online search engine to locate pictures of Niagara Falls. Did the pictures help you understand the passage better? Explain your answer.

   _____
   _____
   _____
   _____

3. Use the Internet resource of your choice to find the nationality and real name of **Charles Blondin**, who walked across the Falls on a tightrope in 1859. Briefly report your findings.

   _____
   _____
   _____
   _____

Name _____ Date _____

Language Arts **Reading**

1.H # Recording the Year's Reading

DIRECTIONS: Pick at least two reading goals for the year. For example, you might want to read all of the books in the Harry Potter series, or you may wish to learn one new word every week.

The grid below will help you keep a record of all of the reading you've done over the year. Remember to fill it in regularly to show what you've read. Place a star beside the titles of the books that helped you reach your goals.

Reading Goal #1: _____

_____

Reading Goal #2: _____

_____

	Title	Author	Date Completed	Genre (biography, science fiction, western, etc.)
1.				
2.				
3.				
4.				
5.				
6.				
7.				
8.				
9.				
10.				
11.				
12.				
13.				
14.				
15.				
16.				
17.				
18.				
19.				
20.				
21.				
22.				
23.				
24.				

© Carson-Dellosa Publishing

Language Arts 1.0

For pages 8–19

Mini-Test 1

Reading

DIRECTIONS: Read the passage. Then, answer questions 1 and 2.

The Brooklyn Bridge

When the Brooklyn Bridge was opened on May 24, 1883, it was declared to be the "Eighth Wonder of the World." The Brooklyn Bridge joins the boroughs of Brooklyn and Manhattan and spans the East River of New York City. At its opening, it was the longest suspension bridge on earth. The bridge has a span of 1,595 feet and cost a total of $15 million to build.

The Brooklyn Bridge is suspended from huge steel cables that are approximately 16 inches thick. The cables are fastened to two gothic-style towers, which stand 275 feet high at each end of the bridge. The bridge holds six lanes of traffic in addition to a unique walkway down the center.

The building of the Brooklyn Bridge was one of the greatest architectural achievements ever. The credit belonged to a father and son, John A. Roebling and Colonel Washington A. Roebling. The Roeblings were pioneer builders of big suspension bridges. Prior to the Brooklyn Bridge, wrought iron had been used to support bridges. The Roeblings' plan called for their new bridge to be built with steel-wire cables. To hold the cables, the Roeblings had to first construct two large towers. These towers were built on foundations sunk in the riverbed and filled with concrete.

By 1877, the towers were completed and work had begun on "spinning the cables." This involved bunching steel wires together in bundles to form four, 16-inch cables. These cables were used to hold more than 1,500 smaller cables. By the time the bridge opened in 1883, 20 workers had died in accidents on the bridge. John A. Roebling had also died as the result of an injury he had received at the site. His son continued the project, but developed the bends from working deep inside the bridge towers' bases. He was confined to bed but still managed to supervise the completion of the bridge with the help of his wife.

1. Which sentence best states the main idea of this passage?
   - (A) The Brooklyn Bridge is considered to be among the greatest engineering feats of all time.
   - (B) The Roeblings were pioneer builders of suspension bridges.
   - (C) Twenty workers died in accidents while building the bridge.
   - (D) Construction of the Brooklyn Bridge began with two large towers.

2. Which detail supports the main idea?
   - (F) With the help of his wife, he still managed to supervise the completion of the bridge.
   - (G) The credit belonged to a father and son, John A. Roebling and Colonel Washington A. Roebling.
   - (H) By 1877, the towers were completed and work had begun on the cables.
   - (J) When it opened, it was the longest suspension bridge on earth.

DIRECTIONS: Choose the best answer.

3. Kim is about to begin reading a book titled *Let Liberty Ring.* Where in the book should Kim look to get a general overview of the book's contents?
   - (A) the title page
   - (B) the introduction
   - (C) the glossary
   - (D) the index

4. Which of these references would provide another word for *beautiful*?
   - (F) encyclopedia
   - (G) book of quotations
   - (H) thesaurus
   - (J) almanac

20

© Carson-Dellosa Publishing

Language Arts Standards

2.0 Grammar and Usage of the English Language
By the end of the school year, students should demonstrate correct use of:
- **2.A** Grammar, including irregular verbs. *(See pages 22–23.)*
- **2.B** Paragraph structure, including opening, middle, and closing sentences. *(See pages 24–25.)*
- **2.C** Punctuation, including quotation marks, commas, and colons. *(See page 26.)*
- **2.D** Sentence construction, including correct subject/verb agreement and verb tense. *(See page 27.)*
- **2.E** Spelling strategies for fifth grade content-area vocabulary. *(See page 28.)*

By the end of the school year, students should be able to revise work by:
- **2.F** Making their writing easier to understand. *(See page 29.)*
- **2.G** Rearranging the sequence of words, sentences, and paragraphs. *(See page 30.)*
- **2.H** Adding or deleting details and explanations. *(See page 31.)*
- **2.I** Using dictionaries and reference books to assist in editing. *(See pages 32–33.)*

© Carson-Dellosa Publishing

Name _____ Date _____

Language Arts

Grammar

Grammar and Usage of the English Language

DIRECTIONS: Write the correct form of the verb *lie* or *lay* in each blank.

1. Peter and Zach _____ their towels on the sand.

2. "Zach, where have you _____ our picnic basket?" asked Peter.

3. "I _____ it under the umbrella," replied Zach.

4. Peter decided to _____ on his towel.

DIRECTIONS: Circle the correct underlined word in each sentence.

5. The library is open every day <u>accept/except</u> Sunday.

6. How did the speech <u>affect/effect</u> the students?

7. Mr. Randolph <u>accepted/excepted</u> Mr. Greer's resignation.

8. Everyone <u>accept/except</u> my little sister stayed up late.

DIRECTIONS: Choose the best answer.

9. Jeremy taught _____ to play the guitar.
   - Ⓐ hisself
   - Ⓑ itself
   - Ⓒ themselves
   - Ⓓ himself

10. Sheila is _____ than I am.
    - Ⓕ more hungrier
    - Ⓖ hungriest
    - Ⓗ most hungry
    - Ⓙ hungrier

11. The twins can take care of _____ .
    - Ⓐ themselves
    - Ⓑ herself
    - Ⓒ himself
    - Ⓓ yourselves

12. He was the _____ member of the club.
    - Ⓕ more louder
    - Ⓖ louder
    - Ⓗ loudest
    - Ⓙ most loud

13. Lena hurt _____ climbing a tree.
    - Ⓐ itself
    - Ⓑ themselves
    - Ⓒ she
    - Ⓓ herself

14. He is _____ in history than I am.
    - Ⓕ interested
    - Ⓖ interesting
    - Ⓗ most interested
    - Ⓙ more interested

Name _____ Date _____

15. Carmina _____ left a chocolate bar on the camp table.
- Ⓐ angry
- Ⓑ carelessly
- Ⓒ bravely
- Ⓓ have

16. The water _____ in the fountain.
- Ⓕ splash
- Ⓖ having splashed
- Ⓗ splashing
- Ⓙ splashed

17. My mother _____ for three hours.
- Ⓐ drive
- Ⓑ driven
- Ⓒ has drove
- Ⓓ drove

DIRECTIONS: Choose the line that has a usage error. If there is no error, choose "No mistakes."

18.
- Ⓕ George Washington
- Ⓖ are called the father
- Ⓗ of our country.
- Ⓙ No mistakes

19.
- Ⓐ Binoculars are helpful
- Ⓑ because they let you
- Ⓒ observe things closely.
- Ⓓ No mistakes

20.
- Ⓕ We missed the
- Ⓖ baseball game however
- Ⓗ there was a train crossing.
- Ⓙ No mistakes

21.
- Ⓐ The junior high
- Ⓑ play take place on
- Ⓒ Friday and Saturday night.
- Ⓓ No mistakes

22.
- Ⓕ He hasn't never made
- Ⓖ a mistake on any of
- Ⓗ his reading assignments.
- Ⓙ No mistakes

23.
- Ⓐ We haveta get more
- Ⓑ decorations for the hall
- Ⓒ in order to finish.
- Ⓓ No mistakes

24.
- Ⓕ Mrs. Green give
- Ⓖ her fifth-grade class
- Ⓗ a surprise quiz.
- Ⓙ No mistakes

25.
- Ⓐ Carlos and Jeremy are
- Ⓑ best friends who play
- Ⓒ on the same basketball team.
- Ⓓ No mistakes

Name _____ Date _____

Language Arts

2.B

Paragraph Structure

Grammar and Usage of the English Language

DIRECTIONS: Read each paragraph. Choose the best topic sentence for the paragraph.

 A paragraph should be about one idea. The correct answer is the one that fits best with the rest of the paragraph.

1. _____. Snails produce a liquid on the bottom of their feet. Then, they "surf" on the rippling waves of this sticky liquid. Starfish have slender tube feet with tiny suction cups that help them grip. Dolphins whip their tails up and down to thrust their bodies through the water.

    - (A) Animals eat a variety of foods found in nature.
    - (B) There are many different animals in the United States.
    - (C) Animals move about in many unusual ways.
    - (D) Animals have different kinds of feet.

2. _____. A honeybee collects pollen and nectar from a flower. When the bee goes to the next flower, some of the pollen from the first flower falls onto the second. The second flower uses this pollen to make seeds.

    - (F) It is estimated that honeybees pollinate billions of dollars worth of crops each year.
    - (G) The most important role of the honeybee is to pollinate plants.
    - (H) If you are stung by a bee, remove the stinger carefully.
    - (J) Bees are considered pests.

3. _____. Toads and tree frogs croak in the evenings. Sometimes the chirping of the crickets is so loud that you can't hear the little frogs. But the booming of the big bullfrogs can always be heard. I don't know how Lane Roy sleeps.

    - (A) Crickets are louder than frogs.
    - (B) Swamps are homes to many different creatures.
    - (C) Frogs make a variety of sounds.
    - (D) The swamp behind the house is filled with sound.

DIRECTIONS: Read each paragraph. Choose the sentence that does not belong in the paragraph.

4. (1) In 1567, Francis Drake, John Hawkins, and other English seamen were on a voyage. (2) They hoped to make a profit by selling smuggled goods to some of the Spanish colonies. (3) On their way back from their voyage, they stopped at a Mexican port. (4) By far, Drake is best known as the first Englishman to sail around the world.

    - (F) Sentence 1
    - (G) Sentence 2
    - (H) Sentence 3
    - (J) Sentence 4

© Carson-Dellosa Publishing

Name _____ Date _____

5. **(1) In his book *Over the Top of the World*, Will Steger relates the travels of his research party across the Arctic Ocean from Siberia to Canada in 1994. (2) With a team of 6 people and 33 dogs, Steger set out by dogsled to complete this daring mission. (3) At other times, they boarded their canoes to cross chilly stretches of water. (4) Along the way, the party would exchange dogsleds for canoe sleds because of the breaking ice packs.**

- (A) Sentence 1
- (B) Sentence 2
- (C) Sentence 3
- (D) Sentence 4

6. **(1) The "Great Zimbabwe" is one of many stone-walled fortresses built on the Zimbabwean plateau. (2) The Shona spoke a common Bantu language and all were herdsmen and farmers. (3) Researchers believe that the Shona people built this structure over a course of 400 years. (4) More than 18,000 people may have lived in the "Great Zimbabwe."**

- (F) Sentence 1
- (G) Sentence 2
- (H) Sentence 3
- (J) Sentence 4

DIRECTIONS: Read the paragraph. Use it to answer the questions.

(1) There are many differences between frogs and toads. **(2)** Frogs have narrow bodies and ridges down their backs. **(3)** They have large, round ear membranes and small teeth in their upper jaws. **(4)** Their long hind legs enable them to take long leaps. **(5)** A toad's short legs limit it to only short jumps. **(6)** Frogs have smooth, moist, soft skin. **(7)** Most frogs are water-dwellers.

7. If another paragraph were added that told about toads, what would make a good first sentence for that paragraph?

- (A) Their ear membranes are smaller than frogs'.
- (B) In contrast, toads have chubby bodies and ridges on their heads.
- (C) Toads and frogs are similar to each other in many ways.
- (D) However, they lay their eggs in strings rather than clumps.

8. Which sentence should be left out of this paragraph?

- (F) Sentence 3
- (G) Sentence 4
- (H) Sentence 5
- (J) Sentence 6

9. Choose the best last sentence for this paragraph.

- (A) They lay clumps of eggs in their watery habitat.
- (B) Toads have no teeth.
- (C) Frogs make a loud croaking sound.
- (D) Most toads make their homes on land.

Name _____ Date _____

Language Arts
2.C

Punctuation

Grammar and Usage of the English Language

DIRECTIONS: Fill in the circle next to the punctuation mark that is needed in the sentence. Choose "None" if no additional punctuation marks are needed.

1. The team carried in the bats balls, and gloves.
   - (A) ;
   - (B) ,
   - (C) :
   - (D) None

2. "Great catch" yelled the pitcher.
   - (F) ?
   - (G) .
   - (H) !
   - (J) None

3. Did you see that foul ball
   - (A) ?
   - (B) .
   - (C) ,
   - (D) None

4. Matilda hit a home run.
   - (F) !
   - (G) "
   - (H) ,
   - (J) None

5. That's three strikes," said the umpire.
   - (A) ,
   - (B) "
   - (C) "
   - (D) None

6. Yes the Fifth Grade Firecrackers won the game.
   - (F) ,
   - (G) .
   - (H) !
   - (J) None

DIRECTIONS: Read each item. Fill in the circle next to the choice that has a punctuation error. If there is no mistake, choose "No mistakes."

7.
   - (A) Samuel Clemens had no money
   - (B) He began writing articles
   - (C) for a newspaper called the *Territorial Enterprises*.
   - (D) No mistakes

8.
   - (F) Samuel's newspaper articles
   - (G) were eventually compiled
   - (H) into his first book, Roughing It
   - (J) No mistakes

9.
   - (A) Samuel Clemens
   - (B) first used the pen name:
   - (C) Mark Twain while he worked as a writer in Virginia City, Nevada.
   - (D) No mistakes

10.
   - (F) 742 West Main Street
   - (G) Virginia City, NV, 80235
   - (H) December 12, 2003
   - (J) No mistakes

DIRECTIONS: Choose the word or words that fit best in the blank and show the correct punctuation.

11. Gabriel watched a caterpillar climb up the side of _____ aquarium.
   - (A) its
   - (B) it's
   - (C) its'
   - (D) its's

12. He placed bits of grass, _____ small twigs inside.
   - (F) some lettuce and
   - (G) some lettuce, and
   - (H) some lettuce, and,
   - (J) some lettuce and,

STOP

Name _____ Date _____

Language Arts

2.D

Sentence Construction

Grammar and Usage of the English Language

DIRECTIONS: Choose the answer that is a complete and correctly written sentence.

1. Ⓐ Scientists spends many hours recording the behavior and habits of animals.
   Ⓑ They search for clues to explain why animals act as they do.
   Ⓒ Through careful observation, the behavior of an animal might could be explained.
   Ⓓ Lemmings, however, does an unexplainable thing.

2. Ⓕ Glass snakes ain't snakes at all.
   Ⓖ They is one of several kinds of lizards that inhabitate the earth.
   Ⓗ Most legless lizards resemble worms, but the glass snake looks very much like a true snake.
   Ⓙ It can break off his tail as easily as a pieces of glass.

DIRECTIONS: Read each answer choice. Fill in the circle for the choice that has an error. If there are no errors, choose "No mistakes."

3. Ⓐ A beach vacation and a ski vacation
   Ⓑ is alike in some ways
   Ⓒ and different in others.
   Ⓓ No mistakes

4. Ⓕ Doing the laundry is a big contribution
   Ⓖ to my family, and I get to put away
   Ⓗ my own clothes exactly the way I like them.
   Ⓙ No mistakes

DIRECTIONS: Read the story. Use it to answer the questions.

(1) Last Saturday, the Wilson family drove to Chicago to watch a Cubs baseball game. (2) The bustling streets around the ballpark were filled with activity. (3) The children spotted a booth outside the stadium that was selling Cubs' baseball caps. (4) They begged their dad to buy each of them a hat. (5) He insisted that they wait until they got inside the park. (6) When they got to the front of the line, the children saw a woman handing out free Cubs' hats. (7) It was free hat day. (8) Mr. Wilson smiled and the children cheered.

5. **How is sentence 1 best written?**
   Ⓐ On a drive to Chicago last Saturday, the Wilson family was watching a Cubs baseball game.
   Ⓑ To watch a Cubs baseball game, the Wilson family drove to Chicago last Saturday.
   Ⓒ Last Saturday, the Wilson family was driving to Chicago and watching a Cubs baseball game.
   Ⓓ As it is

6. **What is the best way to combine sentences 4 and 5 without changing their meaning?**
   Ⓕ They begged their dad to buy each of them a hat, but he insisted that they wait until they got inside the park.
   Ⓖ They begged their dad to buy each of them a hat, because he insisted that they wait until they got inside the park.
   Ⓗ They begged their dad to buy each of them a hat; therefore, he insisted that they wait until they got inside the park.
   Ⓙ Since their dad insisted that they wait until they got inside the park, they begged him to buy each of them a hat.

© Carson-Dellosa Publishing

Name _____ Date _____

Language Arts

2.E

Spelling

Grammar and Usage of the English Language

DIRECTIONS: Write the contractions for the words in parentheses.

1. (You are) _____ early, and

    (they are) _____ late.

2. (It will) _____ be easy to do

    this math problem.

3. (Let us) _____ ride our bikes

    to see if (they are) _____ at

    the park.

4. (Do not) _____ worry,

    (I have) _____ got a map.

5. (I will) _____ see

    (what is) _____ going on.

DIRECTIONS: Choose the word that is spelled correctly and best completes the sentence.

6. I'll be there in a _____.
    - Ⓐ minit
    - Ⓑ minite
    - Ⓒ minnute
    - Ⓓ minute

7. Marsha will meet us _____.
    - Ⓕ afterward
    - Ⓖ afterword
    - Ⓗ afterwerd
    - Ⓙ aftirward

8. What a _____ mistake we made!
    - Ⓐ terible
    - Ⓑ terrible
    - Ⓒ terribull
    - Ⓓ terrable

9. My birthday is on the _____.
    - Ⓕ twelth
    - Ⓖ twelfeth
    - Ⓗ twelveth
    - Ⓙ twelfth

DIRECTIONS: Find the underlined word that is spelled incorrectly. If all the underlined words are spelled correctly, choose "All correct."

10.
    - Ⓐ be <u>pateint</u>
    - Ⓑ <u>brightly</u> colored
    - Ⓒ was <u>frightened</u>
    - Ⓓ All correct

11.
    - Ⓕ <u>heavier</u> package
    - Ⓖ <u>special</u> place
    - Ⓗ next <u>century</u>
    - Ⓙ All correct

12.
    - Ⓐ <u>pursue</u> her dream
    - Ⓑ <u>reference</u> section
    - Ⓒ political <u>campaign</u>
    - Ⓓ All correct

13.
    - Ⓕ <u>captan</u> of the team
    - Ⓖ <u>believe</u> in yourself
    - Ⓗ run an <u>errand</u>
    - Ⓙ All correct

STOP

Name _____ Date _____

Language Arts

2.F

Making Writing Easier to Understand

Grammar and Usage of the English Language

DIRECTIONS: Read the letter. Then, answer the questions. If the sentence needs no changes, choose "Correct as is."

> Dear Ms. Wood:
>
> **(1)** Our whole class would like to thank you for the nature trail tour. **(2)** We was amazed at the number of flowers, and animals, on the trail. **(3)** The birds and animals, all of them that we saw, were so beautiful. **(4)** We drew pictures of some of the birds and animals after we got back to school. **(5)** The wildflowers, which we saw on the nature trail, were colorful and interesting. **(6)** Our favorite was the one called Queen Anne's lace. **(7)** We are sending you a drawing of this flower as a thank you for the tour.
>
> Sincerely,
>
> Mrs. Jasper's Third-Grade Class

1. **Sentence 2 is best written—**
    - (A) We were amazed by the number of flowers, and animals, on the trail.
    - (B) The flowers and animals was amazing on the trail.
    - (C) We were amazed by the number of flowers and animals on the trail.
    - (D) Correct as is

2. **Sentence 3 is best written—**
    - (F) The birds and animals that we seen were so beautiful.
    - (G) All of the birds and animals that we saw were so beautiful.
    - (H) All of the birds and all of the animals we saw were so beautiful.
    - (J) Correct as is

3. **Sentence 5 is best written—**
    - (A) The wildflowers that we saw on the nature trail were colorful and interesting.
    - (B) We saw on the trail wildflowers which were colorful and interesting.
    - (C) Wildflowers, colorful and interesting, which we saw on the trail.
    - (D) Correct as is

© Carson-Dellosa Publishing

29

Name _____ Date _____

Language Arts
2.F

Rearranging Text

Grammar and Usage of the English Language

DIRECTIONS: The directions below are not very good. They contain information that is not needed. They do not list the materials you need. The steps are not in order, and there are no signal words to help make the order clear. Improve and rewrite the directions.

 Directions should not sound like a story. They should tell the reader what to do.

> Once, I was playing with an old sock. I put it on my hand and pretended it was a ghost. All of a sudden, I realized I was using the sock like a puppet. So I decided to make some real sock puppets! I drew faces on the socks with felt-tipped markers. First of course, I had to ask my mother for some old socks to use. I got some thread and cotton and pieces of fabric, and I cut out four pieces in the shape of a rabbit's ears. I got a needle and sewed two of the ear pieces together with a hole at the bottom. I sewed the ear together after I stuffed it with cotton. I did the same thing to make another ear. I sewed the ears on the puppet. I had a good time doing this, and I hope you will, too.

Adding and Deleting Text

Language Arts 2.H — Grammar and Usage of the English Language

DIRECTIONS: Read the report, and then answer the questions.

(1) Thomas Jefferson accomplished many great things. (2) He is probably best known as the main author of the Declaration of Independence. (3) Jefferson was a person of integrity, and many people trusted him. (4) He was a member of the Continental Congress and a minister to France. (5) He was made Secretary of State in 1790 and Vice President in 1797. (6) Jefferson served as President of the United States from 1801 to 1809. (7) His wife was not alive to be his first lady. (8) This great man continued to work for his principles until he passed away in 1826.

1. What is the topic sentence of the paragraph?
   - (A) Sentence 1
   - (B) Sentence 2
   - (C) Sentence 3
   - (D) Sentence 4

2. Which of these could be added after sentence 2?
   - (F) Many politicians signed the Declaration.
   - (G) He was only 33 years old when he helped write the Declaration.
   - (H) The Declaration of Independence was the first step in a war against Britain.
   - (J) Benjamin Franklin helped Jefferson with some of the ideas in the document.

3. Which sentence does not belong in the paragraph?
   - (A) Sentence 5
   - (B) Sentence 6
   - (C) Sentence 7
   - (D) Sentence 8

4. Which of these could be added after sentence 6?
   - (F) He was President for seven years.
   - (G) During his presidency, he helped the United States purchase the Louisiana Territories.
   - (H) Some people liked him and some didn't.
   - (J) He was only the eighth President of the United States.

5. Write a Sentence 9 to complete the paragraph.

   _____
   _____
   _____
   _____
   _____
   _____
   _____
   _____
   _____

Name _____ Date _____

Language Arts
2.1

Using Reference Materials

Grammar and Usage of the English Language

DIRECTIONS: Use the sample thesaurus entry below to answer the questions.

> **supine,** *adj.* **1.** flat, flat on one's back, horizontal, lounging, recline.
> **2.** inactive, motionless, lazy, lifeless.
> **supple,** *adj.* **1.** flexible, bendable, pliant; elastic, stretchable.
> **2.** limber, loose-limbed, double-jointed.
> **3.** yielding, unresistant, passive.
> **4.** changeable, movable, agreeable, willing.

1. The words listed in this thesaurus entry are both _____ .

   Ⓐ nouns
   Ⓑ verbs
   Ⓒ adjectives
   Ⓓ adverbs

2. Write three synonyms for the word *supple*.

   _____
   _____

3. Write one antonym for the word *supple*.

   _____

4. Even if you didn't know the meaning of *supine* before looking in the thesaurus, how would you define it after reading this entry? Write a definition.

   _____
   _____

DIRECTIONS: A **bibliography** is a list of the books and articles a writer uses for reference when writing a report. A bibliography tells interested readers where to find more information on the report's topic. The bibliography below was prepared by someone who wrote a report called *The Wild West*. Read the bibliography and use it to answer questions 5–9.

> **Book**
> Alter, Judy. Author
> *Growing Up in the Old West*
> Watts, 1999
>
> **Encyclopedia Article**
> "Pioneers in the Wild West"
> *McMahon Encyclopedia*, 2002 edition
> vol. 12, pp. 278–282.
>
> **Magazine Article**
> Tripp, John R. Author
> "Exploring the American West."
> *The U.S. Experience*
> vol. 114 (April 1998): 25–32.

5. What three types of references did the writer use to write her report?

   _____
   _____
   _____

6. Which of these references was published most recently?

   _____

7. In what volume of the encyclopedia did the writer find her information about pioneers in the Wild West?

   _____

Name _____ Date _____

8. On what pages did the magazine article appear?

_____

9. If you wanted to find out what it was like to be a child in the Old West, what would be the best reference?

_____

DIRECTIONS: Use the sample dictionary entries and the Pronunciation Guide to answer questions 10–15.

> **camp** /'kamp/ *n.* 1. a place, usually away from cities, where tents or simple buildings are put up to provide shelter for people working or vacationing there 2. a place, usually in the country, for recreation or instruction during the summer months [goes to summer camp each July] 3. a group of people who work to promote a certain idea or thought or who work together in support of another person *v.* 4. To live temporarily in a camp or outdoors.
> **cam·paign** /kăm-'pān/ *n.* 1. A series of military operations that make up a distinct period during a war 2. A series of activities designed to bring about a desired outcome [an election campaign] *v.* 3. to conduct a campaign
> **cam·pus** /'kam-pəs/ *n.* 1. The grounds and buildings of a school
>
> Pronunciation Guide:
> **a**sh, st**ay**, ə = a in *alone* and u in *circus*, w**e**t, **ea**sy, h**i**t, h**i**de, f**o**x, g**o**, b**u**t, m**u**sic

10. The "u" in *campus* sounds most like the vowel sound in _____ .

- Ⓕ but
- Ⓖ music
- Ⓗ circus
- Ⓙ wet

11. Which definition best fits the word *camp* as it is used in the sentence below?

The field workers lived in a *camp* a mile away from the farm.

- Ⓐ 1
- Ⓑ 2
- Ⓒ 3
- Ⓓ 4

12. How many syllables are in the word *campaign*?

- Ⓕ 1
- Ⓖ 2
- Ⓗ 3
- Ⓙ 4

13. In which of these sentences is *camp* used as a verb?

- Ⓐ The governor's camp worked through the night to prepare her acceptance speech.
- Ⓑ Della will go to music camp in July.
- Ⓒ The hike back to camp took three hours.
- Ⓓ The family will camp in Yosemite this spring.

14. What part of speech is the word *campus*?

- Ⓕ verb
- Ⓖ noun
- Ⓗ adjective
- Ⓙ adverb

15. Look at the words in the sample dictionary. Which guide words would appear on the dictionary page on which these words are located?

- Ⓐ campground–candle
- Ⓑ camera–campfire
- Ⓒ camisole–canal
- Ⓓ camper–campsite

Name _____ Date _____

Language Arts
2.0
For pages 22–33

Mini-Test 2

Grammar and Usage of the English Language

DIRECTIONS: Read the paragraph. Choose the sentence that does not belong.

1. (1) Niagara Falls, one of the world's biggest waterfalls, is partly in the United States and partly in Canada. (2) My family went there for our vacation last summer. (3) In 1969, scientists did a strange thing at the falls. (4) They shut off the American falls for several months by building a big dam across the river so no water could get to the falls. (5) The scientists wanted to study the rocks underneath the water.

   Ⓐ Sentence 1
   Ⓑ Sentence 2
   Ⓒ Sentence 4
   Ⓓ Sentence 5

DIRECTIONS: Read the paragraph. Choose the sentence that fits best in the blank.

2. One of the nicest things about summer evenings is being able to watch fireflies or try to catch them. _____. Some scientists think the lights are used to scare away birds that might eat the fireflies. Others think the fireflies use their lights to say "Hello" to their future mates.

   Ⓕ My grandma likes to sit on the porch in the evening.
   Ⓖ I usually catch fireflies in a big jar.
   Ⓗ Fireflies need to have lots of air if you catch them and put them in a jar.
   Ⓙ Did you ever wonder why fireflies light up?

DIRECTIONS: Choose the best answer.

3. She is a _____ cheerleader than I am.
   Ⓐ more better
   Ⓑ best
   Ⓒ better
   Ⓓ most better

4. I can't wait for _____ to get here!
   Ⓕ tomorrow
   Ⓖ tommorrow
   Ⓗ tommorow
   Ⓙ tomorow

5. Jason fixed _____ a huge bowl of ice cream.
   Ⓐ him
   Ⓑ himself
   Ⓒ itself
   Ⓓ hisself

6. Which punctuation mark is needed in the following sentence?
   Abby asked, Do you want me to serve dinner now?"
   Ⓕ !
   Ⓖ .
   Ⓗ "
   Ⓙ None

7. If you wanted to find a synonym for the word *attractive,* which reference would you use?
   Ⓐ a dictionary
   Ⓑ an encyclopedia
   Ⓒ an atlas
   Ⓓ a thesaurus

Language Arts Standards

3.0 Literature
Using the literature read during the school year, students should be able to:

- **3.A** Identify similarities and differences in theme from book to book. *(See pages 36–37.)*
- **3.B** Think about how the author's word choices and decisions about content communicate meaning. *(See pages 38–39.)*
- **3.C** Look at what makes one type of literature different from another. *(See pages 40–41.)*
- **3.D** Describe and compare the personalities of different characters, and why they act the way they do. *(See pages 42–43.)*
- **3.E** Develop ideas (for example, draw conclusions, make predictions) about events, characters, and settings. *(See pages 44–49.)*
- **3.F** Select books based on personal needs and interest. *(See page 50.)*
- **3.G** Produce written work in at least one literary genre (e.g., realistic fiction). *(See page 51.)*

Name _____ Date _____

Language Arts
3.A

Literature

Identifying Similarities and Differences in Theme

DIRECTIONS: Read both stories. Then, answer the questions on the next page.

What If?

We were settled in our sleeping bags after a really bad day.

We went fishing in the morning with Toby—after breakfast, of course—just off the dock. But that was enough. The monster of the lake pulled me into the water three times, although Toby says I'm just faking it. I'm not faking! There's a monster fish in this lake. I'm never going to swim here again—ever!

This afternoon, I had archery class. I got two bull's-eyes that didn't count just because they were on another kid's target! Then came camping skills class. We learned how to make a stew over a campfire. How was I supposed to know the can would be so hot? I dropped the can and put out the fire. What a bunch of crybabies those other kids are!

Well, like I said, we had just settled down in bed when I happened to look out the window. It's hard to believe any animal in its right mind would want to live in such a dark, scary place. So, I was checking things out to see if everything was okay. I caught a glimmer of something big and shadowy. It was so big its shadow blotted out all the moonlight.

When I saw that shadow, I got a little bit scared. Well, I was scared enough to poke my head down into my sleeping bag and clamp the top of the bag closed with my fist. And when Toby left us, because he wanted to be with the other counselors, I started worrying.

What would I do if a huge owl swooped down?
What if the owl smashed through the window?
And grabbed me?
And flew away with me in its claws?
Who would tell my parents?

I almost wanted to cry. I used to do that a lot. But I didn't this time. It's not a good idea to cry around other guys. Somebody might laugh.

I was getting a little hot inside my sleeping bag. I opened my fist. I popped my head out. No one else was making a sound, other than the deep-sleep breathing sounds of all the other kids in the cabin. I looked out the window.

And there it was.

I'll Save You

It was just Dollar Lake, the size of five or six backyards filled with water. "Not much bigger than a kiddie pool," my mom always said. But it was deep and cold. Springs fed the small lake, and it was such a dark green that you couldn't see the bottom. Plus, weeds grew thick around the far end of the lake. "Stay away from that end of the lake," my mom always said. "Those weeds are so thick you could drown."

My older brother Jimmy told me a swamp monster lived in those weeds that would come out from the lake at night to hunt little boys. I'd pull my covers over my head and worry that my screen was not solid enough to hold the swamp monster back. Some nights when I got the courage, I'd leap out of bed, run to the window, and slam it shut. When I awakened in the morning, it would be open, and I would be alive. But it never stopped

GO

36 © Carson-Dellosa Publishing

Name _____ Date _____

> me from worrying that one night, Mom and Dad would find me gone with my screen ripped open. A trail of lake weeds would be the only thing left of me. I was just a little kid. I didn't know any better.
>
> One night, just after my eighth birthday, I heard someone shouting.
>
> "Help!" I heard.
>
> Then, "Help!" again.
>
> I pulled my covers over my head thinking it was the swamp monster, and he had finally gotten some unfortunate little boy. I thought of Billy. I imagined him being pulled from his bed and dragged across his back lawn, kicking and screaming.
>
> "Help!" I heard it again. It didn't sound like Billy. More like a girl. More like Mom. "Jim? Steven? Help!" It *was* Mom. The swamp monster had Mom.
>
> In a burst of courage, I leaped from my bed and ran down the stairs. I rushed to the back door shouting, "I'll save you! I'll save you!" I quickly unlocked the door and bounded headfirst into Mom, knocking her over.
>
> "Mom," I said, "What are you doing here? I thought—" but I caught myself before I spilled out, "I thought the swamp monster had you."
>
> "I forgot my keys, and Jim locked the door when he went to bed," she said as she picked herself up from the porch. "I just went to the Watsons to help Mrs. Watson hem a dress. Did I frighten you?"
>
> "No! No!" I stuttered. "I just thought you were hurt. I'm glad you're okay, Mom," I said with a smile. As I looked out into the dark, I thought about the swamp monster. It didn't seem so scary any more. You never knew when one thing might turn out to be something else—something much less scary!

1. **What theme do both of these stories have in common? Explain your answer.**

   _____
   _____
   _____
   _____
   _____
   _____

2. **Who was braver—the narrator of "What If?" or the narrator of "I'll Save You"? Explain your answer.**

   _____
   _____
   _____
   _____
   _____
   _____

3. **Identify one major difference in the theme of each story.**

   _____
   _____
   _____
   _____
   _____
   _____

Name _____ Date _____

Language Arts Literature

3.B # Author's Influence on Meaning

DIRECTIONS: Read the passage and answer the questions on the next page.

Easter Island

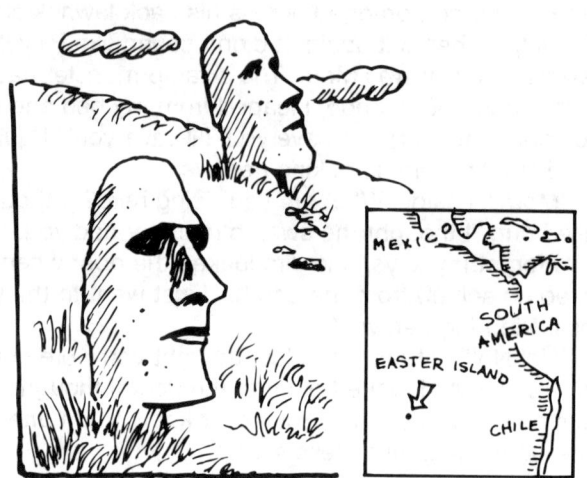

Few places in the world are more intriguing and mystifying than Easter Island, located in the Pacific Ocean 2,300 miles from the coast of Chile. Easter Island has 64 square miles of rugged coastline and steep hills. Scientists believe the island began as a volcano. Three extinct volcanoes remain on the island. The largest one rises 1,400 feet high.

On Easter Sunday of 1722, Dutch Admiral Jacob Roggeveen and his crew landed on Easter Island aboard the Dutch ship *Arena*. The astonished crew found dozens of huge stone figures standing on long stone platforms. The statues, some measuring 40 feet tall, were similar in appearance. Their expressionless faces were without eyes. Huge red stone cylinders were placed on their heads. Since that time, the island has been a source of mystery and intrigue to scientists and explorers.

Archaeologists believe that three different cultures lived on Easter Island. Around 400 A.D., the island was inhabited by a group of people who specialized in making small stone statues.

Years later, another civilization tore down these statues and used them to build long temple platforms called *ahus*. These people carved more than 600 enormous stone busts of human forms and placed them on the *ahus*. Some *ahus* still hold up to 15 statues.

Scientists believe that the statues were carved from hard volcanic rock in the crater walls of the volcano called *Rana Raraku*. The statues were chiseled with stone picks made of basalt. Although the statues weigh many tons each, it is believed that they were moved with ropes and rollers across the island and placed on the *ahus*. This may be the reason for one island legend about the statues "walking" to their site.

About 1670, another group of people invaded the island. These invaders practiced cannibalism. During this time, many people began living in underground caves where they hid their treasures.

Today, Easter Island is governed by Chile, a country of South America. Almost the entire population of 2,000 people lives in the small village of Hanga Roa on the west coast of the island.

 GO

38   © Carson-Dellosa Publishing

Name _____ Date _____

1. **The author believes that Easter Island** _____ .
   - (A) is fascinating to study
   - (B) is not worth scientific study
   - (C) is not a real place
   - (D) is the result of cannibalism

2. **The author's purpose in writing this passage is most likely** _____ .
   - (F) to convince readers to visit Easter Island
   - (G) to tell about a trip to Easter Island
   - (H) to explain why Easter Island is a source of mystery
   - (J) to report the latest scientific findings about Easter Island

3. **Which words most clearly reveal the author's feelings about the subject of Easter Island?**
   - (A) intriguing and mystifying
   - (B) it is believed
   - (C) rugged coastline
   - (D) enormous stone

4. **According to the author, which of the following is true about *ahus*?**
   - (F) People who lived in underground caves built the *ahus*.
   - (G) *Ahus* were chiseled with stone picks.
   - (H) There is no such thing as *ahus*.
   - (J) It is likely that ropes and rollers moved the statues to the *ahus*.

5. **Is the author successful in explaining why Easter Island is mysterious and intriguing? Why or why not?**

   _____
   _____
   _____
   _____
   _____
   _____
   _____
   _____
   _____
   _____
   _____
   _____
   _____
   _____
   _____
   _____
   _____
   _____

STOP

© Carson-Dellosa Publishing

Name _____ Date _____

Language Arts

3.C

Different Forms of Literature

Literature

DIRECTIONS: Read the passage below and answer questions 1–4.

A Doomed Romance

You are my love, my love you are.
I worship you from afar;
I through the branches spy you.

You, Sir, are a climbing thug.
I do not like your fuzzy mug.
Away from me, please take you!

Oh, grant me peace, my love, my dove.
Climb to my home so far above
This place you call your warren.

I like my home in sheltered hollow
Where fox and weasel may not follow.
Please go away, tree rodent!

I love your ears, so soft and tall.
I love your nose, so pink and small.
I must make you my own bride!

I will not climb, I cannot eat
The acorns that you call a treat.
Now shimmy up that oak; hide!

Now I hide up in my bower.
Lonesome still, I shake and cower.
Sadness overtakes me.

I must stay on the lovely ground
With carrots crisp and cabbage round.
I long for gardens, not trees.

1. This passage is which genre (type) of literature?
   - Ⓐ poetry
   - Ⓑ biography
   - Ⓒ nonfiction
   - Ⓓ fable

2. What clues in the passage helped you decide what genre it is?

   _____
   _____
   _____
   _____
   _____

3. Who are the two speakers in this passage? Identify them and write one adjective to describe the tone of each voice.

   A. _____
   _____

   B. _____
   _____

4. What do you think the theme of this passage is? Write it in one phrase or sentence.

   _____
   _____
   _____
   _____
   _____

Name _____ Date _____

DIRECTIONS: Read each story below and write the kind of story it is on the line.

> **Examples:**
>
> The following list tells you about four types of stories, called *genres*.
>
> **Science Fiction**—a make-believe story based on scientific possibilities. Science fiction is also called *fantasy*, but it can include scientific facts.
>
> **Myth**—a make-believe story that explains how something came to be. Myths often describe how the world was created.
>
> **Nonfiction**—factual information. Nonfiction stories are true.
>
> **Realistic Fiction**—a make-believe story that could actually happen. These stories aren't true, but it's easy to believe they are.

5. Juniper trees grow in Arizona. Tiny fairies live in their trunks. During the full moon, the fairies come out and dance at night. While dancing, they place blue berries on each tree for decoration. That's how the juniper gets its berries.

   _____

6. "It's a bird!" Tim shouted. "It's a plane!" Connie said. But it was a spaceship! It landed next to a juniper tree. Little green men got off the spaceship. They clipped off several branches of the tree. "They're collecting tree samples to study on Mars," Connie whispered. They watched amazed as the spaceship disappeared into the sky.

   _____

7. Jason and Patrick went for a hike. Because they were in the high desert, they carried water with them. When they got tired, the two boys sat in the shade of a juniper tree to rest and drink their water. That's when the rattlesnake appeared. "Don't move!" Patrick said to Jason. The boys sat still until the snake moved away. "What an adventure!" Jason said as the two boys returned home.

   _____

8. Juniper trees are small, gnarly trees that grow in many parts of the world. Members of the evergreen family, they remain green year round. Juniper trees can be easily identified by their tiny blue or red berries. There are 13 different kinds of juniper trees in the United States. One kind of juniper tree is called the *alligator juniper* because its bark looks similar to the skin of an alligator. It grows in the Southwest.

   _____

Name _____ Date _____

Language Arts

3.D

Analyzing Characters

Literature

DIRECTIONS: Read the story. Then, complete the character web on the next page.

Save the Day

Tate raced toward the baseball diamond. He greeted his teammates, jumping up and down. "Are you ready to win the championship?" he asked excitedly.

His two best friends, Jeffrey and Alyssa, smiled at his excitement. "It looks like our star batter is ready," Jeffrey said. Jeffrey didn't want to admit that he was pretty nervous. Lately, he'd been in a slump. His average had declined late in the season. He hoped he could pull it back up today when it counted most.

Alyssa was calm, as usual. She never seemed to get butterflies in her stomach, even under pressure. She was the team's pitcher and had a mean fastball.

The players warmed up and took the field. The game was a close one, but Tate and his team were victorious in the end. Afterward, the three buddies went to a nearby ice-cream shop to celebrate.

"Great job today, Alyssa!" Tate complimented his friend. "You kept your cool even when we were behind 2 to 0."

"Thanks." Alyssa said modestly. She licked her black raspberry cone neatly. Not a drip escaped off the cone.

"You were pretty great yourself," Jeffrey said to Tate. "I jumped off the bench, almost knocking it over, when you hit that ball over the fence in the fifth inning!" The two boys gave each other high fives. In their enthusiasm, the boys knocked Tate's ice cream off its cone.

"Oh, no," Tate said, disappointedly.

"Sorry, Tate," Jeffrey said. But Jeffrey couldn't stop smiling. He was in too good a mood. He'd hit the winning run today, and he felt great. He hadn't let his team down. Now, he wouldn't let his friend down.

"I have some money left," he said to Tate. "Let's go back up to the counter so I can save the day again!"

42

© Carson-Dellosa Publishing

Name _____ Date _____

Tate

How he feels before the game _____
Why? _____
_____
_____

What he does during the game
_____
_____
_____

What he probably does next
_____
_____
_____
_____

Jeffrey

How he feels before the game _____
Why? _____
_____
_____

What he does during the game
_____
_____
_____

What he probably does next
_____
_____
_____
_____

Alyssa

How she feels before the game _____
Why? _____
_____
_____

What she does during the game
_____
_____
_____

What she probably does next
_____
_____
_____
_____

STOP

© Carson-Dellosa Publishing

Name _____   Date _____

Language Arts

3.E

Literature

Developing Ideas About Characters and Setting

DIRECTIONS: Read the story. Then, answer the questions on the next page.

The Escape

Into the shady glen the small figure rode on a pony little larger than a dog. The pony's breath misted in the crisp air as the beast blew air out of its nostrils. The green-mantled figure patted the neck of the beast, whispering words of comfort into the animal's ear. In response, the faithful steed nickered, thumped his wide hoofs twice upon the soft bed of the forest floor, and ceased its shaking.

"We've left the raiders behind, old friend," said Rowan, as she removed her hooded mantle and tossed her head back and forth, bringing peace to her own troubled mind. Rowan was one of four daughters of Sylvia, guide of all wood folk.

Suddenly, shouts of rough men cut through the glade's peace.

"In here, I tell ya. The maid's gone to hiding in this grove."

"Nah, ya lunk. She'd never wait for us here. Not after she dunked old Stefan at the marsh. No! She's a gone on to her crazy folk, don'tcha know."

The two gray-cloaked riders dismounted, still arguing as they examined the earth for traces of the child's flight.

"Who was the lout who let her escape?" asked the first.

"'Tis one who no longer breathes the air so freely," returned the second grimly. "The lord nearly choked the fool, even as the knave begged for mercy. Ah, there's little patience for one who lets a mystic escape, to be true!"

Five nobly dressed horsemen wove through the trees to the clearing where these two rustics still squatted. In the lead came the fierce lord, a huge form with scarlet and gray finery worn over his coat of mail.

"What say you?" he roared. "Have you found the trail of Rowan?"

"No, sire," spoke the first gray, trembling, "though I was certain the child headed into this wood. Shall I continue to search, lord?"

"Aye, indeed," replied the master calmly, controlled. "She is here. I know it, too. You have a keen sense for the hunt, Mikkel. Be at ready with your blade. And you too, Short Brush! Though a child, our Rowan is vicious with her weapon."

"Yes, sire," agreed Mikkel and Short Brush.

The two grays beat the bushes in the search. Closer and closer they came to the child's hiding place, a small earthen scoop created when the roots of a wind-blown tree pulled free of the earth.

The evil lord and his lot remained mounted, ready to pursue should the young girl determine to take flight once more.

And so, they were not prepared for the child's play.

GO →

44

© Carson-Dellosa Publishing

> Rowan softly, softly sang, "You wind-whipped branches shudder, shake. You oaks and cedars, tremble. Take these men and beasts who do us wrong. Not in these woods do they belong."
>
> As a mighty gust of wind roared, nearby trees slapped their branches to the point of breaking, reaching out and grasping the five mounted men. An immense gaping cavern opened in the trunk of an ancient oak and swallowed the five surprised mail-clad men whole.
>
> Mikkel and Short Brush, too, were lifted high into the air by a white pine and a blue spruce. Lifted high. Kept high. For a while.
>
> "Return from whence you came. Go to your families, and tell them of the wrath of Sylvia," commanded Rowan. "She would not wish you to come to her land again!"
>
> The pine and spruce tossed the two gray trackers over the trees of the forest and into the field beyond. The field was already harvested and soggy with the rains of autumn. Mikkel and Short Brush, unhurt but shaken by their arboreal flight, rose and fled immediately to tell their master of the strange doings of this wood.

1. What sort of creature is Rowan?

2. What do we know of her kind so far?

3. How many enemies are mentioned in this selection? How are they identified?

4. How do we know of the power of Rowan?

5. Why might the evil lord wish to recapture Rowan?

6. What is the meaning of the word *arboreal*?

7. Why might Rowan have allowed the two rustics to remain alive?

8. What is the setting for the story? How do you know?

Language Arts

3.E

Making Inferences

Literature

DIRECTIONS: Read the story. Then, answer the questions on the next page.

An Inferencing Incident

"Quiet down, students, and please go to your desks," Mr. Chan said to the class. He waited for everyone to get settled. "Now, please take out your writing journals. Today, we will be learning about inferencing."

"Is that like conferencing?" Daphne asked eagerly. The students often held conferences to discuss their stories, and Daphne had just finished a good one.

"No," replied Mr. Chan. "But that's a good guess. In fact, that's what inferencing is—it is making an educated guess based on what you already know. Then, you add to it any new information you receive. Daphne saw that we were using our journals and inferred that we would be doing something that involved writing. Good inferencing, Daphne!"

Just then, a loud clanging noise rang through the room. The students put down their materials and lined up at the door. They walked single file out to the playground. All the other students soon joined them. This had happened many times before, so the students knew what to do.

After waiting a long time on the playground, the restless students began to wonder. They usually did not have to wait this long before returning to their classrooms. All at once, a red truck with a ladder on top drove up to the school. The students began talking anxiously. Some men and women raced around to the side of the building carrying a water hose.

The students became nervous as they saw the men and women direct the hose to where a small puff of smoke was coming out of a window near the school's cafeteria. Mr. Chan went to talk with the principal as the students watched in concern.

"Don't worry," Mr. Chan reassured them a moment later. "Everyone is safe. The situation will be taken care of shortly. But I'm going to make an inference. I infer that we may be eating lunch in our classroom today instead of in the cafeteria!"

Name _____ Date _____

1. **At the beginning of the article the students are _____ .**
   - (A) quietly working on an assignment
   - (B) out of their desks and making noise
   - (C) working on a science experiment
   - (D) eating lunch

   How do you know?

   _____

2. **Daphne feels _____ her finished story.**
   - (F) proud and excited to share
   - (G) dissatisfied with
   - (H) ashamed of
   - (J) bored about

   How do you know?

   _____

3. **The loud noise is _____ .**
   - (A) the children misbehaving
   - (B) a fire alarm
   - (C) a thunderstorm
   - (D) an argument in the hall outside the classroom

   What are the clues?

   _____

4. **The people who arrive at the school are _____ .**
   - (F) police officers
   - (G) firefighters
   - (H) a TV crew
   - (J) teachers

   What are the clues?

   _____

5. **The smoke is most likely caused by _____ .**
   - (A) burnt pizza
   - (B) a science experiment
   - (C) library books burning
   - (D) a truck's exhaust fumes

   How do you know?

   _____

6. **Explain why Mr. Chan says the students will be eating their lunch in the classroom.**

   _____

   _____

   _____

   _____

   _____

   _____

© Carson-Dellosa Publishing

Name _____ Date _____

Language Arts
3.E

Drawing Conclusions

Literature

DIRECTIONS: Read the passage. Then, answer the questions on the next page.

The World Series

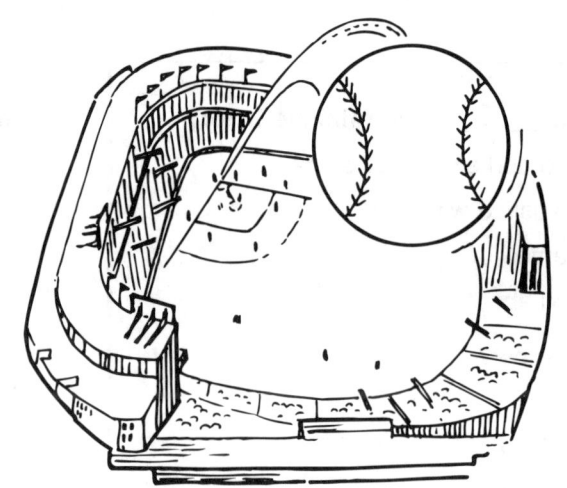

Baseball is an important part of American culture and history. The World Series is the most exciting and important sporting event of the year because it names the national champion in America's favorite pastime.

In spite of what the title says, the World Series is actually not a championship open to the world. The World Series matches the American League champion team against the National League champion team. The first team to win four games out of seven wins the World Series.

The World Series was first played in 1903. The American League champions, the Boston Pilgrims, played the National League champions, the Pittsburgh Pirates. The Boston Pilgrims, now named the Boston Red Sox, won this first World Series.

Although the World Series seemed to be off to a great start in 1903, the next year was a different story. In 1904, the New York Giants refused to play the Boston Pilgrims in the World Series. To this day, no one is sure why they refused, but 1904 was the first year in World Series history that did not have a world championship series (the other was in 1994).

For a team to make it to the World Series takes months of hard work and a lot of talent. Most teams play more than 150 games between April and October of each year. Many great baseball players, such as Babe Ruth, Jackie Robinson, Joe Di Maggio, and Lou Gehrig, have played in the World Series.

Many World Series records have been broken over the years. But in 1956, a little-known player named Don Larsen pitched a no-hitter game for the New York Yankees. His record has never been broken.

The New York Yankees have won more World Series championships than any other team in history. No matter who wins the title, the World Series remains one of the most popular events each year for sport fans. In fact, there is even a World Series for the youngest players. Unlike the adult World Series, the Little League World Series includes teams from other countries. Taiwan has won more than any other foreign country.

48

© Carson-Dellosa Publishing

Name _____ Date _____

1. **Which of the following statements best represents the author's purpose in writing about the World Series?**

   Ⓐ The teams that play in the World Series should both be from the National League.

   Ⓑ The New York Giants did not have a good reason for refusing to play in 1904.

   Ⓒ Teams that get to the World Series have worked hard for months.

   Ⓓ A World Series is not complete without a good snack to eat.

2. **If the headline "World Series Deemed Unnecessary" appeared in a local paper, how might the author of the story on the previous page respond?**

   _____
   _____
   _____
   _____

3. **If you were looking at the following titles in a local bookstore, which would you guess was written by the author of this piece?**

   Ⓕ *Baseball Foul-Ups Through the Ages*

   Ⓖ *A Comprehensive History of Sports*

   Ⓗ *The Most Exciting Games of the World Series*

   Ⓙ *Reasons to Abolish Baseball Leagues*

4. **What is your opinion about the World Series? Do you think it is the most exciting and important sporting event of the year? Write a few sentences in which you support your opinion.**

   _____
   _____
   _____
   _____
   _____
   _____
   _____
   _____
   _____
   _____
   _____
   _____
   _____
   _____
   _____
   _____
   _____
   _____

© Carson-Dellosa Publishing

Name _____ Date _____

Language Arts   Literature

3.F

Finding Favorites

DIRECTIONS: Borrow a fiction, nonfiction, biography, and poetry book from the library. Read them and write a brief summary of each.

1. **Title of fiction book** _____

    Summary: _____
    _____
    _____
    _____
    _____

2. **Title of nonfiction book** _____

    Summary: _____
    _____
    _____
    _____
    _____

3. **Title of biography** _____

    Summary: _____
    _____
    _____
    _____
    _____

4. **Title of poetry book** _____

    Summary: _____
    _____
    _____
    _____
    _____

5. What are the main differences in the books you chose?
    _____
    _____
    _____
    _____
    _____
    _____
    _____

6. In what ways are the books you chose the same?
    _____
    _____
    _____
    _____
    _____
    _____
    _____
    _____
    _____

7. Which genre did you like the most? Why?
    _____
    _____
    _____
    _____
    _____
    _____
    _____

STOP

Name _____ Date _____

Language Arts   **Literature**

3.G   # Creating a Written Work

DIRECTIONS: Use the space below and extra paper as needed to produce a written work in the genre of your choice. Some suggested genres include short story, poem, personal narrative, expository composition, or persuasive essay. Use the following descriptions to help you choose the genre you would like to use.

- A **short story** should include plot, setting, and point of view. Use sensory details to develop characters.
- A **poem** should include literary techniques such as rhythm, rhyme, and imaginative language.
- A **personal narrative** is a true story with a clear beginning, middle, and end.
- An **expository composition** tells about or explains something of interest.
- A **persuasive essay** tries to get others to accept a certain point of view. It should include plenty of supporting details and a convincing conclusion.

_____
_____
_____
_____
_____
_____
_____
_____
_____
_____
_____
_____
_____
_____
_____
_____
_____
_____
_____
_____

© Carson-Dellosa Publishing

Language Arts 3.0

Mini-Test 3

For pages 36–51

Literature

DIRECTIONS: Read the passage. Then, answer the questions.

Survivors

As far as Kiki was concerned, the island had always been her home, and she loved it. She had been just about a year old when the ship she and her family had been on was caught in a great storm. She didn't remember their home in England, where she had been born, or boarding the ship for Australia. Kiki certainly didn't remember how her family and a few dozen others had arrived on the island in lifeboats, or even how they had built houses and made new lives.

The Martin family and the others who had survived the shipwreck had worked hard to make the island livable. In the weeks following the wreck, chests of seeds, tools, and food washed up on the beach. These chests gave the survivors a chance to build a new life on the island. Now, ten years after the disaster, the island was a wonderful place to live. Everyone had a comfortable home and there was plenty of food.

Kiki and the other children explored the island every day. It was on one of these outings that they saw the great ships. The children had climbed to the top of the highest peak on the island to study the sea birds that nested on the cliffs below. When they reached the top of the peak, Kiki spotted the four ships sailing toward the island.

By the time Kiki and her friends climbed down the mountain, the ships had reached the island and the captain and crew were surprised to find English settlers there. They had known about the shipwreck, of course, but they had no idea there were survivors. The ships were heading to Australia, and the survivors were welcomed to join the crew on board.

That, however, was the problem. Almost all the survivors didn't want to leave the island, especially the children like Kiki who had spent most of their lives there or the dozen who had been born there. For them, the island was their world, and they couldn't imagine leaving it.

1. What is the main idea of this story?
   - Ⓐ how people lived after a shipwreck
   - Ⓑ explorers discovering a deserted island
   - Ⓒ children studying sea birds
   - Ⓓ a family's journey to Australia

2. What helped the survivors begin their new lives on the island?
   - Ⓕ having the children explore the island
   - Ⓖ memories of England
   - Ⓗ the captain and crew of the ships sailing to Australia
   - Ⓙ supplies that washed up on the beach

3. How do you suppose Kiki will feel if her family decides to leave the island?
   - Ⓐ disappointed
   - Ⓒ proud
   - Ⓑ excited
   - Ⓓ happy

4. If the children could vote on whether to leave the island or to stay, which of these would probably happen?
   - Ⓕ Most would vote to leave.
   - Ⓖ Most would vote to stay.
   - Ⓗ Most would not vote.
   - Ⓙ There would be a tie.

5. What do you know about the island from reading this passage?
   - Ⓐ The island has a desert climate.
   - Ⓑ There are cliffs on the island.
   - Ⓒ There are palm trees on the island.
   - Ⓓ Dangerous animals live on the island.

52 © Carson-Dellosa Publishing

How Am I Doing?

Mini-Test 1 Page 20 **Number Correct**	4 answers correct	**Great Job!** Move on to the section test on page 54.
	3 answers correct	**You're almost there!** But you still need a little practice. Review the practice pages 8–19 before moving on to the section test on page 54.
	0–2 answers correct	**Oops!** Time to review what you have learned and try again. Review the practice section on pages 8–19. Then, retake the test on page 20. Now, move on to the section test on page 54.

Mini-Test 2 Page 34 **Number Correct**	6–7 answers correct	**Awesome!** Move on to the section test on page 54.
	4–5 answers correct	**You're almost there!** But you still need a little practice. Review the practice pages 22–33 before moving on to the section test on page 54.
	0–3 answers correct	**Oops!** Time to review what you have learned and try again. Review the practice section on pages 22–33. Then, retake the test on page 34. Now, move on to the section test on page 54.

Mini-Test 3 Page 52 **Number Correct**	5 answers correct	**Great Job!** Move on to the section test on page 54.
	3–4 answers correct	**You're almost there!** But you still need a little practice. Review the practice pages 36–51 before moving on to the section test on page 54.
	0–2 answers correct	**Oops!** Time to review what you have learned and try again. Review the practice section on pages 36–51. Then, retake the test on page 52. Now, move on to the section test on page 54.

© Carson-Dellosa Publishing

Name _____ Date _____

Final Language Arts Test
for pages 8–52

DIRECTIONS: Read each passage. Then, answer the questions.

An urban habitat is home to many animals. Birds like pigeons and starlings nest on tall buildings. Mice and rats build their nests in or near buildings. Squirrels, rabbits, and opossums make their homes in the wide-open spaces of city parks. Timid animals like foxes and raccoons search for food in neighborhood garbage cans at night. Perhaps the favorite city animals, though, are the ones that live in the homes of people—cats, dogs, and other animal friends we call pets.

1. **What would be a good title for this passage?**
   - Ⓐ Pests Among Us
   - Ⓑ City Critters
   - Ⓒ A Nocturnal Nuisance
   - Ⓓ An Urban Legend

2. **What is the main idea of this passage?**
   - Ⓕ People should protect city animals.
   - Ⓖ Urban animals cause many problems.
   - Ⓗ Many animals live in the city.
   - Ⓙ People who live in cities should not have pets.

3. **If the author wanted to continue describing urban habitats, what would be a good topic for the next paragraph?**
   - Ⓐ career opportunities in cities
   - Ⓑ urban crime
   - Ⓒ city schools
   - Ⓓ plants that can be found in cities

4. **What is the author's purpose for writing this passage?**
   - Ⓕ to tell people about animals that live in urban habitats
   - Ⓖ to warn people about urban animals
   - Ⓗ to present a plan to city officials about protecting animals
   - Ⓙ to explain how people and animals work together

Today was very busy. Jane, Carl, and I went out around 8:00 to fill our buckets with blackberries. It was hard work, and we didn't get back until it was time for lunch. This afternoon, Aunt Mara showed us how to wash and sort the berries. When it was time to make jam, Aunt Mara did the cooking part. Then, she let us fill the jars and decorate the labels. Now, Aunt Mara is letting me take a jar of jam home for Mom. She'll be surprised that I helped make it. I hope the rest of my stay here is as much fun as today was.

5. **What was the first thing the narrator did?**
   - Ⓐ picked blackberries
   - Ⓑ ate lunch
   - Ⓒ decorated labels
   - Ⓓ washed berries

6. **Who cooked the berries?**
   - Ⓕ the narrator
   - Ⓖ Jane
   - Ⓗ Carl
   - Ⓙ Aunt Mara

7. **How does the narrator feel about this experience?**
   - Ⓐ frustrated
   - Ⓑ surprised
   - Ⓒ happy
   - Ⓓ angry

8. **When did the children pick the berries?**
   - Ⓕ at night
   - Ⓖ in the afternoon
   - Ⓗ in the evening
   - Ⓙ in the morning

Name _____ Date _____

DIRECTIONS: Choose the answer that best completes the sentence.

9. Jeff and Channa _____ us make bread.
   - Ⓐ had help
   - Ⓑ will help
   - Ⓒ helps
   - Ⓓ helping

10. No one _____ him about the change of plans.
    - Ⓕ telled
    - Ⓖ told
    - Ⓗ tells
    - Ⓙ did tell

DIRECTIONS: Choose the answer that uses an incorrect verb.

11.
    - Ⓐ The library have a room for music.
    - Ⓑ In the room, you can listen to tapes.
    - Ⓒ The room has lots of books about music.
    - Ⓓ I love spending time there.

12.
    - Ⓕ Chang has picked up her heavy backpack.
    - Ⓖ She carry that backpack everywhere.
    - Ⓗ It has all her art supplies in it.
    - Ⓙ She also carries her laptop in the backpack.

13.
    - Ⓐ He forgot to take his jacket home.
    - Ⓑ It was a cold day.
    - Ⓒ He shiver without his jacket.
    - Ⓓ He was very glad to get home at last.

14.
    - Ⓕ Nobody is home today.
    - Ⓖ The house are locked up.
    - Ⓗ It looks strange with the shades down.
    - Ⓙ I am not used to seeing it so empty.

DIRECTIONS: Decide which punctuation mark, if any, is needed in the underlined part of each sentence.

15. The puppy couldn't find the food <u>dish</u>
    - Ⓐ ,
    - Ⓑ .
    - Ⓒ ?
    - Ⓓ None

16. "This is <u>fun,</u> answered Lettie.
    - Ⓕ ,
    - Ⓖ ?
    - Ⓗ "
    - Ⓙ None

17. <u>Jeff</u> will you please bring in the newspaper?
    - Ⓐ !
    - Ⓑ ,
    - Ⓒ ?
    - Ⓓ None

18. <u>Lisa</u> brother is studying to be a dentist.
    - Ⓕ .
    - Ⓖ 's
    - Ⓗ ,
    - Ⓙ None

Name _____ Date _____

DIRECTIONS: Find the word that is spelled correctly and fits best in the blank.

19. Please _____ your work.
    - (A) revew
    - (B) reeview
    - (C) review
    - (D) raview

20. He is my best _____ .
    - (F) frind
    - (G) frend
    - (H) friend
    - (J) freind

21. We can _____ the gymnasium.
    - (A) decarate
    - (B) decorait
    - (C) decorrate
    - (D) decorate

22. The store is in a good _____ .
    - (F) locashun
    - (G) locashin
    - (H) locatin
    - (J) location

23. Students were _____ for bravery.
    - (A) honored
    - (B) honord
    - (C) honered
    - (D) honard

DIRECTIONS: Read the paragraph below. Find the sentence that does not belong in the paragraph.

(1) Gregory's father worked for the Wildlife Department. (2) One day, he came to Gregory's class carrying a small cage. (3) When Gregory's father left, the students discussed his visit. (4) When he opened the top of the cage, a furry little raccoon popped out.

24.
   - (F) Sentence 1
   - (G) Sentence 2
   - (H) Sentence 3
   - (J) Sentence 4

DIRECTIONS: Read the paragraph below. Find the sentence that best fits the blank in the paragraph.

The first comic books were made in 1911. But it wasn't until 1933 that they really became popular. The first best-selling comic books were created by two high school students named Jerry Siegel and Joe Schuster. _____. He performed amazing feats.

25.
   - (A) Some people are comic book collectors.
   - (B) They wrote their own science fiction magazine about a superhero.
   - (C) Nowadays, comic books are created by publishing companies.
   - (D) Comic books are sold in stores all over the world.

Name _____ Date _____

DIRECTIONS: Read each passage. Then, answer the questions.

Police officers carry equipment that helps them to protect themselves and other people. They carry guns, nightsticks, flashlights, and handcuffs on their belts. Some wear bullet-proof vests. They also carry two-way radios so they can call other officers for assistance.

26. **The above passage is _____ .**
    - (F) a poem
    - (G) nonfiction
    - (H) fiction
    - (J) a play

27. **Why would police officers need equipment for protection?**
    - (A) because they teach people about the laws
    - (B) because they are trained to use the equipment
    - (C) because sometimes their work can be dangerous
    - (D) because they need to write reports

I was so nervous. I hadn't seen Abbie in three years, not since my mom got that new job. I remember the day we moved away. Abbie brought me our photograph in a frame. I gave her a necklace with a friendship charm on it. We promised to stay friends forever. Now that I was finally going to see her again, I wondered if we would still like the same kinds of things and laugh at the same kinds of jokes. I rubbed my sweaty palms on my jeans as we pulled into Abbie's driveway.

28. **Why hasn't the narrator seen Abbie for three years?**
    - (F) they were best friends
    - (G) because they didn't like each other's gifts
    - (H) because they had a fight
    - (J) because the narrator had to move away

29. **Why are the narrator's palms sweaty?**
    - (A) because she is nervous
    - (B) because she has a fever
    - (C) because she feels sick
    - (D) because she doesn't want to move

30. **The passage gives you enough information to believe that the narrator _____ .**
    - (F) was angry at her mom for making her move
    - (G) had a special friendship with Abbie
    - (H) liked her new school
    - (J) doesn't keep her promises

31. **The narrator will feel happy if _____ .**
    - (A) Abbie is not home
    - (B) Abbie has changed a lot
    - (C) she gets to move again
    - (D) she and Abbie still get along

Name _____ Date _____

Final Language Arts Test
Answer Sheet

1. Ⓐ Ⓑ Ⓒ Ⓓ
2. Ⓕ Ⓖ Ⓗ Ⓙ
3. Ⓐ Ⓑ Ⓒ Ⓓ
4. Ⓕ Ⓖ Ⓗ Ⓙ
5. Ⓐ Ⓑ Ⓒ Ⓓ
6. Ⓕ Ⓖ Ⓗ Ⓙ
7. Ⓐ Ⓑ Ⓒ Ⓓ
8. Ⓕ Ⓖ Ⓗ Ⓙ
9. Ⓐ Ⓑ Ⓒ Ⓓ
10. Ⓕ Ⓖ Ⓗ Ⓙ

11. Ⓐ Ⓑ Ⓒ Ⓓ
12. Ⓕ Ⓖ Ⓗ Ⓙ
13. Ⓐ Ⓑ Ⓒ Ⓓ
14. Ⓕ Ⓖ Ⓗ Ⓙ
15. Ⓐ Ⓑ Ⓒ Ⓓ
16. Ⓕ Ⓖ Ⓗ Ⓙ
17. Ⓐ Ⓑ Ⓒ Ⓓ
18. Ⓕ Ⓖ Ⓗ Ⓙ
19. Ⓐ Ⓑ Ⓒ Ⓓ
20. Ⓕ Ⓖ Ⓗ Ⓙ

21. Ⓐ Ⓑ Ⓒ Ⓓ
22. Ⓕ Ⓖ Ⓗ Ⓙ
23. Ⓐ Ⓑ Ⓒ Ⓓ
24. Ⓕ Ⓖ Ⓗ Ⓙ
25. Ⓐ Ⓑ Ⓒ Ⓓ
26. Ⓕ Ⓖ Ⓗ Ⓙ
27. Ⓐ Ⓑ Ⓒ Ⓓ
28. Ⓕ Ⓖ Ⓗ Ⓙ
29. Ⓐ Ⓑ Ⓒ Ⓓ
30. Ⓕ Ⓖ Ⓗ Ⓙ

31. Ⓐ Ⓑ Ⓒ Ⓓ

© Carson-Dellosa Publishing

New York Mathematics Content Standards

The mathematics section of the New York City Standards measures knowledge in five different areas.

1. Arithmetic and Number Concepts
2. Geometry and Measurement Concepts
3. Function and Algebra Concepts
4. Statistics and Probability Concepts
5. Mathematical Process

The mathematics section of the New York State Standards measures knowledge in two different areas:

1. **Analysis, Inquiry, and Design**
   - *1.1:* Mathematical Analysis
3. **Mathematics**
   - *3.1:* Mathematical Reasoning
   - *3.2:* Number and Numeration
   - *3.3:* Operations
   - *3.4:* Modeling/Multiple Representation
   - *3.5:* Measurement
   - *3.6:* Uncertainty
   - *3.7:* Patterns/Functions

New York Mathematics Table of Contents

Arithmetic and Number Concepts
- Standards and What They Mean 60
- Practice Pages 62
- Mini-Test 1 87

Geometry and Measurement Concepts
- Standards and What They Mean 89
- Practice Pages 90
- Mini-Test 2 104

Function and Algebra Concepts
- Standards and What They Mean 105
- Practice Pages 106
- Mini-Test 3 115

Statistics and Probability Concepts
- Standards and What They Mean 116
- Practice Pages 117
- Mini-Test 4 128

Mathematical Process
- Standards and What They Mean 129
- Practice Pages 130
- Mini-Test 5 136

How Am I Doing? 137

Final Mathematics Test 139

Answer Sheet 143

Mathematics Standards

1.0 Arithmetic and Number Concepts
By the end of the school year, students should:

1.A Use knowledge of place value and expanded notation to read and write numbers up to one billion and decimal numbers through thousandths. *(See pages 62–63.)*

What it means:
- Students should be able to identify place values on both sides of a decimal point (ones, tens, hundreds, and thousands to the left of the decimal point, and tenths, hundredths, and thousandths to the right of the decimal point).

1.B Explore powers of ten as another way of naming large numbers. *(See page 64.)*

1.C Estimate whole numbers by rounding to the nearest thousand and ten thousand and decimals to the nearest tenth and hundredth. *(See page 65.)*

1.D Use estimation to check the reasonableness of results. *(See page 66.)*

What it means:
- Students should be able to estimate an answer and recognize when the answer is not reasonable. For instance, students should be able to estimate that 3 dozen eggs is about 30 and that 300 is not a reasonable answer.

1.E Identify differences between prime and composite numbers. *(See page 67.)*

What it means:
- A **prime number** is divisible only by itself and one. For example, *11* is prime.
- A **composite number** is divisible by other numbers. For example, *24* is composite.

1.F Use addition, subtraction, multiplication, and division facts efficiently and accurately. *(See page 68.)*

What it means:
- Students should be able to use multiplication to check answers to division problems (e.g., $6 \div 2 = 3$; $3 \times 2 = 6$) and use division to check answers to multiplication problems (e.g., $4 \times 2 = 8$; $8 \div 2 = 4$). They should know that any number multiplied or divided by *1* is that number (e.g., $432 \times 1 = 432$; $432 \div 1 = 432$). They should also know that any number multiplied by *0* is *0* (e.g., $432 \times 0 = 0$) and that dividing a number by *0* is not possible.

1.G Add and subtract large numbers. *(See page 69.)*

1.H Multiply by 3-digit numbers. *(See page 70.)*

1.I Divide by 2-digit divisors. *(See page 71.)*

1.J Understand the difference between proper and improper fractions. *(See page 72.)*

What it means:
- A **proper fraction** is one in which the numerator is less than the denominator (e.g., $\frac{1}{2}$). An improper fraction is one in which the numerator is larger than or equal to the denominator (e.g., $\frac{5}{3}$).

1.K Change improper fractions to equivalent mixed numbers and vice-versa. *(See page 72.)*

1.L Find the greatest common factor and least common multiple of a set of numbers. *(See page 73.)*

What it means:
- **Common factors** are numbers that are factors for more than one number. For example, the factors of 12 are 1, 2, 3, 4, 6, and 12. The factors for 15 are 1, 3, 5, and 15. The common factors for 12 and 15 would be 1 and 3.
- The **lowest common multiple** is the smallest number that 2 or more numbers will divide into evenly. For example, the least common multiple for 3 and 4 is 12.

1.M Use factor trees to find the prime factorization of a number. *(See page 74.)*

What it means:
- **Prime factorization** is showing any number as the product of its primes. For example, $16 = 2 \times 2 \times 2 \times 2$ or 2^4 or $36 = 2 \times 2 \times 3 \times 3$ or $2^2 \times 3^2$.

1.N Add and subtract fractions and mixed numbers with like and unlike denominators and express fractions in simplest form. *(See pages 75–76.)*

1.O Multiply with fractions. *(See page 77.)*

1.P Explore division with fractions. *(See page 77.)*

1.Q Find equivalent fractions. *(See page 78.)*

1.R Add and subtract decimal numbers. *(See page 79.)*

1.S Multiply decimals to the hundredths place. *(See page 80.)*

1.T Explore dividing decimals without remainders (to hundredths). *(See page 80.)*

1.U Relate dividing decimals to the monetary system (e.g., $4.50 divided by 3). *(See page 81.)*

1.V Compare relationships among fractions, decimals, and percents (e.g., $\frac{1}{4} = \frac{25}{100} = 0.25 = 25\%$). *(See page 82.)*

1.W Compare decimals and fractions using the terms less than, greater than, between, and equivalent. *(See page 83.)*

1.X Use positive and negative numbers to represent changes in quantities in real situations. *(See page 84.)*

1.Y Use a number line to identify and compare positive and negative numbers. *(See page 85.)*

1.Z Explore adding integers using the number line (positive and negative numbers). *(See page 86.)*

Name _____ Date _____

Mathematics

Using Place Value and Expanded Notation

Arithmetic and Number Concepts

DIRECTIONS: Choose the best answer.

1. 597,346 =
   - (A) five million, ninety-seven thousand, three hundred forty-six
   - (B) five hundred ninety-seven million, three hundred forty-six
   - (C) five hundred ninety-seven, three hundred forty-six
   - (D) five hundred ninety-seven thousand, three hundred forty-six

2. Which of these is 7,207,354?
   - (F) seven million, two hundred thousand, three hundred fifty-four
   - (G) seven hundred twenty-seven thousand, three hundred fifty-four
   - (H) seven million, two hundred seven thousand, three hundred fifty-four
   - (J) seven million, twenty-seven thousand, three hundred fifty-four

3. Which is the numeral for six million, three hundred seventy-nine thousand, five hundred forty-one?
   - (A) 637,541
   - (B) 6,379,541
   - (C) 6,397,541
   - (D) 637,941

4. In which numeral is there a 5 in both the tens and the ten thousands place?
   - (F) 1,505,925
   - (G) 5,501,658
   - (H) 7,356,259
   - (J) 2,459,519

5. Which of these lists shows the numbers in order from smallest to largest?
   - (A) 562,423   85,264   9,156
   - (B) 56   891   3,210
   - (C) 653   74   89
   - (D) 9,547   5,632   3,527

6. Which of these has a 4 in the hundredths place?
   - (F) 4.523
   - (G) 8.634
   - (H) 3.844
   - (J) 7.498

7. Which of these is 56.84?
   - (A) fifty-six and eighty-four hundredths
   - (B) fifty-six hundred and eighty-four
   - (C) fifty-six and eighty-four tenths
   - (D) fifty-six and eighty-four

62 © Carson-Dellosa Publishing

Name _____ Date _____

8. **Which group of decimals is ordered from least to greatest?**
   - (F) 4.482, 4.483, 4.481, 4.408
   - (G) 4.576, 4.432, 4.678, 4.104
   - (H) 4.978, 4.652, 4.331, 4.320
   - (J) 4.269, 4.692, 4.699, 4.732

9. **Which decimal shows how much of the shape is shaded?**

   - (A) 0.23
   - (B) 0.27
   - (C) 0.49
   - (D) 0.72

10. **What is the value of 6 in 89.634?**
    - (F) 6 tens
    - (G) 6 hundreds
    - (H) 6 tenths
    - (J) 6 hundredths

DIRECTIONS: The following numbers are written in expanded form. Write each number in standard form.

11. $100{,}000 + 2{,}000 + 300 + 70 + 5 + \frac{3}{10} + \frac{4}{100}$

    _____

12. $20{,}000 + 5{,}000 + 40 + 3 + \frac{2}{10}$

    _____

13. $700{,}000 + 80{,}000 + 2{,}000 + 400 + 60 + \frac{2}{10{,}000}$

    _____

14. $200{,}000{,}000 + 100{,}000 + 4{,}000 + 30 + 1 + \frac{4}{100{,}000}$

    _____

15. $9{,}000{,}000 + 600{,}000 + 50{,}000 + 300$

    _____

DIRECTIONS: Write each whole number in expanded form.

16. 1,200,341 _____

17. 10,650.003 _____

18. 238,200.05 _____

19. 563.00201 _____

20. 4,070,004 _____

Name _____ Date _____

Mathematics 1.B

Using Powers of Ten

Arithmetic and Number Concepts

DIRECTIONS: Choose the best answer.

1. The 7 in 68,745 means _____ .
   - Ⓐ 7×10^1
   - Ⓑ 7×10^2
   - Ⓒ 7×10^3
   - Ⓓ 7×10^4

2. 4,000,000 = _____
   - Ⓕ 4×10^6
   - Ⓖ 4×10^7
   - Ⓗ 4×10^8
   - Ⓙ 4×10^9

3. 3×10^5 = _____
   - Ⓐ 30,000,000
   - Ⓑ 3,000,000
   - Ⓒ 300,000
   - Ⓓ 30,000

4. 7,813 = _____
   - Ⓕ $(7 \times 10^2) + (8 \times 10^2) + 10^2 + 3^2$
   - Ⓖ $(7 \times 10^4) + (8 \times 10^3) + 10^2 + 3$
   - Ⓗ $(7 \times 10^3) + (8 \times 10^2) + 10^1 + 3$
   - Ⓙ $(7 \times 10^4) + (8 \times 10^3) + 10^2 + (3 \times 10^1)$

5. One billion is the same as _____ .
   - Ⓐ 10^9
   - Ⓑ 10^{10}
   - Ⓒ 10^{11}
   - Ⓓ 10^{12}

6. The 5 in 54,112 means _____ .
   - Ⓕ 1×10^5
   - Ⓖ 5×10^4
   - Ⓗ 10×5^5
   - Ⓙ 5×10^3

7. 60,000 = _____
   - Ⓐ 6×10^3
   - Ⓑ 6×10^4
   - Ⓒ 6×10^5
   - Ⓓ 6×10^6

8. 2×10^3 = _____
   - Ⓕ 20
   - Ⓖ 200
   - Ⓗ 2,000
   - Ⓙ 20,000

9. 51,940 = _____
   - Ⓐ $(5 \times 10^4) + (1 \times 10^3) + (9 \times 10^2) + 4$
   - Ⓑ $(5 \times 10^5) + (1 \times 10^4) + (9 \times 10^3) + (4 \times 10^2)$
   - Ⓒ $(5 \times 10^6) + (1 \times 10^5) + (9 \times 10^4) + 4^3$
   - Ⓓ $(5 \times 10^4) + (1 \times 10^3) + (9 \times 10^2) + (4 \times 10^1)$

10. The 3 in 3,981 means _____ .
    - Ⓕ 3×10^1
    - Ⓖ 10×3^4
    - Ⓗ 3×10^2
    - Ⓙ 3×10^3

11. One million is the same as _____ .
    - Ⓐ 10^5
    - Ⓑ 10^6
    - Ⓒ 10^7
    - Ⓓ 10^8

12. 9×10^8 = _____
    - Ⓕ 9,000,000
    - Ⓖ 90,000,000
    - Ⓗ 900,000,000
    - Ⓙ 9,000,000,000

Name _____ Date _____

Mathematics
1.C

Rounding Numbers

Arithmetic and Number Concepts

DIRECTIONS: Choose the best answer.

1. What is 385,001 rounded to the nearest ten thousand?
   - (A) 100,000
   - (B) 350,000
   - (C) 390,000
   - (D) 400,000

2. What is 455,398 rounded to the nearest thousand?
   - (F) 455,390
   - (G) 455,400
   - (H) 450,000
   - (J) 455,000

3. What is 138,981 rounded to the nearest ten thousand?
   - (A) 100,000
   - (B) 139,000
   - (C) 140,000
   - (D) 200,000

4. What is 138,981 rounded to the nearest thousand?
   - (F) 100,000
   - (G) 139,000
   - (H) 140,000
   - (J) 200,000

5. What is 0.19 rounded to the nearest tenth?
   - (A) 0.2
   - (B) 0.3
   - (C) 0.4
   - (D) 0.5

6. What is 0.467 rounded to the nearest hundredth?
   - (F) 0.40
   - (G) 0.45
   - (H) 0.46
   - (J) 0.47

7. What is 0.234 rounded to the nearest hundredth?
   - (A) 0.20
   - (B) 0.22
   - (C) 0.23
   - (D) 0.24

8. What is 26,489 rounded to the nearest thousand?
   - (F) 26,490
   - (G) 26,000
   - (H) 26,500
   - (J) 27,000

9. What is 0.32 rounded to the nearest tenth?
   - (A) 0.2
   - (B) 0.3
   - (C) 0.33
   - (D) 0.4

10. What is 0.783 rounded to the nearest hundredth?
    - (F) 0.79
    - (G) 0.80
    - (H) 0.70
    - (J) 0.78

STOP

© Carson-Dellosa Publishing

Name _____ Date _____

Mathematics

Estimating

Arithmetic and Number Concepts

DIRECTIONS: Choose the best answer by estimating.

1. It costs $15.75 per student to take a field trip to the aquarium. If 10 students go on the trip, what is the estimated total cost?
   - (A) $255
   - (B) $260
   - (C) $190
   - (D) $160

2. A Tasmanian devil weighs 12,025 grams. A mole weighs about $\frac{1}{200}$ of what a Tasmanian devil weighs. About how much does a mole weigh?
   - (F) 60 grams
   - (G) 600 grams
   - (H) 240,000 grams
   - (J) 2,400,000 grams

3. Stacey spent $14.83 at the store. Harry spent $35.32 at the store. Approximately how much more did Harry spend than Stacey?
   - (A) $21
   - (B) $20
   - (C) $50
   - (D) $44

4. Golden lion tamarins are an endangered species. Only about 416 still live in the wild. They live in groups of 8. About how many groups still live in the wild if there are 416 golden lion tamarins?
   - (F) 50
   - (G) 55
   - (H) 40
   - (J) 35

5. I am a number. I am the smallest number that can become 500 when it's rounded to the nearest 10. What number am I?
   - (A) 495
   - (B) 501
   - (C) 450
   - (D) 549

6. I am a number. I am the largest whole number that must equal two thousand when rounded to the nearest thousand. What number am I?
   - (F) 1,999
   - (G) 2,999
   - (H) 2,499
   - (J) 1,499

7. Nadia sailed 3.8 hours a day for 5 days. About how many hours did Nadia sail all together?
   - (A) 25 hours
   - (B) 20 hours
   - (C) 18 hours
   - (D) 15.5 hours

8. I am an amount of U.S. money. I am the cost of five $0.88 hamburgers rounded to the nearest dollar. How much money am I?
   - (F) $4
   - (G) $5
   - (H) $3
   - (J) $6

Name _____ Date _____

Mathematics 1.E — Prime and Composite Numbers

Arithmetic and Number Concepts

DIRECTIONS: Choose the best answer.

> **Clue:** A **composite number** is divisible by other numbers besides 1 and itself.

1. Does this figure represent a prime number?
   - (A) yes
   - (B) no

2. Which factors are *not* represented by the figure?
   - (F) 4 × 5
   - (G) 2 × 2 × 5
   - (H) 2 × 10
   - (J) 3 × 5

3. Does this figure represent a prime number?

   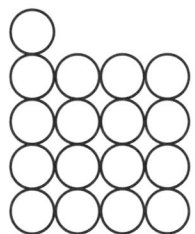

   - (A) yes
   - (B) no

4. Which number is a factor of both of the numbers represented by the figures?

   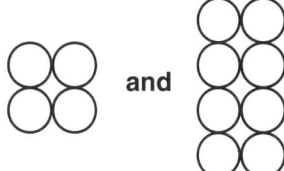 and

   - (F) 3
   - (G) 4
   - (H) 5
   - (J) 6

5. Does this figure represent a prime number?
   - (A) yes
   - (B) no

6. A prime number has exactly two factors, Itself and _____.
   - (F) 2
   - (G) 4
   - (H) 0
   - (J) 1

7. Does this figure represent a prime number?
   - (A) yes
   - (B) no

© Carson-Dellosa Publishing

Name _____ Date _____

Mathematics

Using Arithmetic Facts

Arithmetic and Number Concepts

DIRECTION: Choose the best answer.

1. 76 people live in Harold's apartment building. In Mike's apartment building, there are 85 people. How many more people live in Mike's building than in Harold's building?
   - (A) 161
   - (B) 9
   - (C) 76
   - (D) 85

2. Each new bus can carry 66 passengers. How many passengers can ride on 85 new buses?
   - (F) 561
   - (G) 151
   - (H) 19
   - (J) 5,610

3. The stakes in Jack's croquet set are 2 feet long. He drove one stake $\frac{3}{4}$ foot into the ground. How much of the stake is above ground?
   - (A) $1\frac{1}{4}$ feet
   - (B) 2 feet
   - (C) $\frac{3}{4}$ foot
   - (D) 1 foot

4. There are 336 cases on a truck. The truck will make 12 stops and leave the same number of cases at each stop. How many cases will be left at each stop?
   - (F) 4,032
   - (G) 324
   - (H) 28
   - (J) 48

5. Mrs. Robins drives 19 miles every working day. How many miles does she drive in a five-day workweek?
   - (A) 24
   - (B) 95
   - (C) 14
   - (D) 4

6. There are 160 packages on 4 large carts. Each cart holds the same number of packages. How many packages are on each cart?
   - (F) 640
   - (G) 40
   - (H) 156
   - (J) 164

7. Sarah's father worked 36 hours one week and 47 hours the next week. How many hours did he work during these two weeks?
   - (A) 11
   - (B) 83
   - (C) 1,692
   - (D) 80

STOP

Name _____ Date _____

Mathematics

Adding and Subtracting Large Numbers

Arithmetic and Number Concepts

DIRECTIONS: Find the correct answers.

Examples:

```
  584        297     Check addition by
+ 297      + 584     adding in reverse.
  881        881

  701        235     Check subtraction
- 466      + 466     with addition.
  235        701
```

1.
   28,153
− 17,745

2.
   49,853
+ 83,289

3.
  8,466
+ 7,907

4.
  84,542
− 9,368

5.
  642,017
− 568,726

6.
  7,431
+ 6,214

7.
  52,814
+ 7,623

8.
  74,222
+ 6,787

9.
  872
− 593

10.
  8,466
+ 7,907

11.
  3,001
−   597

12.
  7,210
+ 6,143

© Carson-Dellosa Publishing

Mathematics 1.H — Multiplying by 3-Digit Numbers

Arithmetic and Number Concepts

DIRECTIONS: Find the correct answer.

Examples:

```
    468    Multiplicand            987              850
  × 375    Multiplier            × 645            × 470
   2340    1st Partial Product    4935              000
  32760    2nd Partial Product   39480            59500
 140400    3rd Partial Product  592200           340000
175,500    Product              636,615          399,500
```

1. 804
   × 408

2. 700
   × 840

3. 500
   × 902

4. 678
   × 386

5. 762
   × 691

6. 398
   × 421

7. 703
   × 307

8. 843
   × 658

9. 504
   × 405

10. 874
   × 981

11. 426
   × 721

12. 638
   × 247

Name _____ Date _____

Mathematics
1.1

Dividing by 2-Digit Numbers

Arithmetic and Number Concepts

DIRECTIONS: Find the correct answers.

1. 89)25276
2. 27)743
3. 15)405
4. 62)984
5. 45)28260

6. 35)7623
7. 12)7641
8. 65)8125
9. 81)71037
10. 96)81312

11. 79)75208
12. 27)6529
13. 42)28182
14. 44)38412
15. 81)48114

16. 56)5178
17. 84)4361
18. 36)5436
19. 97)3522
20. 61)5536

© Carson-Dellosa Publishing

Name _____ Date _____

Mathematics

1.J/1.K **Proper and Improper Fractions**

Arithmetic and Number Concepts

DIRECTIONS: Write a **P** beside each of the proper fractions. Write an **I** beside each of the improper fractions.

A **proper fraction** is one in which the numerator is less than the denominator. An **improper fraction** is one in which the numerator is equal to or greater than the denominator.

1. $\frac{1}{4}$ _____
2. $\frac{4}{1}$ _____
3. $\frac{7}{8}$ _____
4. $\frac{3}{4}$ _____
5. $\frac{13}{15}$ _____

6. $\frac{10}{3}$ _____
7. $\frac{6}{4}$ _____
8. $\frac{4}{7}$ _____
9. $\frac{9}{17}$ _____
10. $\frac{5}{2}$ _____

11. $\frac{11}{7}$ _____
12. $\frac{1}{2}$ _____
13. $\frac{2}{3}$ _____
14. $\frac{5}{3}$ _____
15. $\frac{2}{2}$ _____

DIRECTIONS: Change each improper fraction to a mixed number. Reduce each fraction part to its simplest form.

16. $\frac{25}{9} =$
17. $\frac{18}{3} =$
18. $\frac{8}{7} =$
19. $\frac{26}{4} =$
20. $\frac{11}{6} =$

21. $\frac{7}{3} =$
22. $\frac{27}{6} =$
23. $\frac{9}{4} =$
24. $\frac{8}{5} =$
25. $\frac{14}{3} =$

DIRECTIONS: Change each mixed number to an improper fraction. Use the same denominator for the improper fraction as shown in the mixed number.

26. $3\frac{1}{4}$
27. $4\frac{1}{4}$
28. $1\frac{5}{7}$
29. $5\frac{3}{10}$
30. $4\frac{4}{7}$

31. $6\frac{5}{6}$
32. $5\frac{5}{8}$
33. $7\frac{2}{5}$
34. $7\frac{1}{3}$
35. $3\frac{4}{15}$

STOP

72

© Carson-Dellosa Publishing

Name _____ Date _____

Mathematics

Greatest Common Factors and Least Common Multiples

Arithmetic and Number Concepts

DIRECTIONS: Choose the best answer.

Example:

Common factors are numbers that are factors for more than one number. For example: **Factors of 12:** 1, 2, 3, 4, 6, 12; **Factors of 15:** 1, 3, 5, 15; The common factors for 12 and 15 are 1 and 3.

The **least common multiple** is the smallest number that two or more numbers will divide into evenly. For example: **Multiples of 3:** 3, 6, 9, 12, 15, and so on; **Multiples of 4:** 4, 8, 12, 16, 20, and so on; The least common multiple of 3 and 4 is 12.

1. What is the greatest common factor of 42 and 54?
    - (A) 6
    - (B) 7
    - (C) 4
    - (D) 9

2. What is the greatest common factor of 16 and 64?
    - (F) 4
    - (G) 8
    - (H) 16
    - (J) 2

3. What is the greatest common factor of 20 and 48?
    - (A) 10
    - (B) 12
    - (C) 6
    - (D) 4

4. What is the greatest common factor of 32 and 80?
    - (F) 4
    - (G) 8
    - (H) 16
    - (J) 10

5. What is the least common multiple of 3, 6, and 8?
    - (A) 6
    - (B) 12
    - (C) 18
    - (D) 24

6. What is the least common multiple of 4, 5, and 10?
    - (F) 20
    - (G) 15
    - (H) 10
    - (J) 5

7. What is the least common multiple of 4, 6, and 9?
    - (A) 12
    - (B) 24
    - (C) 36
    - (D) 48

8. What is the least common multiple of 5 and 3?
    - (F) 3
    - (G) 5
    - (H) 15
    - (J) 30

© Carson-Dellosa Publishing

73

Name _____ Date _____

Mathematics

Prime Factorizations

Arithmetic and Number Concepts

DIRECTIONS: Find the prime factorization of each composite number. Write the prime factors in numerical order on the leaves of the factor tree. Check your answers by completing the factor tree.

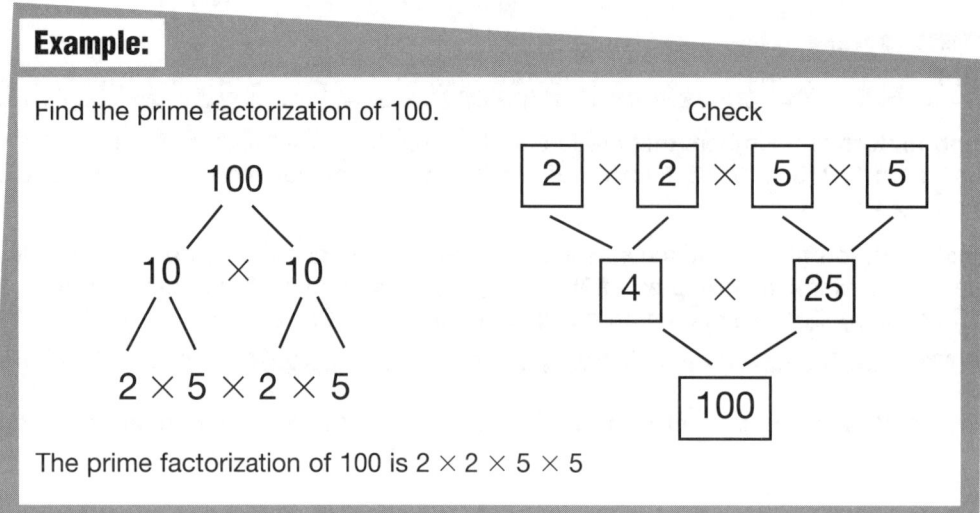

The prime factorization of 100 is $2 \times 2 \times 5 \times 5$

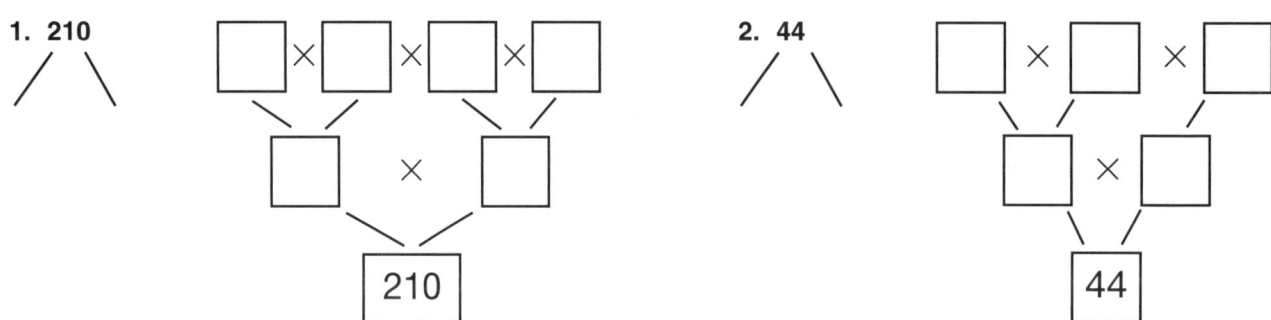

1. 210

Prime Factorization = _____

2. 44

Prime Factorization = _____

3. 1,050

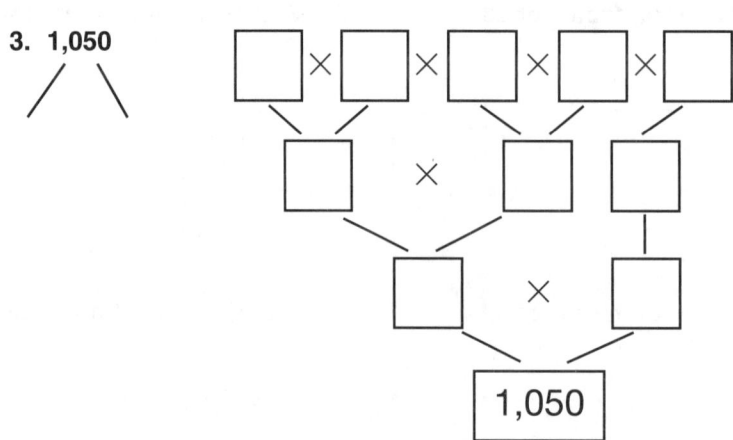

Prime Factorization = _____

Name _____ Date _____

Mathematics

Adding Fractions

Arithmetic and Number Concepts

DIRECTIONS: Add the following fractions. Reduce answers to lowest terms or write as mixed numbers.

1. $\dfrac{3}{8}$
    $+\dfrac{2}{8}$

2. $\dfrac{1}{4}$
    $+\dfrac{1}{4}$

3. $\dfrac{4}{12}$
    $+\dfrac{5}{12}$

4. $\dfrac{1}{10}$
    $+\dfrac{4}{5}$

5. $\dfrac{3}{4}$
    $+\dfrac{1}{5}$

6. $\dfrac{1}{5}$
    $+\dfrac{1}{3}$

7. $\dfrac{2}{3}$
    $+\dfrac{1}{4}$

8. $\dfrac{2}{5}$
    $+\dfrac{9}{20}$

9. $52\dfrac{4}{9}$
    $+8\dfrac{7}{8}$

10. $16\dfrac{2}{7}$
    $+14\dfrac{1}{3}$

11. $40\dfrac{1}{2}$
    $+50\dfrac{2}{3}$

12. $84\dfrac{5}{6}$
    $+94\dfrac{2}{3}$

STOP

Name _____ Date _____

Mathematics

Subtracting Fractions

Arithmetic and Number Concepts

DIRECTIONS: Subtract the following fractions. Reduce answers to lowest terms or write as mixed numbers.

1. $\dfrac{7}{8} - \dfrac{3}{8}$

2. $\dfrac{5}{9} - \dfrac{3}{9}$

3. $\dfrac{1}{2} - \dfrac{1}{5}$

4. $\dfrac{1}{3} - \dfrac{1}{4}$

5. $\dfrac{2}{3} - \dfrac{2}{5}$

6. $\dfrac{5}{9} - \dfrac{1}{2}$

7. $\dfrac{2}{3} - \dfrac{1}{2}$

8. $\dfrac{5}{6} - \dfrac{1}{5}$

9. $\dfrac{4}{5} - \dfrac{5}{10}$

10. $3\dfrac{4}{7} - 1\dfrac{1}{14}$

11. $8\dfrac{5}{6} - 3\dfrac{3}{8}$

12. $7\dfrac{7}{8} - 2\dfrac{1}{4}$

76

Mathematics

1.0/1.P

Multiplying and Dividing Fractions

Arithmetic and Number Concepts

DIRECTIONS: Multiply the fractions to complete this table.

×	$\frac{3}{5}$	$\frac{1}{2}$	$\frac{2}{3}$	$\frac{1}{6}$	$\frac{1}{8}$
$\frac{1}{2}$	$\frac{3}{10}$				
$\frac{3}{8}$					
$\frac{4}{7}$					
$\frac{5}{8}$					
$\frac{1}{10}$					

DIRECTIONS: Work the problems. Show your work like this:

$$6 \div \frac{1}{4} = \frac{6}{1} \div \frac{1}{4} = \frac{6}{1} \times \frac{4}{1} = \frac{24}{1} = 24$$

1. $7 \div \frac{1}{3} =$	5. $8 \div \frac{1}{2} =$
2. $16 \div \frac{1}{3} =$	6. $2\frac{1}{2} \div \frac{1}{2} =$
3. $6 \div \frac{1}{2} =$	7. $18 \div \frac{1}{7} =$
4. $3\frac{1}{9} \div \frac{1}{3} =$	8. $5\frac{1}{4} \div \frac{3}{8} =$

Name _____ Date _____

Mathematics
1.Q

Finding Equivalent Fractions

Arithmetic and Number Concepts

DIRECTIONS: Choose the best answer.

1. Which of the following is *not* equivalent to $\frac{3}{4}$?
   - (A) $\frac{34}{100}$
   - (B) $\frac{9}{12}$
   - (C) $\frac{15}{20}$
   - (D) $\frac{75}{100}$

2. The puzzle had 100 pieces. Eight of the pieces were solid white. Which fraction does *not* show how many of the pieces were solid white?
   - (F) $\frac{8}{100}$
   - (G) $\frac{4}{50}$
   - (H) $\frac{2}{25}$
   - (J) $\frac{1}{10}$

3. Which of the following is *not* equivalent to $\frac{1}{2}$?
   - (A) $\frac{50}{100}$
   - (B) $\frac{2}{10}$
   - (C) $\frac{2}{4}$
   - (D) $\frac{5}{10}$

4. Which of the following is equivalent to $\frac{3}{10}$?
   - (F) $\frac{1}{3}$
   - (G) $\frac{2}{9}$
   - (H) $\frac{6}{20}$
   - (J) None of the above

5. This fraction picture shows that $\frac{1}{2}$ means the same as which other fraction?
   - (A) $\frac{1}{4}$
   - (B) $\frac{1}{8}$
   - (C) $\frac{2}{8}$
   - (D) $\frac{4}{8}$

   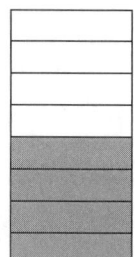

6. Which figure is less than $\frac{3}{4}$ shaded?
   - (F)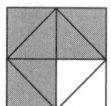
   - (G)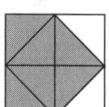
   - (H)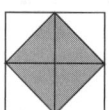
   - (J)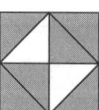

STOP

Name _____ Date _____

Mathematics
1.R

Adding and Subtracting Decimal Numbers

Arithmetic and Number Concepts

DIRECTIONS: Choose the best answer.

Clue: When adding and subtracting decimals, remember to line up the decimal points so that the place values line up.

1. 28.95 + 17.39 =
   - Ⓐ 36.64
   - Ⓑ 9.56
   - Ⓒ 46.25
   - Ⓓ 46.34

2. 28.1 − 26.9 =
   - Ⓕ 1.2
   - Ⓖ 2.2
   - Ⓗ 55
   - Ⓙ 1.19

3. 0.711 − 0.462 =
   - Ⓐ 1.173
   - Ⓑ 0.349
   - Ⓒ 0.249
   - Ⓓ 0.351

4. 56.32 + 2.1 =
   - Ⓕ 58.42
   - Ⓖ 77.32
   - Ⓗ 56.53
   - Ⓙ 54.22

5. A book 0.75 inch thick is placed on a book 0.813 inch thick. What is the combined thickness of the books?
   - Ⓐ 1.563
   - Ⓑ 0.063
   - Ⓒ 1.0
   - Ⓓ 0.50

6. Yesterday 0.333 inch of rain fell. Today 0.68 inch of rain fell. How much rain fell during the two days?
   - Ⓕ 0.347 inch
   - Ⓖ 0.50 inch
   - Ⓗ 1.013 inch
   - Ⓙ 1 inch

7. A rock weighs 0.563 pound. Suppose 0.25 pound is chipped away. How much would the remaining rock weigh?
   - Ⓐ 0.313 pound
   - Ⓑ 0.813 pound
   - Ⓒ 0.538 pound
   - Ⓓ 0.588 pound

8. Mr. Anthony and Mr. Androtti completed 0.75 of a job. Mr. Androtti completed 0.222 of the job. What part of the job did Mr. Anthony complete?
   - Ⓕ 0.972
   - Ⓖ 0.147
   - Ⓗ 0.528
   - Ⓙ 0.297

© Carson-Dellosa Publishing

Multiplying and Dividing Decimal Numbers

Mathematics 1.S/1.T

Arithmetic and Number Concepts

DIRECTIONS: Choose the best answer.

Clue: To determine the decimal point in the product (the answer for a multiplication problem), count the number of decimal places in the factors.

1. 3.6
   × 6
   - (A) 2.16
   - (B) 216
   - (C) 21.6
   - (D) None of the above

2. 0.13 × 4 =
   - (F) 0.52
   - (G) 0.50
   - (H) 0.59
   - (J) None of the above

3. 6.87 × 4 =
   - (A) 27.48
   - (B) 2.748
   - (C) 274.8
   - (D) None of the above

4. 2.03
   × 0.02
   - (F) 0.406
   - (G) 0.0406
   - (H) 2.006
   - (J) None of the above

5. 3)7.2
   - (A) 2.4
   - (B) 2.12
   - (C) 2.89
   - (D) None of the above

6. 0.12 × 6 =
   - (F) 0.84
   - (G) 0.96
   - (H) 0.72
   - (J) None of the above

7. 0.32 × 2 =
   - (A) 0.36
   - (B) 0.70
   - (C) 0.66
   - (D) None of the above

8. 0.37 ÷ 5 =
   - (F) 0.086
   - (G) 0.074
   - (H) 0.065
   - (J) None of the above

9. 11.13 ÷ 5.3 =
   - (A) 5.83
   - (B) 16.43
   - (C) 2.10
   - (D) None of the above

10. 28.86 ÷ 3.9 =
    - (F) 112.554
    - (G) 7.4
    - (H) 24.96
    - (J) None of the above

Name _____   Date _____

Mathematics
1.U

Decimals and Money

Arithmetic and Number Concepts

DIRECTIONS: Choose the best answer.

1. Triplets Brad, Chad, and Tad received a birthday card from their grandmother. She included a check for $45.75 and told them that each of them should get the same amount after the check is cashed. How much will each boy get if they divide the check equally?

    (A) $15.00
    (B) $15.15
    (C) $15.25
    (D) $15.50

2. Keisha and Darlene split a pizza. The pizza cost $18.98. If they both chipped in the same amount to pay for the pizza, how much did each one contribute?

    (F) $9.49
    (G) $9.50
    (H) $8.49
    (J) $8.50

3. Randy bought five boxes of his favorite cereal—Sugar Spazzers—at the grocery store. The total cost of the five boxes was $18.65. How much does one box of Sugar Spazzers cost?

    (A) $5.73
    (B) $4.72
    (C) $3.93
    (D) $3.73

4. Isaiah bought $2\frac{1}{2}$ gallons of gasoline for his lawn mower. He paid $3.95 for the $2\frac{1}{2}$ gallons. How much would one gallon of gasoline have cost him?

    (F) $1.98
    (G) $1.58
    (H) $2.63
    (J) $1.95

5. Jamie made $12.75 for three hours of babysitting last Saturday evening. How much was she paid per hour?

    (A) $3.75
    (B) $4.00
    (C) $4.25
    (D) $4.55

6. The total purchase price of Barbara's DVD player was $180.65. If she makes five equal payments to the store to buy the DVD player, what will be the amount of each payment?

    (F) $30.11
    (G) $36.13
    (H) $60.22
    (J) $66.13

STOP

Name _____ Date _____

Mathematics

1.V

Fractions, Decimals, and Percents

Arithmetic and Number Concepts

DIRECTIONS: Choose the best answer.

> **Example:**
>
> **If 0.87 represents how many students passed the test, what percentage passed if there were 100 students?**
>
> Ⓐ 13%
> Ⓑ 87%
> Ⓒ 100%
> Ⓓ 43%
>
> Answer: B

1. 30 people at the concert left early. There were a total of 100 people there at the beginning of the concert. Which of the following shows how many people left early?

   Ⓐ $\frac{3}{10}$
   Ⓑ 30%
   Ⓒ 0.30
   Ⓓ All of the above

2. Which of the following is equivalent to 35%?

   Ⓕ $\frac{1}{3}$
   Ⓖ 0.35
   Ⓗ $\frac{35}{50}$
   Ⓙ 0.035

3. Which of the following is *not* equivalent to $\frac{1}{2}$?

   Ⓐ $\frac{50}{100}$
   Ⓑ 0.5
   Ⓒ $\frac{25}{100}$
   Ⓓ 50%

4. Which of the following is *not* equivalent to $\frac{3}{4}$?

   Ⓕ $\frac{9}{12}$
   Ⓖ 75%
   Ⓗ 0.75
   Ⓙ 0.34

5. Which of the following is equivalent to $\frac{38}{100}$?

   Ⓐ 3.8%
   Ⓑ 03.8
   Ⓒ $\frac{3}{8}$
   Ⓓ 0.38

6. Another way to write 0.20 is _____ .

   Ⓕ $\frac{1}{20}$
   Ⓖ 25%
   Ⓗ $\frac{1}{5}$
   Ⓙ 2%

STOP

82 © Carson-Dellosa Publishing

Name _____ Date _____

Mathematics
1.W

Comparing Decimals and Fractions

Arithmetic and Number Concepts

DIRECTIONS: For each problem, write the term *less than, greater than, between,* or *equivalent to* to make the expression true.

Examples:

1.3 is <u>greater than</u> $1\frac{1}{4}$

$\frac{3}{4}$ is <u>equivalent to</u> .75

$\frac{5}{6}$ is <u>less than</u> .85

1. $\frac{1}{2}$ is _____ 0.6

2. $\frac{5}{4}$ is _____ 1.1

3. $\frac{2}{3}$ is _____ 0.5 and 0.7

4. $\frac{7}{8}$ is _____ 0.9

5. $\frac{4}{5}$ is _____ 0.3 and 0.5

6. $\frac{1}{5}$ is _____ 0.2

7. $1\frac{1}{2}$ is _____ 1.7

8. $\frac{9}{13}$ is _____ 0.9

9. 1.25 is _____ $1\frac{1}{4}$

10. 0.5 is _____ $\frac{3}{6}$

11. 0.25 is _____ $\frac{2}{5}$

12. 2.333 is _____ $2\frac{1}{3}$

13. 0.4 is _____ $\frac{4}{8}$ and $\frac{8}{10}$

14. 1.8 is _____ $\frac{1}{8}$

15. 0.3 is _____ $\frac{1}{6}$ and $\frac{1}{2}$

16. 0.1 is _____ $\frac{2}{20}$

17. 0.7 is _____ $\frac{7}{8}$

18. $\frac{6}{9}$ is _____ 0.666

19. $\frac{5}{8}$ is _____ 0.5 and 0.8

20. 0.75 is _____ $\frac{8}{10}$

© Carson-Dellosa Publishing

Name _____ Date _____

Mathematics

Representing Changes in Quantity

Arithmetic and Number Concepts

DIRECTIONS: Choose the best answer.

1. Chandler is playing a card game with his friends. His total score is currently 60 points. Suppose he is dealt some unlucky cards on the next round and scores −80 points for the round. What is his total score now?

    - Ⓐ −20 points
    - Ⓑ 0 points
    - Ⓒ −60 points
    - Ⓓ 140 points

2. If you have a pizza divided into 8 equal slices and you remove two slices, what fraction of the pizza have you removed?

    - Ⓕ $\frac{1}{4}$
    - Ⓖ $\frac{1}{8}$
    - Ⓗ $\frac{2}{8}$
    - Ⓙ $\frac{2}{4}$

3. The mileage reading on Jaqui's car is 30,569. It is 43 miles from her home to her grandmother's house in Siler City. If she drives from her home to her grandmother's house and back again, without making any side trips on the way, what will the mileage reading be on her car?

    - Ⓐ 30,483
    - Ⓑ 30,526
    - Ⓒ 30,612
    - Ⓓ 30,655

4. This morning, Alyssa has a $53.00 balance in her checkbook. Today, she writes the following checks: $14.00 to the bakery, $6.50 to her friend Tony, $28.75 to the computer store, and $7.50 to her father. She made no deposits in her account today. What is her checkbook balance at the end of the day?

    - Ⓕ $109.75
    - Ⓖ −$5.75
    - Ⓗ −$3.75
    - Ⓙ $0

5. Including himself, there were six people at Noah's party. He bought a dozen cupcakes for the party. Everyone ate one cupcake except Noah. He ate three cupcakes. How many cupcakes were left at the end of the party?

    - Ⓐ 3
    - Ⓑ 4
    - Ⓒ 5
    - Ⓓ 6

6. Rachel completely filled the gas tank of her car before running her errands today. Her car's gas tank holds 15 gallons of gasoline. If she used exactly $\frac{1}{3}$ of the amount of gas in the tank to run her errands, how many gallons of gasoline are left in the tank?

    - Ⓕ 3 gallons
    - Ⓖ 5 gallons
    - Ⓗ 10 gallons
    - Ⓙ 13 gallons

Number Lines

DIRECTIONS: Use this number line for questions 1–5.

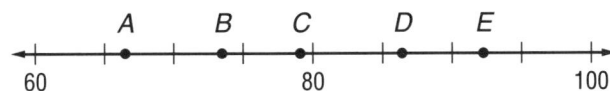

1. Which point on the number line shows 79.1?
   - (A) B
   - (B) C
   - (C) D
   - (D) E

2. Which point on the number line shows $\frac{277}{3}$?
   - (F) B
   - (G) C
   - (H) D
   - (J) E

3. Which point on the number line shows 66.5?
   - (A) A
   - (B) B
   - (C) C
   - (D) D

4. Which point on the number line shows 86.4?
   - (F) B
   - (G) C
   - (H) D
   - (J) E

5. Which point on the number line shows $73\frac{1}{2}$?
   - (A) A
   - (B) B
   - (C) C
   - (D) D

DIRECTIONS: Use this number line for questions 6–10.

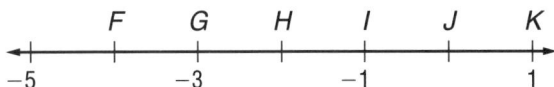

6. Which point on the number line shows −4?
   - (F) F
   - (G) G
   - (H) H
   - (J) I

7. Which point on the number line shows 0?
   - (A) H
   - (B) I
   - (C) J
   - (D) K

8. Which point on the number line shows −2?
   - (F) F
   - (G) G
   - (H) H
   - (J) I

9. Which point on the number line shows 1?
   - (A) H
   - (B) I
   - (C) J
   - (D) K

10. Which point on the number line shows −3?
    - (F) F
    - (G) G
    - (H) H
    - (J) I

STOP

Adding Integers Using the Number Line

Mathematics 1.Z — Arithmetic and Number Concepts

DIRECTIONS: Use the number line to choose the best answer.

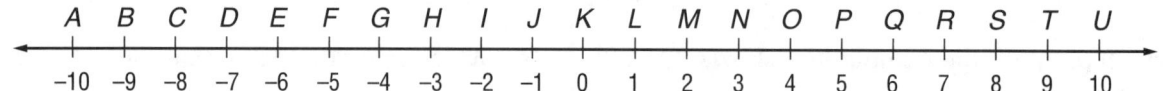

1. Which point on the number line shows $-5 + 2$?
   - (A) D
   - (B) H
   - (C) N
   - (D) R

2. Which point on the number line shows $-1 + 2$?
   - (F) I
   - (G) J
   - (H) K
   - (J) L

3. Which point on the number line shows $3 + 7$?
   - (A) U
   - (B) G
   - (C) R
   - (D) N

4. Start at point D on the number line and add 5. Which number do you get?
   - (F) -4
   - (G) -3
   - (H) -2
   - (J) -1

5. Start at point K on the number line and add 3. Which number do you get?
   - (A) 0
   - (B) 1
   - (C) 2
   - (D) 3

6. Start at point A on the number line and add 10. Which number do you get?
   - (F) -1
   - (G) 0
   - (H) 9
   - (J) 10

7. If you added the numbers at point C and point N, which number would you get?
   - (A) 11
   - (B) 5
   - (C) -5
   - (D) 3

8. If you added the numbers at point M and point P, which letter would you be on?
   - (F) Q
   - (G) R
   - (H) S
   - (J) T

STOP

Name _____ Date _____

Mathematics

1.0

For pages 62–86

Mini-Test 1

Arithmetic and Number Concepts

DIRECTIONS: Choose the best answer.

1. What is the value of 6 in 89.634?
   - (A) 6 tens
   - (B) 6 hundreds
   - (C) 6 tenths
   - (D) 6 hundredths

2. Which of these is the same as the number in the place value chart?

thousands	hundreds	tens	ones
4	3	8	0

   - (F) 4,830
   - (G) four thousand, thirty-eight
   - (H) 4,000 + 380 + 80
   - (J) 4,380

3. What number makes these number sentences true?

   $9 + \square = 15$

   $42 \div 7 = \square$

   - (A) 6
   - (B) 4
   - (C) 12
   - (D) 9

4. $2\frac{33}{100}$
   - (F) 23.3
   - (G) 0.233
   - (H) 233
   - (J) 2.33

5. What point on the number line shows 1.5?

   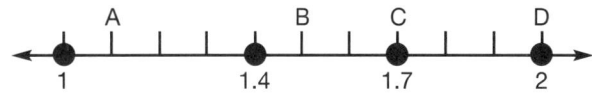

   - (A) A
   - (B) B
   - (C) C
   - (D) D

6. Which of these is a prime number?
   - (F) 19
   - (G) 21
   - (H) 32
   - (J) 48

7. What are all of the factors of the product 5×4?
   - (A) 2, 4, 5, and 10
   - (B) 1, 2, 4, 5, 10, and 20
   - (C) 1, 4, 5, and 9
   - (D) 1, 2, 3, 4, 5, 6, 10, and 20

8. Which of the following is an improper fraction?
   - (F) $\frac{7}{6}$
   - (G) $\frac{1}{2}$
   - (H) $\frac{3}{4}$
   - (J) $\frac{2}{3}$

9. What is 0.568 rounded to the nearest hundredth?
   - (A) 0.50
   - (B) 0.55
   - (C) 0.56
   - (D) 0.57

GO

© Carson-Dellosa Publishing

10. The 6 in 762,341 means _____ .
    - F) 6×10^3
    - G) 6×10^4
    - H) 6×10^5
    - J) 6×10^6

11. The sum of 631 and 892 is closest to _____ .
    - A) 1,600
    - B) 1,500
    - C) 1,400
    - D) 1,300

12. What is the decimal equivalent of 5/8?
    - F) 0.58
    - G) 0.625
    - H) 1.6
    - J) 0.6

13. The mileage reading on Mr. Lee's car is 14,142. On Mr. Cook's car, the reading is 14,319. How many more miles does Mr. Cook have on his car than Mr. Lee?
    - A) 177
    - B) 1,462
    - C) 180
    - D) 460

14. Which of these is another way to write $\frac{7}{11}$?
    - F) $\frac{21}{35}$
    - G) $\frac{35}{66}$
    - H) $\frac{28}{44}$
    - J) $\frac{11}{15}$

15. Which number shows the value of the shaded portion of this figure?
    - A) $\frac{2}{5}$
    - B) 60%
    - C) 0.5
    - D) 2.1

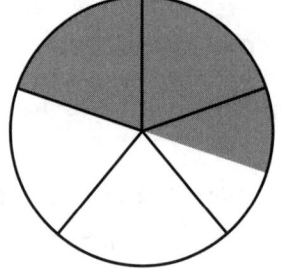

16. 1,222
    2,907
    5,745
    + 4,306
    - F) 14,270
    - G) 14,320
    - H) 14,180
    - J) None of the above

17. $7\frac{1}{4} - 5\frac{1}{5}$
    - A) $1\frac{2}{5}$
    - B) $2\frac{1}{20}$
    - C) $1\frac{19}{20}$
    - D) None of the above

18. $24\overline{)1,246}$
    - F) 50 R23
    - G) 52 R16
    - H) 51 R20
    - J) None of the above

19. 1.576
    + 2.33
    - A) 4.102
    - B) 3.906
    - C) 3.889
    - D) None of the above

20. $0.33 \times 2.4 =$
    - F) 0.792
    - G) 0.927
    - H) 0.872
    - J) None of the above

STOP

Mathematics Standards

2.0 Geometry and Measurement Concepts
By the end of the school year, students should:

2.A Estimate and measure length, distance, mass, volume, and capacity using customary and metric units (e.g., in., ft., mm, cm, m). *(See page 90.)*

2.B Identify equivalent units of measure within a system (e.g., 3 ft. = 1 yd., 5 m = 500 cm, 2 cups = 1 pint). *(See page 91.)*

2.C Estimate and weigh familiar objects in customary and metric units. *(See page 92.)*

2.D Identify the relationships among seconds, minutes, and hours. *(See page 93.)*

2.E Develop the formulas for the perimeter of a rectangle and a square. *(See page 94.)*

2.F Develop the formulas for the area of a rectangle and a square. *(See page 94.)*

What it means:
- **Perimeter** is the distance around an object.
- **Area** is the amount of space contained in a surface.

2.G Measure area and perimeter of triangles and polygons by using graph paper and/or square tiles. *(See page 95.)*

2.H Identify a plane as a flat surface which extends endlessly in all directions. *(See page 96.)*

2.I Identify and define the parts of a circle and define circumference as the distance around a circle. *(See page 96.)*

2.J Draw/construct a radius, chord, diameter, and circumference of a circle. *(See page 97.)*

2.K Explore the relationships among diameter, radius, and circumference of circles. *(See page 98.)*

2.L Read and name the coordinates of a given point on a four-quadrant grid. *(See page 99.)*

2.M Plot coordinates of given points on a four-quadrant grid. *(See page 100.)*

2.N Investigate three-dimensional shapes to begin to develop a method for finding the volume of rectangular prisms. *(See page 101.)*

What it means:
- **Volume** is the measure of the inside of a space figure. Volume of a rectangular prism = length × width × height.

2.O Represent and create models of two- and three-dimensional shapes including cubes and prisms. *(See page 102.)*

2.P Use centimeter graph paper to explore scale drawings and relate scale to ratio. *(See page 103.)*

© Carson-Dellosa Publishing

Name _____ Date _____

Mathematics 2.A

Estimating and Measuring Length, Distance, Mass, Volume, and Capacity

Geometry and Measurement Concepts

DIRECTIONS: Choose the best answer.

1. Mr. Green drove 243 miles yesterday and 175 miles today. Ms. Baxter drove 271 miles yesterday and 170 miles today. Miss Washington drove 250 miles yesterday and 178 miles today. Mrs. Kent drove 189 miles yesterday and 230 miles today. Which person drove the farthest distance?

    A Mr. Green
    B Ms. Baxter
    C Miss Washington
    D Mrs. Kent

2. About how long is this drawing of a carrot?

    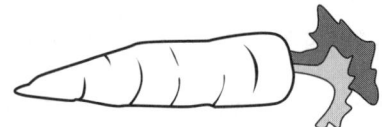

    F 0.5 feet
    G 0.5 yard
    H 5 centimeters
    J 5 inches

3. Which of these is closest to the length of the line above this ruler?

    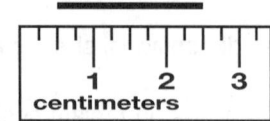

    A 2.25 centimeters
    B 2 centimeters
    C 1.5 centimeters
    D 1 centimeter

4. A broken pipe in a factory is leaking water at the rate of 2 pints per hour. It leaks for 2 days before it can be repaired. How many gallons of water were lost because of the leak?

    F 96 gallons
    G 12 gallons
    H 4 gallons
    J 24 gallons

5. Which of the following can hold the greatest amount of liquid?

    A a one-gallon jug
    B a one-pint measuring cup
    C a one-quart bucket
    D a one-liter bottle

6. How long is one side of the cube?

    F 1.5 cm
    G 2.5 cm
    H 4 cm
    J 3.5 cm

    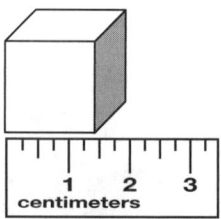

7. What is the volume of the cube above?

    A 3.375 cm³
    B 15.625 cm³
    C 64 cm³
    D 42.875 cm³

8. A rectangle is 5 feet wide and 8 feet long. What is the area?

    F 40 ft.²
    G 13 ft.²
    H 3 ft.²
    J 26 ft.²

90 © Carson-Dellosa Publishing

Name _____ Date _____

Mathematics
2.B

Identifying Equivalent Units of Measure

Geometry and Measurement Concepts

DIRECTIONS: Choose the best answer.

1. A recipe calls for 6 quarts of water. How many gallons is that?
   - (A) 1 gallon
   - (B) $1\frac{1}{2}$ gallons
   - (C) 2 gallons
   - (D) $2\frac{1}{2}$ gallons

2. Kenny's book is 30 mm thick. How many centimeters thick is the book?
   - (F) 0.3 cm
   - (G) 3 cm
   - (H) 33 cm
   - (J) 300 cm

3. 1 kilogram = _____
   - (A) 100 milligrams
   - (B) 10 grams
   - (C) 100 grams
   - (D) 1,000 grams

4. A hair comb weighs about 35 grams. How many milligrams does that equal?
   - (F) 3.5 milligrams
   - (G) 35,000 milligrams
   - (H) 350 milligrams
   - (J) 3,500 milligrams

5. 30 ft. = _____
   - (A) 5 yd.
   - (B) 10 yd.
   - (C) 15 yd.
   - (D) 20 yd.

6. A football field is 100 yards long. About how many inches is that?
   - (F) 800 inches
   - (G) 3,600 inches
   - (H) 33 inches
   - (J) 400 inches

7. 4 gallons = _____
   - (A) 40 cups
   - (B) 8 quarts
   - (C) 16 pints
   - (D) 64 cups

8. 16 cups is equivalent to all of the following except _____ .
   - (F) 8 pints
   - (G) 1 gallon
   - (H) 4 quarts
   - (J) 100 fluid ounces

STOP

© Carson-Dellosa Publishing

91

Name _____ Date _____

Mathematics
2.C

Estimating Weights

Geometry and
Measurement
Concepts

DIRECTIONS: Choose the best answer.

1. Mr. Werner bought a roast that weighed 3,500 grams. How many kilograms did the roast beef weigh?
    - (A) 35 kilograms
    - (B) 3.5 kilograms
    - (C) .35 kilograms
    - (D) 350 kilograms

2. The load limit on a small bridge is 8 tons. What is the load limit in pounds?
    - (F) 16,000 pounds
    - (G) 1,600 pounds
    - (H) 160 pounds
    - (J) 8,000 pounds

3. A dime weighs about 2 grams. Find the weight in grams of a roll of 50 dimes.
    - (A) 100 grams
    - (B) 150 grams
    - (C) 200 grams
    - (D) 20 grams

4. Jackie's baby weighed 112 ounces when it was born. How many pounds did the baby weigh?
    - (F) 6 pounds
    - (G) 7 pounds
    - (H) 8 pounds
    - (J) 9 pounds

5. A shipping crate was loaded with 600 kilograms of cargo. How many grams were on the crate?
    - (A) 6,000 grams
    - (B) 60,000 grams
    - (C) 600,000 grams
    - (D) 60 grams

6. What is the best estimate for the weight of a library book?
    - (F) 4 ounces
    - (G) 2 pounds
    - (H) 25 pounds
    - (J) 10 pounds

7. There are 30 tons of ore on a freight car. How many pounds of ore are on the freight car?
    - (A) 6,000 pounds
    - (B) 600 pounds
    - (C) 60,000 pounds
    - (D) 60 pounds

STOP

Name _____ Date _____

Mathematics

2.D

Identifying Relationships Among Time Elements

Geometry and Measurement Concepts

DIRECTIONS: Choose the best answer.

1. What time will this clock show in 45 minutes?
   - (A) 4:05
   - (B) 4:00
   - (C) 4:15
   - (D) 4:20

2. What time will the clock above show in 300 seconds?
   - (F) 3:37
   - (G) 3:40
   - (H) 4:00
   - (J) 4:35

3. Baxter begins his guitar lesson at 3:00 P.M. His lesson lasts for 45 minutes. Before going home, he plays basketball for 35 minutes. It will take him 20 minutes to walk home. At what time will Baxter arrive at home?
   - (A) 4:55
   - (B) 4:40
   - (C) 5:15
   - (D) 5:05

4. Luca finished his homework at 8:37 P.M. If he started his homework 92 minutes earlier, at what time did Luca begin his homework?
   - (F) 7:05 P.M.
   - (G) 7:09 P.M.
   - (H) 7:35 P.M.
   - (J) 11:09 P.M.

5. Jaime read for half an hour on Monday, 47 minutes on Tuesday, 1 hour and 4 minutes on Wednesday, and 81 minutes on Thursday. Which statement describes Jaime's pattern for reading?
   - (A) Add 15 minutes each day
   - (B) Subtract 17 minutes each day
   - (C) Add 12 minutes each day
   - (D) Add 17 minutes each day

6. How many seconds are there in an hour?
   - (F) 3600
   - (G) 3000
   - (H) 360
   - (J) 300

7. Jenna will be leaving on vacation in 28 hours. If it is 8:00 A.M. on the 23rd, what day and time will she be leaving?
   - (A) 8:00 A.M. on the 24th
   - (B) 8:00 P.M. on the 24th
   - (C) 12:00 A.M. on the 24th
   - (D) 12:00 P.M. on the 24th

© Carson-Dellosa Publishing

Finding the Perimeter and Area of Rectangles and Squares

Mathematics 2.E/2.F

Geometry and Measurement Concepts

DIRECTIONS: Choose the best answer.

1. How do you find the perimeter of a rectangle?
   - A. square the length of one side
   - B. subtract the length of the shortest side from the length of the longest side
   - C. multiply the base times the height
   - D. add the lengths of all sides

2. How do you find the area of a square?
   - F. square the length of one side
   - G. subtract the length of the shortest side from the length of the longest side
   - H. multiply the length times the width
   - J. add the lengths of all sides

3. How do you find the area of a rectangle?
   - A. square the length of one side
   - B. subtract the length of the shortest side from the length of the longest side
   - C. multiply the length times the width
   - D. add the lengths of all sides

[Park: 150 yards by 325 yards]

4. What is the perimeter of the park?
   - F. 950 yards
   - G. 950 square yards
   - H. 48,750 yards
   - J. 48,750 square yards

5. What is the area of the park?
   - A. 950 yards
   - B. 950 square yards
   - C. 48,750 yards
   - D. 48,750 square yards

DIRECTIONS: Use the figure of the lid of a rectangular box for questions 6 and 7.

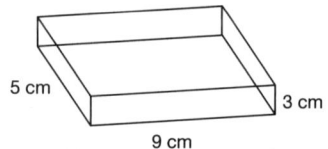

6. What is the perimeter of the box lid?
   - F. 28 cm²
   - G. 28 cm
   - H. 45 cm²
   - J. 135 cm³

7. What is the area of the box lid?
   - A. 45 cm²
   - B. 45 cm
   - C. 28 cm²
   - D. 135 cm³

Name _____ Date _____

Mathematics
2.G

Measuring Area Using Square Tiles

Geometry and Measurement Concepts

DIRECTIONS: Find the area of each shape by counting the square tiles.

1.
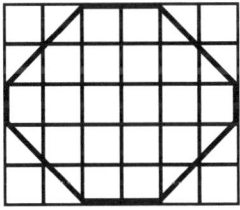
_____

2.
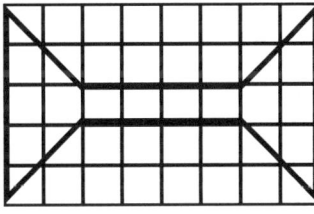
_____

3.
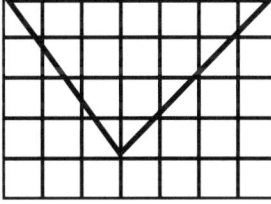
_____

4.
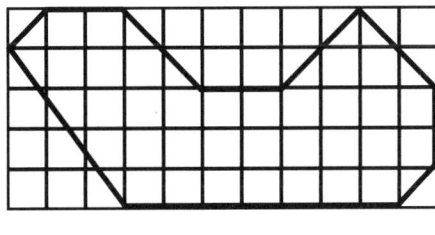
_____

5.
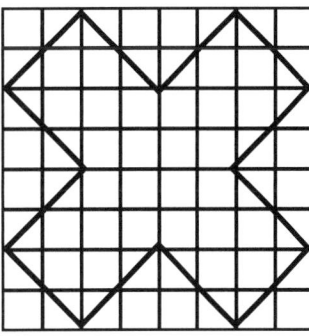
_____

6.
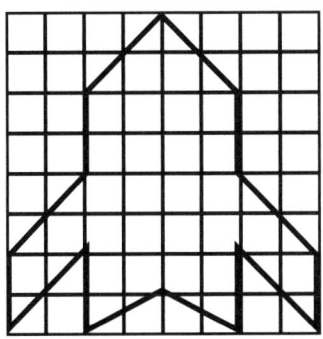
_____

7.
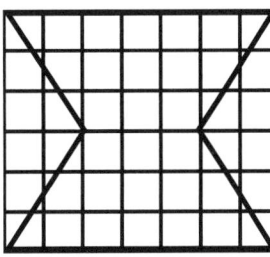
_____

8.
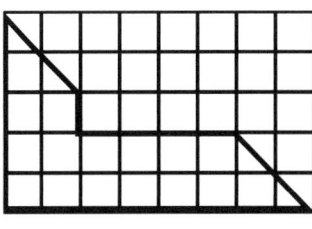
_____

STOP

© Carson-Dellosa Publishing

Circles and Planes

DIRECTIONS: Write the part of the circle that matches each of the terms below. Use correct mathematical notation. For example, for segment AB, write $\overline{AB}$.

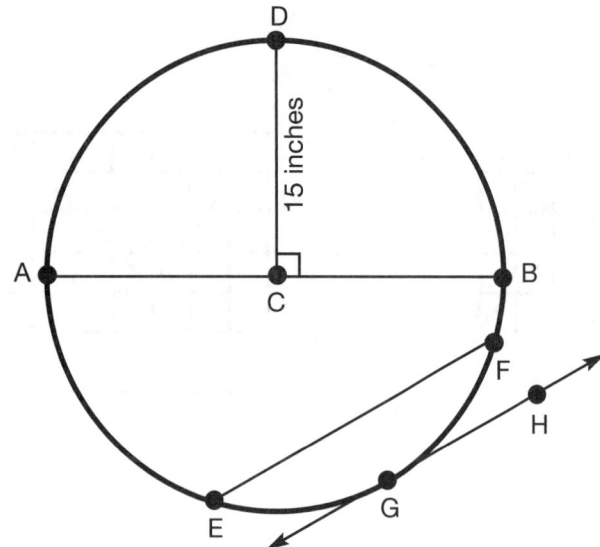

1. diameter =

2. chord =

3. arc =

4. central angle =

5. radius =

6. tangent =

DIRECTIONS: Choose the best answer.

7. A flat surface that extends endlessly in all directions is called a _____ .
   - Ⓐ square
   - Ⓑ plane
   - Ⓒ circle
   - Ⓓ cube

8. A straight line segment joining and included between two points on a circle is called a(n) _____ .
   - Ⓕ arc
   - Ⓖ plane
   - Ⓗ chord
   - Ⓙ tangent

9. The term for the distance around a circle is _____ .
   - Ⓐ radius
   - Ⓑ diameter
   - Ⓒ circumference
   - Ⓓ area

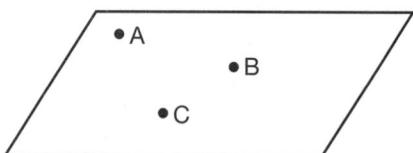

10. The figure above is a _____ .
    - Ⓕ plane
    - Ⓖ central angle
    - Ⓗ tangent
    - Ⓙ circumference

Name _____   Date _____

Mathematics
2.J

Constructing a Circle

Geometry and Measurement Concepts

DIRECTIONS: Use a straight edge and the circle below to construct the various parts of a circle as indicated.

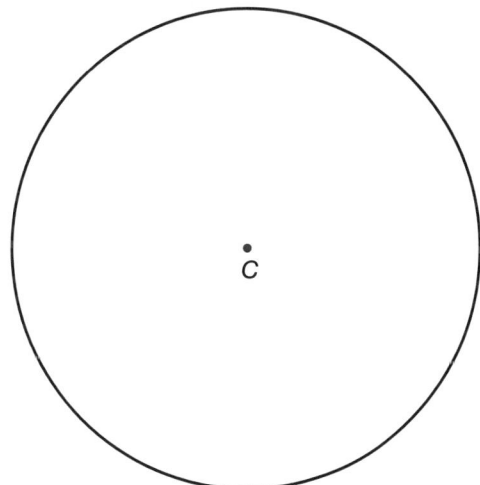

1. Construct a diameter for the circle; it should pass through point C. Label the diameter $\overline{AB}$.

2. Construct a radius $\overline{DC}$ for the circle.

3. Construct a chord for the circle. Label the chord $\overline{EF}$.

DIRECTIONS: In the space below, use a compass to create a circumference of a circle. Then, construct a diameter, radius, and chord. Label the parts of the circle as you choose.

Name _____ Date _____

Mathematics 2.K

Relationship Between Diameter, Radius, and Circumference

Geometry and Measurement Concepts

DIRECTIONS: Select the best answer. Use the provided circle for reference as needed.

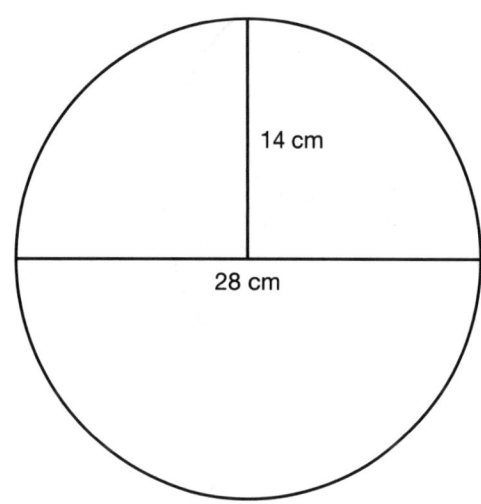

Diameter: 28 cm
Radius: 14 cm
Pi (π): 3.14
Circumference: 87.92 cm

1. The circumference of a circle is _____ times its diameter.
   - Ⓐ 2
   - Ⓑ 3.14
   - Ⓒ 14
   - Ⓓ None of the above

2. The radius of a circle is _____ times its diameter.
   - Ⓕ 14
   - Ⓖ 3.14
   - Ⓗ 2
   - Ⓙ 0.5

3. Pi (π) represents _____.
   - Ⓐ the circumference of a circle divided by its radius
   - Ⓑ the diameter of a circle multiplied by its radius
   - Ⓒ the circumference of a circle divided by its diameter
   - Ⓓ the radius of a circle divided by its diameter

4. Diameter = _____
   - Ⓕ 2 × Radius
   - Ⓖ 3.14 × Radius
   - Ⓗ Circumference ÷ Radius
   - Ⓙ 2 × Pi

5. Diameter = _____
   - Ⓐ Pi × Radius
   - Ⓑ Circumference ÷ Pi
   - Ⓒ Circumference × Pi
   - Ⓓ None of the above

Name _____ Date _____

Mathematics
2.L

Reading and Naming Coordinates

Geometry and Measurement Concepts

DIRECTIONS: Use the following graph for question 1.

1. What point shows (−4, 6)?

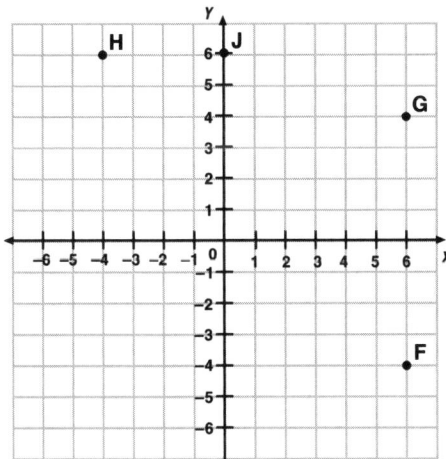

- Ⓐ F
- Ⓑ G
- Ⓒ H
- Ⓓ J

DIRECTIONS: Use the following graph for questions 2–4.

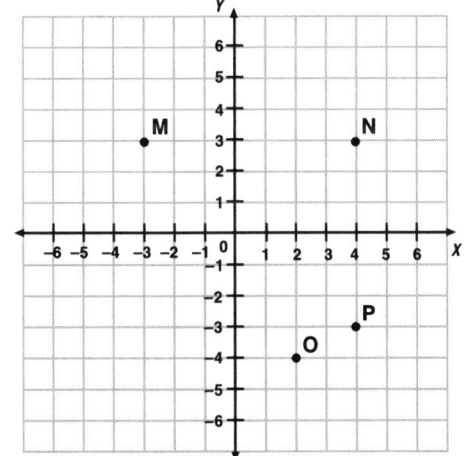

2. Which point is at (4, −3)?
   - Ⓕ M
   - Ⓖ N
   - Ⓗ O
   - Ⓙ P

3. Which point is at (−3, 3)?
   - Ⓐ M
   - Ⓑ N
   - Ⓒ O
   - Ⓓ P

4. What are the coordinates of O?
   - Ⓕ (−3, 3)
   - Ⓖ (2, −4)
   - Ⓗ (−2, 4)
   - Ⓙ (−2, −4)

DIRECTIONS: Use the grid for questions 5–6.

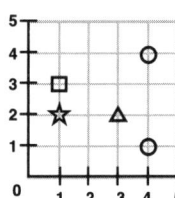

5. Which of these are the coordinates of the square?
   - Ⓐ (1, 2)
   - Ⓑ (3, 2)
   - Ⓒ (1, 3)
   - Ⓓ (4, 4)

6. Which of these are the coordinates of the star?
   - Ⓕ (1, 2)
   - Ⓖ (3, 2)
   - Ⓗ (1, 3)
   - Ⓙ (4, 4)

STOP

© Carson-Dellosa Publishing

Name _____ Date _____

Mathematics
2.M

Plotting Coordinates

Geometry and Measurement Concepts

DIRECTIONS: Plot the points to create four figures on the graph. Connect points with line segments in the order given (go down the columns).

Figure 1	**Figure 2**
(−7, 1)	(7, 1)
(−5, 1)	(7, 3)
(−5, 3)	(5, 3)
(−3, 3)	(5, 5)
(−3, 1)	(7, 5)
(−1, 1)	(7, 7)
(−1, 7)	(1, 7)
(−3, 7)	(1, 5)
(−3, 5)	(3, 5)
(−5, 5)	(3, 3)
(−5, 7)	(1, 3)
(−7, 7)	(1, 1)
(−7, 1)	(7, 1)

Figure 3	**Figure 4**
(−7, −2)	(5, −5)
(−7, −5)	(5, −4)
(−6, −5)	(4, −4)
(−6, −4)	(4, −3)
(−5, −4)	(5, −3)
(−5, −5)	(5, −2)
(−4, −5)	(2, −2)
(−4, −2)	(2, −3)
(−5, −2)	(3, −3)
(−5, −3)	(3, −4)
(−6, −3)	(2, −4)
(−6, −2)	(2, −5)
(−7, −2)	(5, −5)

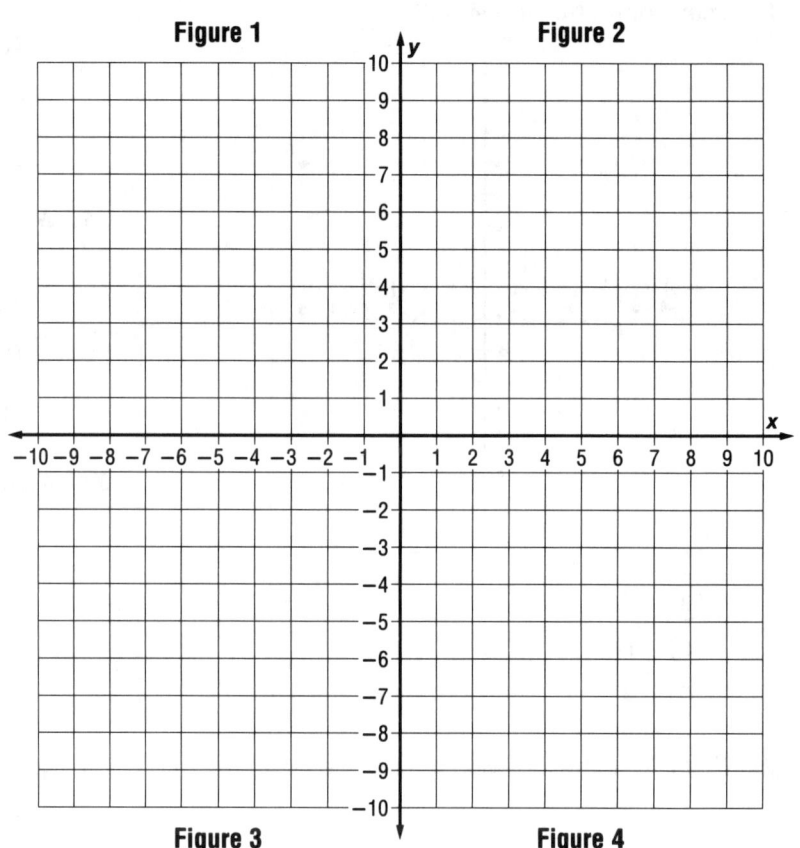

1. What shape is Figure 1?
   _____

2. What shape is Figure 2?
   _____

3. What shape is Figure 3?
   _____

4. What shape is Figure 4?

100

© Carson-Dellosa Publishing

Name _____ Date _____

Mathematics

Finding Volume

Geometry and Measurement Concepts

DIRECTIONS: Choose the best answer.

Clue: Find the volume of each space figure by counting the cubes.

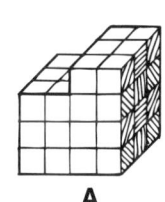  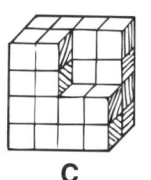 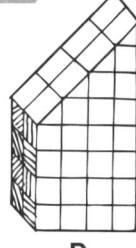

A   B   C   D

1. What is the volume of Shape A?
   - Ⓐ 38
   - Ⓑ 14
   - Ⓒ 42
   - Ⓓ 50

2. What is the volume of Shape B?
   - Ⓕ 38
   - Ⓖ 19
   - Ⓗ 10
   - Ⓙ 26

3. What is the volume of Shape C?
   - Ⓐ 26
   - Ⓑ 16
   - Ⓒ 32
   - Ⓓ 28

4. What is the volume of Shape D?
   - Ⓕ 48
   - Ⓖ 46
   - Ⓗ 40
   - Ⓙ 38

DIRECTIONS: Find the volume of the following rectangular prisms. Include the appropriate units in your answer.

5. 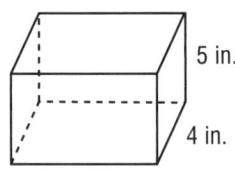 5 in., 4 in., 9 in.   Volume: _____

7. 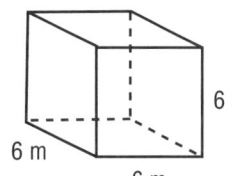 6 m, 6 m, 6 m   Volume: _____

6. 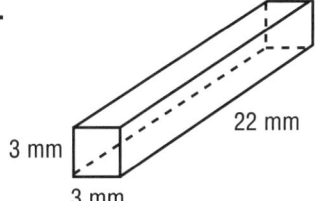 3 mm, 3 mm, 22 mm   Volume: _____

8. 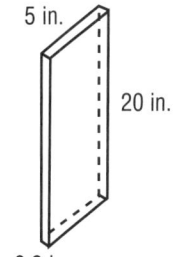 5 in., 20 in., 0.2 in.   Volume: _____

STOP

Name _____ Date _____

Mathematics 2.0

Two-Dimensional and Three-Dimensional Views

Geometry and Measurement Concepts

DIRECTIONS: Draw the front, top, and side views of the shapes for questions 1 and 2.

1. 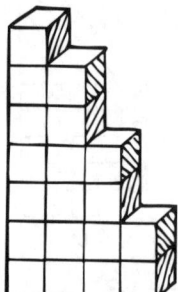   **Front:**   **Top:**   **Side:**

2. 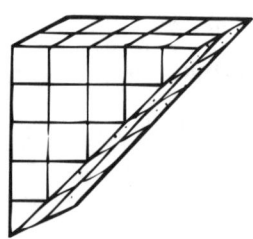   **Front:**   **Top:**   **Side:**

DIRECTIONS: Choose the best answer for questions 3 and 4.

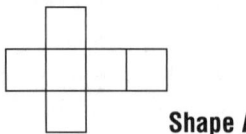
Shape A

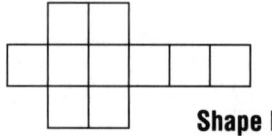
Shape B

3. If Shape A were cut out and folded to construct a three-dimensional figure, what would the figure be?

   Ⓐ cube
   Ⓑ rectangular box

4. If the Shape B were cut out and folded to construct a three-dimensional figure, what would the figure be?

   Ⓕ cube
   Ⓖ rectangular box

STOP

102   © Carson-Dellosa Publishing

Name _____   Date _____

Mathematics
2.P

Scale Drawings and Ratio

Geometry and Measurement Concepts

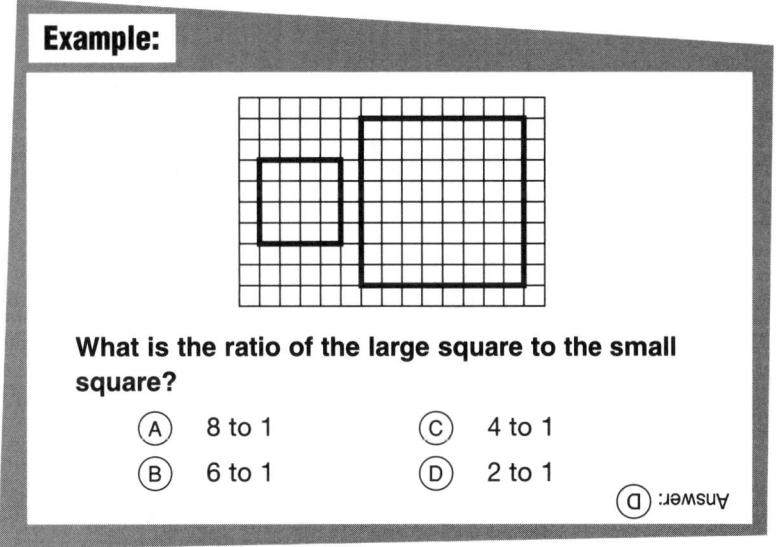

Example:

What is the ratio of the large square to the small square?

- (A) 8 to 1
- (B) 6 to 1
- (C) 4 to 1
- (D) 2 to 1

Answer: D

DIRECTIONS: Use the drawing below to choose the best answer.

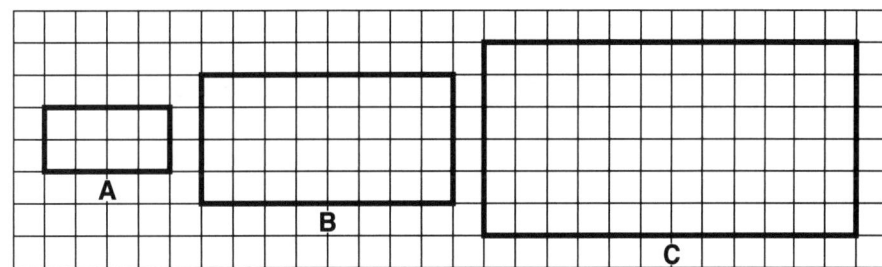

1. What is the ratio of rectangle C to rectangle A?
   - (A) 2 to 1
   - (B) 3 to 1
   - (C) 4 to 1
   - (D) 6 to 1

2. Rectangle B is _____ as large as rectangle A.
   - (F) five times
   - (G) four times
   - (H) three times
   - (J) two times

3. Suppose you drew another rectangle that was three squares high. To keep it in scale with the other rectangles shown, how many squares long would your rectangle need to be?
   - (A) 3
   - (B) 4
   - (C) 5
   - (D) 6

4. Suppose that one of the squares of the graph paper represents four inches. How long is rectangle C?
   - (F) 48 inches
   - (G) 24 inches
   - (H) 12 inches
   - (J) 4 inches

© Carson-Dellosa Publishing

103

Name _____ Date _____

Mathematics
2.0
For pages 90–103

Mini-Test 2

Geometry and Measurement Concepts

DIRECTIONS: Choose the best answer.

1. Which of these is the closest to the length of the sandwich?
   - (A) 5 3/4 inches
   - (B) 6 inches
   - (C) 6 3/4 inches
   - (D) 6 1/4 inches

   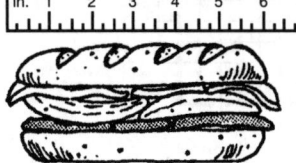

2. Raymond finished his homework at 7:42 P.M. If he started his homework 54 minutes earlier, at what time did he begin his homework?
   - (F) 7:48 P.M.
   - (G) 6:48 P.M.
   - (H) 6:42 P.M.
   - (J) 6:36 P.M.

3. Eric can throw a ball about 2,300 cm. How many meters can he throw the ball?
   - (A) 2.3 meters
   - (B) 23,000 meters
   - (C) 230 meters
   - (D) 23 meters

4. About how long is a baseball bat?
   - (F) 3 inches long
   - (G) 3 feet long
   - (H) 3 yards long
   - (J) 3 miles long

5. What is the area of the figure?
   - (A) 20 square feet
   - (B) 8 square feet
   - (C) 16 square feet
   - (D) 12 square feet

   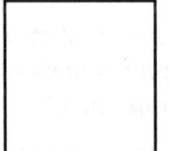
   4 feet / 4 feet

6. What is the perimeter of the figure?
   - (F) 13 meters
   - (G) 42 meters
   - (H) 26 meters
   - (J) 52 meters

   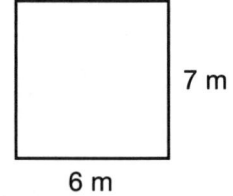
   7 m / 6 m

7. Look at the circle. What does the line segment AB represent?
   - (A) radius
   - (B) diameter
   - (C) perimeter
   - (D) volume

   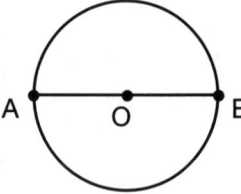

8. Which numbered rectangle is drawn to the same scale as rectangle A?
   - (F) rectangle 1
   - (G) rectangle 2
   - (H) rectangle 3
   - (J) rectangle 4

9. What is the volume of this figure?
   - (A) 18 cubic units
   - (B) 192 cubic units
   - (C) 32 cubic units
   - (D) 48 cubic units

   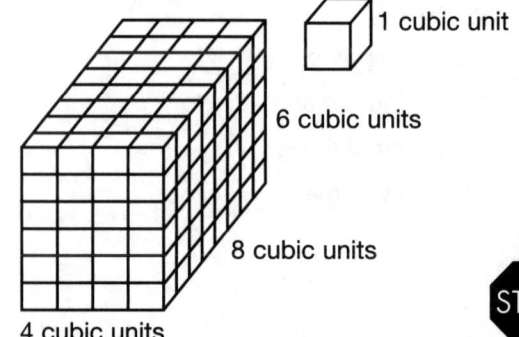
   1 cubic unit
   6 cubic units
   8 cubic units
   4 cubic units

   STOP

104
© Carson-Dellosa Publishing

Mathematics Standards

3.0 Function and Algebra Concepts
By the end of the school year, students should:

3.A Recognize, describe, and generalize a wide variety of patterns and functions. *(See page 106.)*

3.B Use tables, charts, and graphs to help identify patterns. *(See page 107.)*

3.C Use patterns and functions to represent and solve problems. *(See page 108.)*

3.D Use letters (variables) or boxes to stand for any number or object. *(See page 109.)*

What it means:
- A **variable** is an amount that is not known.

3.E Show how one quantity determines another in a functional relationship (e.g., how square numbers grow: 1, 4, 9, 16, …). *(See page 110.)*

3.F Understand that the relationship between two quantities remains the same as long as the same change is made to both quantities. *(See page 111.)*

3.G Write open sentences using letters as placeholders (e.g., $x + 4 = 10$). *(See page 112.)*

3.H Solve open sentences using letters as placeholders (e.g., $x + 4 = 10$; $x = 6$). *(See page 112.)*

3.I Explain the correct sequence for order of operations. *(See page 113.)*

What it means:
- Students should know the order of operations (parentheses, exponents, multiplication, division, addition, subtraction) and know that expressions in parentheses are performed first.

3.J Read and write addition and multiplication inequalities. *(See page 114.)*

What it means:
- Students should know the symbols for less than (**<**) and greater than (**>**).

3.K Solve inequalities involving addition and multiplication and write the solution sets. *(See page 114.)*

© Carson-Dellosa Publishing

Name _____ Date _____

Mathematics

Recognizing and Describing Patterns and Functions

Function and Algebra Concepts

DIRECTIONS: Draw the next three figures in the patterns.

1.

2.

DIRECTIONS: Draw the next shape in the pattern. Then, fill in the table and answer the questions.

Shape	1st	2nd	3rd	4th	5th	6th	7th	8th	9th	10th
Number of Triangles	2	4	6							

3. Describe the pattern for the number of triangles.

   _____
   _____

4. Explain how you can figure out the number of triangles if you know which shape it is.

   _____
   _____

5. How many triangles will be in the 15th shape? _____ the 20th? _____

6. Explain how you can figure out the number of triangles in the next shape if you know the number of triangles in the current shape.

   _____
   _____

Name _____ Date _____

Mathematics
3.B

Identifying Patterns and Relationships

Function and Algebra Concepts

DIRECTIONS: Choose the best answer.

	C1	C2	C3	C4	C5
R1	20	40	60	80	100
R2	18	36	54	72	90
R3	15	30	45	60	75
R4	11	22	33	44	55
R5	6	12	18	24	30

1. Which column has the rule of: Subtract by increasing consecutive integers?
   - Ⓐ C1
   - Ⓑ C2
   - Ⓒ C3
   - Ⓓ C4

2. Which column has the rule of: Subtract by integers increasing by threes?
   - Ⓕ C1
   - Ⓖ C2
   - Ⓗ C3
   - Ⓙ C4

3. Which column has the rule of: Subtract by integers increasing by fives?
   - Ⓐ C2
   - Ⓑ C3
   - Ⓒ C4
   - Ⓓ C5

4. What is the rule for the rows?
   - Ⓕ The numbers increase across by a factor of two.
   - Ⓖ The numbers increase across by the first number in the row.
   - Ⓗ The numbers increase across by a factor of three.
   - Ⓙ The numbers increase across by the sum of the first two numbers.

5. Doug is planning a party. He has to plan where to seat people. He can seat one guest on each open end of a table. He must group the tables in rectangles. Look for a pattern and fill in the table below. Then, make a graph showing how the number of tiles increases for each shape. Plot a point to represent each ordered pair (number of tables, number of guests) in your table from problem number 5. You may have to estimate the location of the point.

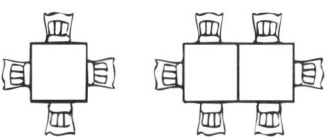

1 table   2 tables

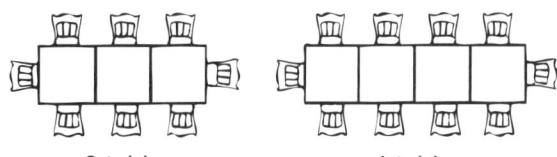

3 tables   4 tables

Number of Tables	1	2	3	4	5	6	7	8
Number of Guests	4	6	8	10				

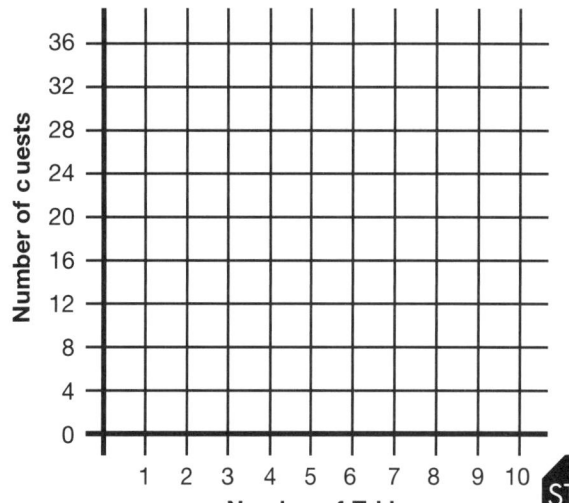

© Carson-Dellosa Publishing

Name _____ Date _____

Mathematics 3.C

Using Patterns and Functions to Solve Problems

Function and Algebra Concepts

DIRECTIONS: Choose the best answer. Mr. Pontario's students are making number charts and labeling the squares from 1 to 100.

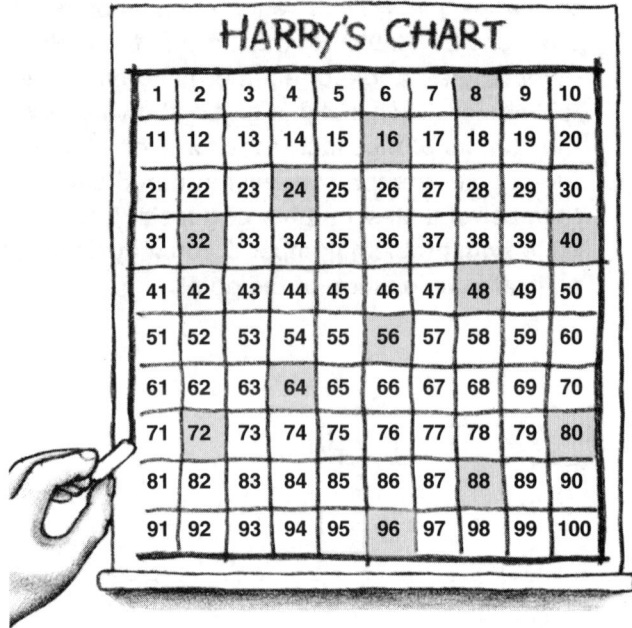

1. Liza is making a number chart. If she shades only the multiples of 4, her chart will have _____ .

    Ⓐ about three-fourths as many shaded numbers as Harry's
    Ⓑ about two-thirds as many shaded numbers as Harry's
    Ⓒ about one-half as many shaded numbers as Harry's
    Ⓓ about twice as many shaded numbers as Harry's

2. Tenisha just made a number chart on which she shaded all the multiples of 5. Which pattern shows the shading on her number chart?

    Ⓕ 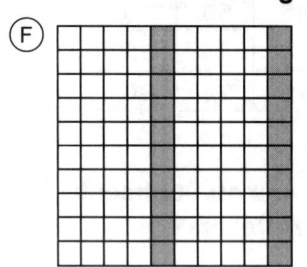   Ⓖ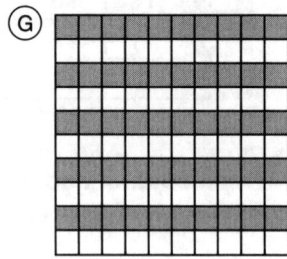

    Ⓗ 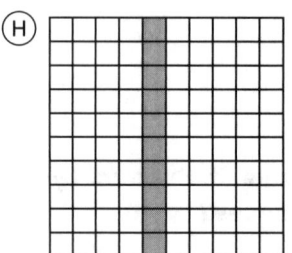   Ⓙ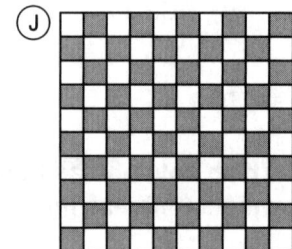

3. Which of these number sentences would help you find the total number of flags?

     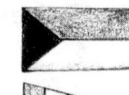 

     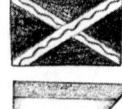 
    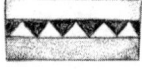  

    Ⓐ 5 + 3 = ■
    Ⓑ 5 − 3 = ■
    Ⓒ 5 × 3 = ■
    Ⓓ 5 ÷ 3 = ■

Name _____ Date _____

Mathematics

Using Variables

Function and Algebra Concepts

DIRECTIONS: Choose a variable for the unknown amount. Then, write a number sentence to represent the problem. Finally, draw a model for the equation and find the solution.

Example:

A **variable** is an amount that is not known. It is often represented by a letter. Variables are used in number sentences that represent a situation. A model is a picture of the situation.

Kyle made a dozen cookies. His little sister ate 5 of them. How many cookies are left?

Variable: Let c = number of cookies left.

Number Sentence: $c + 5 = 12$

Model: a. [plate] + [5 circles] = [12 circles]   b. [plate] = [12 circles with 5 grouped]

Solution: [plate] = [7 circles] $c = 7$

1. Julie is playing a board game. She rolls a 3 on the first die. What must she roll to move 9 spaces?

   Number sentence: _____

   Model:

   Solution: _____

2. Jacob has a bag with 4 pieces of candy. His father puts another handful into the bag. Jacob then has 13 pieces. How many pieces did his father give him?

   Number sentence: _____

   Model:

   Solution: _____

Functional Relationships

Mathematics 3.E — Function and Algebra Concepts

DIRECTIONS: Find the pattern in each row of numbers. Then, write the rule for each row.

> **Example:**
> **Pattern:** 1, 3, 5, 7, 9, 11, 13, 15
> **Rule:** +2

Rule

1. 71, 68, 65, _____, _____, _____, _____, _____   _____

2. 11, 22, 33, _____, _____, _____, _____, _____   _____

3. 17, 25, 33, _____, _____, _____, _____, _____   _____

4. 8, 28, 48, _____, _____, _____, _____, _____   _____

5. 1, 2, 4, 8, _____, _____, _____, _____, _____   _____

6. 128, 64, 32, _____, _____, _____, _____, _____   _____

7. 2, 20, 200, 2,000, _____, _____, _____, _____, _____   _____

8. 130, 115, 100, _____, _____, _____, _____, _____   _____

9. 1, 4, 16, _____, _____, _____, _____, _____   _____

10. 5000, 1000, 200, _____, _____, _____, _____, _____   _____

Name _____ Date _____

Mathematics

3.F

Understanding the Relationship Between Two Quantities

Function and Algebra Concepts

DIRECTIONS: Choose the best answer.

1. Wallid and Hayden each have $5. Wallid finds $2. How much does Hayden need so they both have the same amount?
   - (A) $5
   - (B) $4
   - (C) $3
   - (D) $2

2. If $c = d$, then $c + 7 = \blacksquare$.
   - (F) $d + 7$
   - (G) $d + c$
   - (H) $d + 5$
   - (J) $d + 9$

3. If the first frog took 10 hops and then 2 more, how far would the second frog have to hop to get to the same point?
   - (A) $5 + 4$
   - (B) $6 + 3$
   - (C) $7 + 5$
   - (D) $9 + 5$

4. John and Keisha each have an apple. If John gets an orange, what does Keisha need in order to have the same thing?
   - (F) apple
   - (G) banana
   - (H) strawberry
   - (J) orange

5. If $a = b$, then $a + 10 = b + \blacksquare$.
   - (A) a
   - (B) b
   - (C) 10
   - (D) 7

6. If $c = d$, then $c + 4 = \blacksquare$.
   - (F) $d + 4$
   - (G) $d + c$
   - (H) 4
   - (J) d

7. If $a = b$, then $a + 12 = b + \blacksquare$.
   - (A) 10
   - (B) 12
   - (C) a
   - (D) b

8. If $c = d$, then $c + 15 = \blacksquare + 15$.
   - (F) 15
   - (G) c
   - (H) d
   - (J) 5

9. If $a = b$, then $a + 3 = \blacksquare$.
   - (A) $b + 1$
   - (B) $b + a$
   - (C) $b + 3$
   - (D) $b + 5$

STOP

© Carson-Dellosa Publishing

Writing and Solving Open Sentences

Mathematics 3.G/3.H

Function and Algebra Concepts

DIRECTIONS: Write and solve an open sentence to find the beginning number for each situation. The first one is done for you.

	Equation	Beginning Number
1. After a 6 is added, the result is 11.	$n + 6 = 11$	$n = 5$
2. After 4 is subtracted, the result is 8.		
3. After a 1 is added, the result is −5.		
4. After a 5 is added, the result is −2.		
5. After the number is tripled, the result is 12.		
6. After the number is multiplied by −4, the result is 64.		
7. After the number is divided by 8, the result is 2.		
8. After the number is divided by 4, the result is 20.		
9. After the number is doubled and increased by 1, the result is 17.		
10. After the number is tripled and decreased by 2, the result is 10.		

Mathematics 3.1
Order of Operations

Function and Algebra Concepts

DIRECTIONS: Follow the order of operations explained below to find the solutions. Show your work.

The order in which you do mathematical operations may change your answer. Mathematicians have agreed on a standard order of operations. The following phrase may help you remember the order. Each letter in the phrase stands for a mathematical operation.

Please — **P**arentheses
Excuse — **E**xponents
My — **M**ultiplication
Dear — **D**ivision
Aunt — **A**ddition
Sally — **S**ubtraction

1. $35 + 50 + \dfrac{25}{5} \times 5 - (8 + 11)$

2. $(^-16 + 20) \times 6 \div (6 + 2) + 31$

3. $3 + 2(4 + 9 \div 3)$

4. $5 - [48 \div (12 + 4)] - 16$

5. $\dfrac{1}{2}(^-16 - 4)$

6. $50 \div (4 \times 5 - 36 \div 2) + {}^-9$

7. $4[^-4(3 - 12) - 17]$

8. $[5(20 - 2)] \div \dfrac{30}{2} + 6 - 3$

9. $15 - 8 \times 2 + 11 - 5 \times 2$

10. $2^3 - 6 + [29 - 2 \times 3(1 + 4)]$

Name _____ Date _____

Mathematics 3.J/3.K
Writing and Solving Addition and Multiplication Inequalities

Function and Algebra Concepts

DIRECTIONS: Write and solve the inequalities for each situation.

Examples:

To write and solve an addition inequality:
$n + 10$ is less than 15
Write:
$n + 10 < 15$

Add the opposite of 10 to both sides:
$n + 10 - 10 < 15 + -10$
Solve:
$n < 5$

To write and solve a multiplication inequality:
7 times n is greater than 70
Write:
$7n > 70$

Divide by 7 on both sides:
$7n \div 7 > 70 \div 7$
Solve:
$n > 10$

                                        Equation   **Solution**

1. $n + 17$ is less than 29   _____   _____

2. $n + 4$ is greater than 16   _____   _____

3. $n + 45$ is less than 164   _____   _____

4. $n + 23$ is greater than 38   _____   _____

5. $n + 146$ is less than 255   _____   _____

6. 5 times n is greater than 25   _____   _____

7. 4 times n is less than 42   _____   _____

8. 10 times n is greater than 140   _____   _____

9. 2 times n is less than 18   _____   _____

10. 8 times n is greater than 92   _____   _____

STOP

© Carson-Dellosa Publishing

Name _____   Date _____

Mathematics
3.0
For pages 106–114

Mini-Test 3

Function and Algebra Concepts

DIRECTIONS: Choose the best answer.

1. What is the missing number in this pattern: 1, 4, 9, 16, x, 36, 49?

   (A) 17
   (B) 25
   (C) 26
   (D) 30

2. What is the value of x in the following equation: $x + 17 = 27$?

   (F) 10
   (G) −10
   (H) 20
   (J) −20

3. Which of the following correctly lists the order of mathematical operations?

   (A) parentheses, exponents, division, multiplication, addition, subtraction
   (B) multiplication, division, addition, subtraction, parentheses, exponents
   (C) parentheses, exponents, multiplication, division, addition, subtraction
   (D) exponents, parentheses, multiplication, division, addition, subtraction

4. What is the value of x in the following equation: $x + 5 > 13$?

   (F) $x > 8$
   (G) $x > 13$
   (H) $x < 5$
   (J) $x = 8$

5. What is the value of x in the following equation: $3x < 15$?

   (A) $x > 15$
   (B) $x = 5$
   (C) $x > 5$
   (D) $x < 5$

6. Look for a pattern. Which numbers are missing?

   (F) 14, 19
   (G) 3, 11
   (H) 18, 13
   (J) 20, 15

   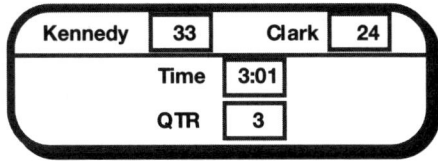

A	B
2	10
5	13
8	16
11	?
?	22

7. The scoreboard for Kennedy vs. Clark is shown. Which of the following equations would show how many points have been scored by both teams?

   Kennedy 33   Clark 24
   Time 3:01
   QTR 3

   (A) $33 + 24 = \blacksquare$
   (B) $33 - 24 = \blacksquare$
   (C) $33 \times 24 = \blacksquare$
   (D) None of the above

8. During the rest of the game, Kennedy scored 10 more points and Clark scored 12 more points. Which scoreboard shows the final information?

   (F)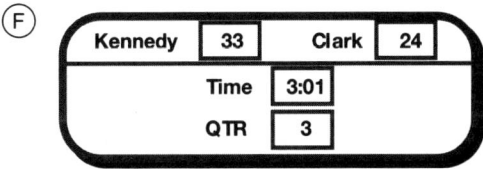
   Kennedy 33   Clark 24
   Time 3:01   QTR 3

   (G) Kennedy 43   Clark 36
   Time 3:01   QTR 4

   (H)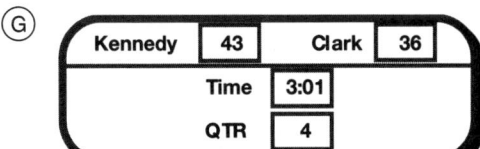
   Kennedy 43   Clark 36
   Time 0:00   QTR 4

   (J)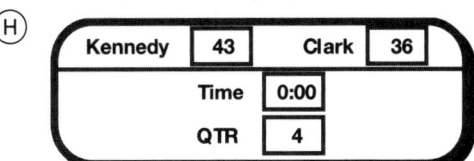
   Kennedy 43   Clark 36
   Time 0:00   QTR 3

   STOP

Mathematics Standards

4.0 Statistics and Probability Concepts
By the end of the school year, students should:

4.A Use different ways of collecting, organizing, and displaying data, such as tally tables, graphs, and Venn diagrams. *(See page 117.)*

4.B Construct, read, and interpret line graphs, bar graphs, pictographs, and line plots. *(See page 118.)*

4.C Read and interpret double bar graphs and circle graphs. *(See page 119.)*

4.D Use circle graphs to explore the concept of percent. *(See page 120.)*

4.E Select, compare, and use appropriate graphs to represent data. *(See page 121.)*

4.F Understand and identify differences among mean, median, mode, and range. *(See page 122.)*

What it means:
Students should know that:
- the **range** of a set of data is the difference between the greatest value and the lowest value of the set.
- the **mean** of a set of data is the sum of the data divided by the number of pieces of data (average).
- the **median** of a set of data is the number in the middle when the numbers are put in order.
- the **mode** of a set of data is the one that occurs most often.

4.G Conduct probability experiments and compare results with predictions. *(See page 123.)*

4.H Predict, represent, and explain probability using fractions, ratio, and percents. *(See page 124.)*

4.I Identify events that are impossible (that have a chance or probability of happening equal to zero), events that are certain (that have a chance or probability of happening equal to one), and events that occur sometimes (expressed as a proper fraction). *(See page 124.)*

4.J Use organized lists, tree diagrams, models to count arrangements and combinations. *(See pages 125–126.)*

What it means:
- Students should know that a **tree diagram** shows all possible outcomes. For example, if you have one pair of pants, and two different shirts, a tree diagram shows all combinations (outcomes) possible. The following diagram shows two possible combinations.

```
                       red shirt
         blue pants  <
                       green shirt
```

4.K Examine random and unbiased samples such as market surveys. *(See page 127.)*

Name _____ Date _____

Mathematics

4.A

Displaying Data

Statistics and Probability Concepts

DIRECTIONS: The tally chart shows the hair color of some fifth-grade students. Choose the best answer.

Brown	Black	Blond	Red

1. Which of these questions could you answer using the information on the tally chart?
   - (A) How often do the students get their hair cut?
   - (B) How many students dye their hair?
   - (C) Which students have long hair?
   - (D) How many more brown-haired students are there than blond-haired students?

2. Which graph below shows the data on the tally chart?

   (F)    (G)    (H) 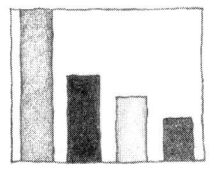   (J)

3. Which circle shows the shaded fraction of the students on the tally chart that have black hair?

   (A) 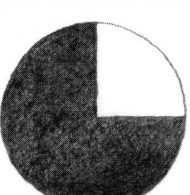   (B) 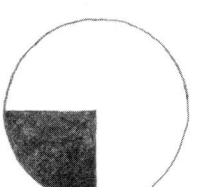   (C) 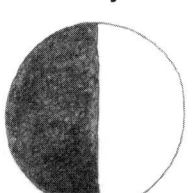   (D)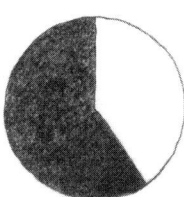

© Carson-Dellosa Publishing

117

Name _____ Date _____

Mathematics 4.B

Interpreting Graphs

Statistics and Probability Concepts

DIRECTIONS: Choose the best answer.

There are five classes of fifth-graders at the Tropicana School: Classes 5-1, 5-2, 5-3, 5-4, and 5-5. A different teacher teaches each class. The number of students in each class is represented by the pictograph below. Each ☺ means 8 students. Use the following pictograph for questions 1–4.

Class	Teacher	Number of Students
5-1	Miss Apple	☺ ☺ ☺ ◖
5-2	Mr. Kiwi	☺ ☺ ☺ ◗
5-3	Ms. Melon	☺ ☺ ☺ ◿
5-4	Mr. Cranberry	☺ ☺ ◖
5-5	Miss Mango	☺ ☺ ☺ ☺

1. How many students does ☺ ☺ represent?
   - (A) 16
   - (B) 8
   - (C) 4
   - (D) 2

2. Which teacher has 30 students?
   - (F) Miss Apple
   - (G) Mr. Kiwi
   - (H) Ms. Melon
   - (J) Mr. Cranberry

3. How many more students are in Miss Apple's class than in Ms. Melon's class?
   - (A) 1
   - (B) 2
   - (C) 3
   - (D) 4

4. Mr. Kiwi divides his students into 5 equal teams. How many students are in each team?
   - (F) 8
   - (G) 5
   - (H) 6
   - (J) 4

DIRECTIONS: The line graph shows the number of points Freda scored in her first five games. Use it to answer questions 5 and 6.

5. Which of the following tables could have been used to make this graph?

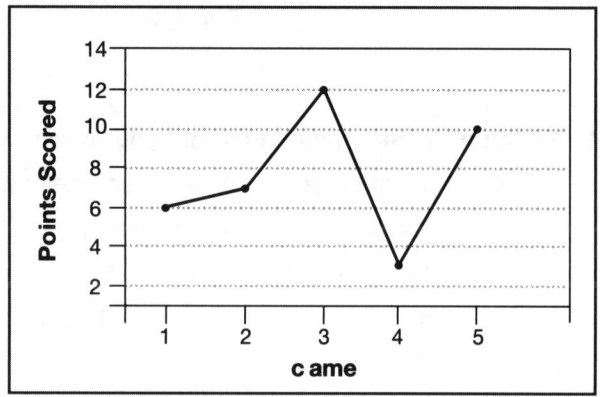

Freda's First Five Games

(A)
Game	Points
1	10
2	3
3	12
4	7
5	6

(B)
Game	Points
1	1
2	2
3	3
4	4
5	5

(C)
Game	Points
1	6
2	7
3	12
4	3
5	10

(D)
Game	Points
1	8
2	9
3	14
4	6
5	10

6. In which game did Freda score the fewest points?
   - (F) Game 1
   - (G) Game 4
   - (H) Game 3
   - (J) Game 2

Name _____   Date _____

Mathematics
4.C **Interpreting Double Bar Graphs**   Statistics and Probability Concepts

DIRECTIONS: The school drama club hopes to raise enough money to buy costumes for their first play. Each of the 10 members was given 15 tins of popcorn and 15 bags of pretzels to sell. The bar graph below shows the results of the sale.

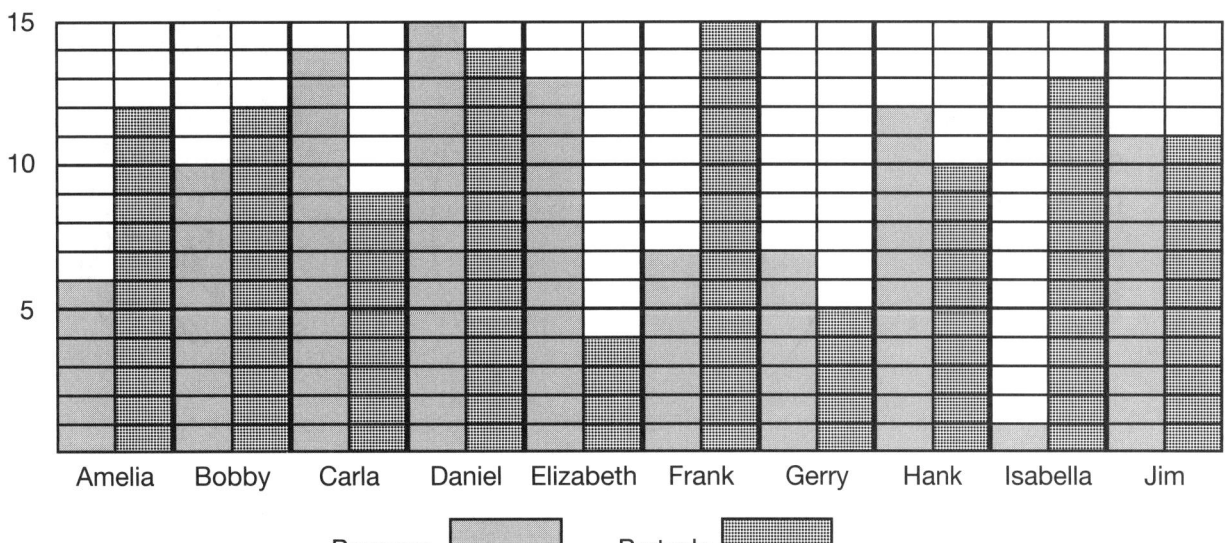

Member	Popcorn	Pretzels
Amelia		
Bobby		
Carla		
Daniel		
Elizabeth		
Frank		
Gerry		
Hank		
Isabella		
Jim		

1. Use the bar graph to complete the data table above.

2. Who sold the most popcorn? _____ The most pretzels? _____

3. Who sold the least popcorn? _____ The least pretzels? _____

4. Which sold best, the tins of popcorn or the bags of pretzels? _____

5. Who made the most total sales? _____

6. Who made the least total sales? _____

© Carson-Dellosa Publishing

Name _____ Date _____

Mathematics
4.D

Interpreting Circle Graphs

Statistics and Probability Concepts

DIRECTIONS: The charts below represent surveys of students' favorites. Show the information in each chart in the circle graphs.

1. Favorite Candy

   Chocolate 30%
   Butterscotch 5%
   Sour Balls 10%
   Licorice 20%
   Jelly Beans 10%
   Suckers 25%

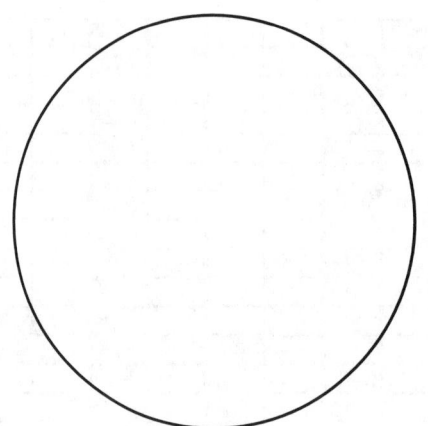

2. What is the favorite candy of the students surveyed? _____

3. What is the least favorite candy of the students surveyed? _____

4. Favorite Types of Movies

   Animated 15%
   Comedy 20%
   Action 25%
   Drama 10%
   Horror 30%

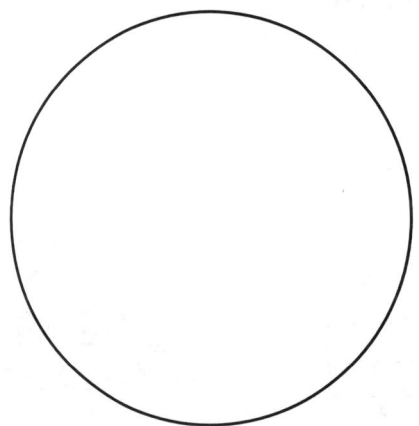

5. Based on this survey, which type of movie should be shown in the theater with the most seats? _____

6. Based on this survey, which type of movie should be in the smallest theater? _____

© Carson-Dellosa Publishing

Name _____ Date _____

Mathematics 4.E

Using Appropriate Graphs

Statistics and Probability Concepts

DIRECTIONS: The same data can be represented different ways depending on which style of chart is used. Use the information in the following table to fill in the bar graph and circle chart below.

School Election Results			
Grade	Votes for Blue Party	Votes for Red Party	Total Votes by Grade
Third	25	5	30
Fourth	10	16	26
Fifth	15	21	36
Total Votes by Party	50	42	

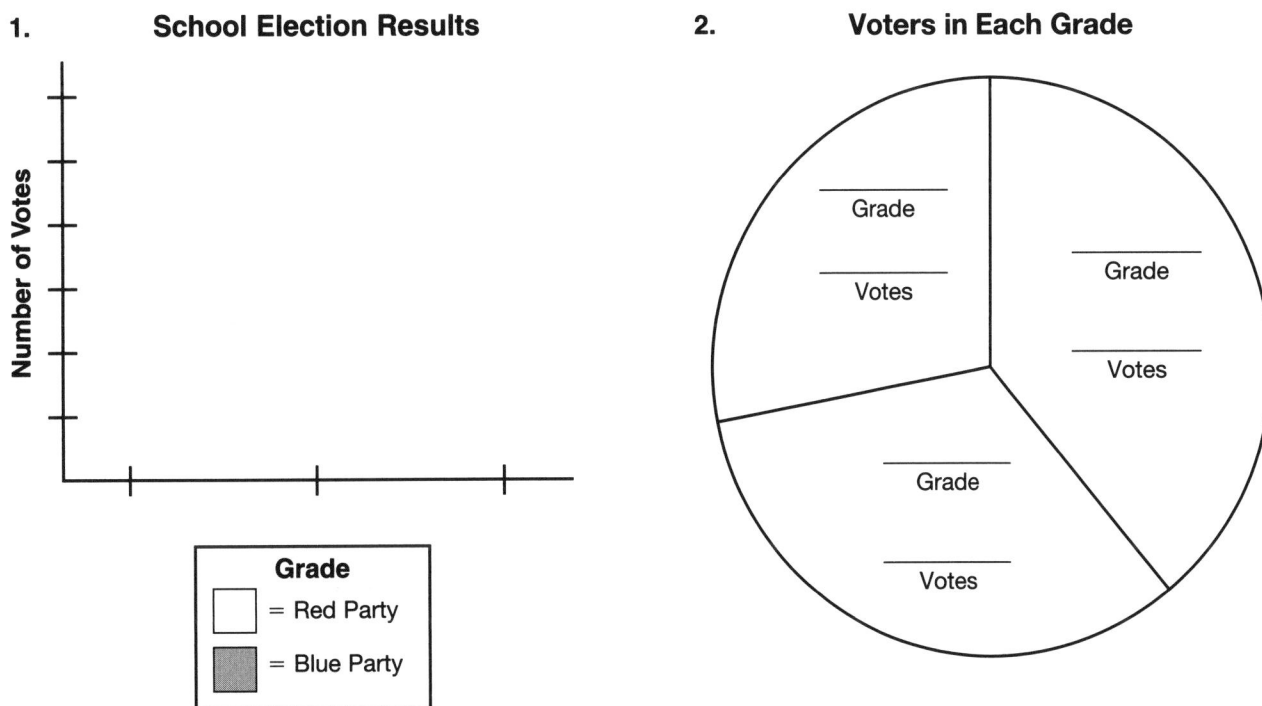

1. **School Election Results**

2. **Voters in Each Grade**

DIRECTIONS: Use the data below to construct a graph of your choice. Then, briefly explain why this is an appropriate graph to use for this data.

3.

Favorite Musical Styles Among Fifth Graders	
Pop	25%
Rock	10%
Rap	30%
Country	20%
Other	15%

STOP

© Carson-Dellosa Publishing

121

Name _____ Date _____

Mathematics

4.F

Range, Mean, Median, and Mode

Statistics and Probability Concepts

DIRECTIONS: Use this data set for questions 1–4.

The average number of rainy days per month in Sun City, Florida, are: 8, 5, 8, 8, 10, 13, 17, 17, 25, 20, 7, 9.

1. What is the range of the data?
   - (A) 8
   - (B) 9.5
   - (C) 12.25
   - (D) 20

2. What is the mean of the data?
   - (F) 8
   - (G) 9.5
   - (H) 12.25
   - (J) 20

3. What is the median of the data?
   - (A) 8
   - (B) 9.5
   - (C) 12.25
   - (D) 20

4. What is the mode of the data?
   - (F) 8
   - (G) 9.5
   - (H) 12.25
   - (J) 20

DIRECTIONS: Use this data set for questions 5–8.

The average basketball attendance per game for the season was: 80, 100, 60, 120, 120, 100, 140.

5. What is the range of the data?
   - (A) 80
   - (B) 100
   - (C) 100, 120
   - (D) 102.9

6. What is the mean of the data?
   - (F) 80
   - (G) 100
   - (H) 100, 120
   - (J) 102.9

7. What is the median of the data?
   - (A) 80
   - (B) 100
   - (C) 100, 120
   - (D) 102.9

8. What is the mode of the data?
   - (F) 80
   - (G) 100
   - (H) 100, 120
   - (J) 140

Name _____ Date _____

Mathematics

Predicting

Statistics and Probability Concepts

DIRECTIONS: Choose the best answer.

1. Which spinner would give you the best chance of landing on the number 2?

   Ⓐ   Ⓑ

   Ⓒ   Ⓓ

2. Which spinner would give you the best chance of landing on the number 4?

   Ⓕ   Ⓖ

   Ⓗ   Ⓙ

3. A bag of jelly beans contains 5 cherry jelly beans, 3 licorice jelly beans, 6 lime jelly beans, and 6 lemon jelly beans. When randomly pulling a jelly bean from the bag, which two colors are equally likely to be pulled out?

   Ⓐ cherry and licorice
   Ⓑ licorice and lime
   Ⓒ lime and lemon
   Ⓓ cherry and lime

4. Carol wants a cherry jelly bean. Without looking, she reaches into the bag and grabs a lime jelly bean. She puts the jelly bean back in the bag. Again, she randomly chooses a jelly bean. How does her chance of getting a cherry jelly bean on the second grab compare to her first grab?

   Ⓕ better
   Ⓖ worse
   Ⓗ same
   Ⓙ None of the above

DIRECTIONS: Perform the experiment as described.

5. Set up a probability experiment as follows: In a box, place 4 red crayons, 5 blue crayons, and 3 yellow crayons. Suppose you reach into the box and randomly choose a crayon, record the color crayon you choose, then put that crayon back and randomly choose again. Make a prediction: If you reach into the box 20 times, how many times will you choose a red crayon? A blue crayon? A yellow crayon? Record your answers in the table below.

Number of times red will be chosen	
Number of times blue will be chosen	
Number of times yellow will be chosen	

Now perform the experiment and record your actual results in the table below.

Number of times red was chosen	
Number of times blue was chosen	
Number of times yellow was chosen	

6. What differences did you find between your predictions and actual results?

   _____
   _____
   _____
   _____
   _____

Probability

Mathematics 4.H/4.I — Statistics and Probability Concepts

DIRECTIONS: For questions 1–4, suppose you wrote the word VACATION on a strip of paper and cut the paper into pieces with one letter per piece. If you put the pieces into a hat and pulled out one piece without looking, determine the probability of each situation.

1. What is the probability that you would pick out the letter A?
   - (A) 1 out of 8
   - (B) 2 out of 8
   - (C) 4 out of 5
   - (D) 2 out of 7

2. Without returning the A to the hat, what is the probability that you would pick out the letter C?
   - (F) 1 out of 8
   - (G) 1 out of 7
   - (H) 2 out of 8
   - (J) 1 out of 6

3. Without returning the A or the C to the hat, what is the probability of picking a vowel?
   - (A) 4 out of 8
   - (B) 3 out of 7
   - (C) 3 out of 5
   - (D) 3 out of 6

4. Given the original word, what is the probability of picking a consonant?
   - (F) 1 out of 8
   - (G) 4 out of 8
   - (H) 2 out of 8
   - (J) 4 out of 6

DIRECTIONS: There are ten white tennis balls and ten green tennis balls in a box. Tony reaches into the box without looking.

5. What is the probability that he will pick a white ball?
   - (A) $\frac{1}{10}$
   - (B) $\frac{1}{2}$
   - (C) $\frac{1}{20}$
   - (D) $\frac{1}{5}$

6. What is the probability that he will pick a green ball?
   - (F) 10%
   - (G) 20%
   - (H) 5%
   - (J) 50%

DIRECTIONS: A bag contains 10 nickels, 10 dimes, and 5 quarters. You reach into the bag and take out one coin. For questions 7 and 9, write a **1** in the blank if the probability is certain; write a **0** if the probability is impossible; express other probabilities as a proper fraction.

7. What is the probability that the coin will be silver? _____

8. What is the probability that you will take a nickel? _____

9. What is the probability that the coin will be worth 50 cents? _____

10. What is the probability that the coin will be worth more than 5 cents? _____

STOP

Name _____ Date _____

Mathematics

4.J

Using Models

Statistics and Probability Concepts

DIRECTIONS: Think about rolling two six-sided dice. Which sum(s) are you most likely to roll? Least likely to roll? Complete the following activity to find out.

Make a probability chart by following the directions. Make three columns on a piece of paper. The first column lists the sums 2 through 12. The second column is all possible combinations of dice pairs that will make the sums 2 through 12. For example, to get 11 you could role a 5 and a 6, or a 6 and then a 5. Next, count the number of different ways you found the sum. Write this number in a "# of ways" column. You should find a total of 36 different pair combinations. Once you have completed the chart, answer the following questions.

1. Which sum is most likely to occur?

   _____

2. Which sums are least likely to occur?

   _____

3. Which sums have the greatest chance of happening (meaning there are 5 possible ways to make the sum out of 36 total combinations)?

   _____

4. What is the probability of rolling a sum of 9?

   _____

5. What is the probability of rolling a sum of 9 or a sum of 5?

   _____

6. In many games, rolling doubles allows you to take another turn. How many different ways can you roll doubles?

   _____

7. What is the probability of rolling doubles?

   _____

Name _____ Date _____

DIRECTIONS: Venita is making a sandwich. She has white, wheat, and Italian bread. She can choose from ham, roast beef, and turkey for the meat. Use the following tree diagram to answer questions 8–10.

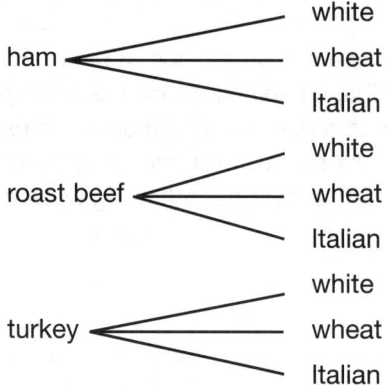

8. How many choices does Venita have?
   - (A) 12
   - (B) 9
   - (C) 3
   - (D) 6

9. If Venita decides she doesn't want wheat bread, how many choices does she have?
   - (F) 12
   - (G) 9
   - (H) 3
   - (J) 6

10. Which of the following is *not* an option Venita can choose?
    - (A) roast beef on rye
    - (B) turkey on Italian
    - (C) ham on wheat
    - (D) turkey on white

DIRECTIONS: Use the following information for questions 11–14.

Scott was choosing what to wear one morning. He has jeans and khakis for pants and red, blue, and green shirts.

11. Draw a tree diagram that shows Scott's choices for outfit combinations.

12. How many options does Scott have for outfits?
    - (F) 6
    - (G) 3
    - (H) 8
    - (J) 2

13. Which of the following is *not* an option?
    - (A) jeans with red shirt
    - (B) khakis with blue shirt
    - (C) jeans with yellow shirt
    - (D) khakis with green shirt

14. If Scott decides he wants to wear his blue shirt, how many options does he have?
    - (F) 6
    - (G) 3
    - (H) 8
    - (J) 2

Name _____ Date _____

Mathematics

Using Samples

Statistics and Probability Concepts

DIRECTIONS: Explain your answers in complete sentences.

1. In a random sample of 35 students in the school cafeteria, Marsha found that 15 ordered spaghetti. If there are 525 students who eat the cafeteria lunch, how many will likely order spaghetti?

2. Is the sample in question 1 a good sampling of the population? Explain.

3. Why might you choose to use the sample survey rather than survey the entire population? Explain.

4. Mickey took a survey of sweatshirt sizes from a random sample of 25 students. The shirts are to be sold in a bookstore at a school with 950 students. Should the sample be larger? Explain.

5. A pre-election poll predicted that a certain candidate for county treasurer would receive 25% of the vote. He actually received 75%. Was this poll useful? Explain.

6. Give two reasons why the pre-election poll could have been so far off in question 5.

7. If a survey is taken of students at a basketball camp, would the results be biased if the questions concern favorite sports? Explain.

8. Would the students at a basketball camp be a good sample population to represent a school's student population? Explain.

Name _____ Date _____

Mathematics 4.0

For pages 117–127

Mini-Test 4

Statistics and Probability Concepts

DIRECTIONS: Choose the best answer.

1. If each 😊 stands for 3 people, how would you show 12 people?

   Ⓐ 😊 😊
   Ⓑ 😊 😊 😊 😊
   Ⓒ 😊 😊 😊 😊 😊
   Ⓓ None of the above

DIRECTIONS: The graph below shows the cost of a ticket to the movies in five different cities. Use the graph for numbers 2–4.

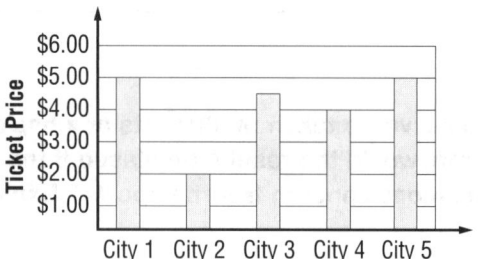

2. What is the mean ticket price?

   Ⓕ $3.90
   Ⓖ $4.00
   Ⓗ $4.10
   Ⓙ $4.30

3. Which ticket price is the mode?

   Ⓐ $4.00
   Ⓑ $10.00
   Ⓒ $2.00
   Ⓓ $5.00

4. What is the range of ticket prices?

   Ⓕ $5.00
   Ⓖ $3.00
   Ⓗ $2.00
   Ⓙ $4.00

DIRECTIONS: Choose the best answer.

Edison was wrapping a present. He had blue, silver, and gold ribbon and white, red, and black wrapping paper. Use the information to answer questions 5–6.

5. Draw a tree diagram that shows Edison's wrapping options.

6. Which of the following is *not* an option?

   Ⓐ silver ribbon on white paper
   Ⓑ blue ribbon on yellow paper
   Ⓒ blue ribbon on red paper
   Ⓓ gold ribbon on black paper

DIRECTIONS: Use the following information for questions 7 and 8. A bag contains 7 red marbles, 5 green marbles, 3 white marbles, and 2 gold marbles.

7. If you reach into the bag without looking, what is the probability of picking a red marble?

   Ⓕ $\frac{7}{10}$ Ⓖ $\frac{7}{8}$
   Ⓗ $\frac{7}{17}$ Ⓙ $\frac{7}{9}$

8. What is the probability of picking a gold marble?

   Ⓐ $\frac{2}{17}$ Ⓑ $\frac{2}{5}$
   Ⓒ $\frac{2}{7}$ Ⓓ $\frac{2}{3}$

STOP

Mathematics Standards

5.0 Mathematical Process
By the end of the school year, students should:

5.A Understand word problems, identifying pertinent, extraneous, and missing information. *(See page 130.)*

What it means:
- When presented with a math problem, students should be able to gather the correct information, in the correct order, and apply relevant mathematical concepts. For example, given the problem: *Six cases of pears and five cases of peaches are delivered to the school cafeteria. Each case contains 12 cans. The peaches are in 32-ounce cans and the pears are in 64-ounce cans. How many cans of pears are there?* Students should determine that they will need to use multiplication to determine the answer. Extraneous information includes the number of cases of peaches and the size of the cans.

5.B Use a variety of strategies to solve and represent problems/solutions (e.g., logical thinking, estimation, number sense, pictures, diagrams, and charts). *(See page 131.)*

5.C Work individually and collaboratively to discuss, justify, and write about solutions to problems using content-specific mathematical language. *(See page 132.)*

5.D Solve problems systematically and logically, and develop an awareness of when estimating is more appropriate than finding an exact answer. *(See page 133.)*

What it means:
- Students should understand that sometimes an exact answer is needed (how much change is received on a purchase) and sometimes an estimate is adequate (how much time it takes to get to a friend's house).

5.E Recognize the use of mathematics in other subject areas, such as science, social studies, and music. *(See page 134.)*

5.F Explore the use of appropriate mathematical tools and technology (e.g., computers, basic four-function or fraction calculators, measuring cups, scales, and rulers—metric and U.S. Standard, thermometers, tape measures, and protractors). *(See page 135.)*

© Carson-Dellosa Publishing

Name _____ Date _____

Mathematics
5.A

Analyzing Word Problems

Mathematical Process

DIRECTIONS: Choose the best answer.

1. Monica ate $\frac{1}{8}$ of her sandwich for lunch, Sam ate $\frac{2}{3}$ of his apple, and Rick drank all of his milk. How much of her milk did Monica drink?
   - (A) $\frac{1}{8}$ of the milk
   - (B) $\frac{2}{3}$ of the milk
   - (C) All of the milk
   - (D) Not enough information

2. There were 258 cans of soup on the grocery store shelf in the morning. At 1:00 P.M., there were 156 cans of soup on the shelf. By the time the store closed at 7:00 P.M., several more cans of soup had been sold. How many cans of soup did the store sell in the entire day?
   - (F) 102 cans
   - (G) 288 cans
   - (H) 414 cans
   - (J) Not enough information

3. Sasha went to the park at 9:30 A.M. She played for 45 minutes and then started soccer practice. She had soccer practice for 90 minutes. At what time did soccer practice end?
   - (A) 10:45 A.M.
   - (B) 11:15 A.M.
   - (C) 11:45 A.M.
   - (D) Not enough information

4. Cora went to the park on Tuesday, Wednesday, and Saturday. She went to the library on Monday and Sunday. On Friday, she went to the museum. On what days did Cora not go to the park or library?
   - (F) Thursday and Sunday
   - (G) Thursday
   - (H) Tuesday and Friday
   - (J) Thursday and Friday

5. Jessica must find the area of a square with one side that is 12 inches long. How can Jessica figure it out?
   - (A) She can add all the sides together.
   - (B) She can multiply 2 sides together.
   - (C) She can divide 2 sides by each other.
   - (D) She cannot figure out the area with the information she has.

6. Lance and Heath collected cans for a school fund-raiser. Lance collected 128 cans and Heath collected 95 cans. If each can is worth five cents, how much money did they raise for the school fund-raiser all together?
   - (F) $11.15
   - (G) $6.40
   - (H) $4.75
   - (J) $2.23

Name _____ Date _____

Mathematics

5.B

Solving Problems

Mathematical Process

DIRECTIONS: Choose the best answer.

 You might find it helpful to use scratch paper to draw pictures or record information to solve many of these problems.

1. Two numbers have a product of 108 and a quotient of 12. What are the two numbers?

   - (A) 9, 12
   - (B) 7, 16
   - (C) 36, 3
   - (D) 54, 6

2. There are several uninvited ants at a picnic in the park. Among the 9 guests that are ants or people, there are 30 legs altogether. How many ants are at the picnic?

   - (F) 9 ants
   - (G) 6 ants
   - (H) 4 ants
   - (J) 3 ants

3. Mr. Grace found three programs that he wanted to buy for the classroom. *Math Busters* was $21.80. *Spelling Practice* was $16.85. *Reading Classics* was $13.65. He spent a total of $35.45. What programs did he buy?

   - (A) *Math Busters* and *Spelling Practice*
   - (B) *Math Busters* and *Reading Classics*
   - (C) *Spelling Practice* and *Reading Classics*
   - (D) None of the above

4. Carla has 6 hockey cards. Ed and Carla together have 16 hockey cards. Judith and Ed together have 25 hockey cards. How many hockey cards does Judith have?

   - (F) 6
   - (G) 9
   - (H) 15
   - (J) 20

5. The number of people watching a hockey game is 900 when rounded to the nearest hundred and 850 when rounded to the nearest ten. Which of these could be the number of people watching the game?

   - (A) 847
   - (B) 849
   - (C) 856
   - (D) 852

6. The Card Shop receives a shipment of trading cards each month. There are 8 hockey cards in a pack, 12 packs in a box, and 16 boxes in a shipping crate. Which is the total number of hockey cards in the shipping crate?

   - (F) 1,536
   - (G) 672
   - (H) 1,436
   - (J) 662

7. After the hockey game, each of these players bought a can of soda from a machine that takes both coins and bills. The soda costs 70¢ per can.

   > Luke used only dimes.
   > Jacques used only quarters.
   > Pierre used only half-dollars.
   > Roland used a dollar bill.

   Which two players got the same amount of change?

   - (A) Luke and Jacques
   - (B) Jacques and Pierre
   - (C) Pierre and Roland
   - (D) Roland and Luke

© Carson-Dellosa Publishing

131

Name _____   Date _____

Mathematics
5.C

Explaining How to Solve Problems

Mathematical Process

DIRECTIONS: Choose the best answer.

1. There are 324 students in the fifth grade. Each student pledged to read 50 books during the year. Which number sentence shows how to find the number of books the fifth graders pledged to read?

   (A) 324 ÷ 50 = ■
   (B) 324 × 50 = ■
   (C) 324 + 50 = ■
   (D) 324 − 50 = ■

2. The amounts below show how much a student earned during a six-week time period. What operations are necessary to find out the student's average weekly earnings?

$41.87	$36.23	$25.90
$42.36	$34.21	$27.83

   (F) subtraction and addition
   (G) addition and multiplication
   (H) addition and division
   (J) multiplication and division

3. What is the number sentence for determining the volume of a rectangular prism that measures 3 units long, 5 units wide, and 8 units high?

   (A) 3 × 5 × 8 = ■
   (B) 3 + 5 + 8 = ■
   (C) (3 × 5) + 8 = ■
   (D) (3 + 5) × 8 = ■

4. The art instructor is paid $15 per hour. She works for 6 hours a day. Which number sentence shows how to find the amount she earns in one day?

   (F) 15 + 6 = ■
   (G) 15 − 6 = ■
   (H) 15 × 6 = ■
   (J) 15 ÷ 6 = ■

5. Suppose you wanted to double the number 8 and then add 10 to it. Which number sentence would you use?

   (A) (8 × 2) + 10 = ■
   (B) 8 + 2 + 10 = ■
   (C) 8 × 2 × 10 = ■
   (D) (2 × 10) + 8 = ■

6. How do you find the perimeter of a rectangle?

   (F) square the length of one side
   (G) subtract the length of the shortest side from the length of the longest side
   (H) multiply the base times the height
   (J) add the lengths of all sides

© Carson-Dellosa Publishing

Name _____ Date _____

Mathematics
5.D **Exact and Approximate Answers**

Mathematical Process

DIRECTIONS: Choose the best answer.

1. Jay took a test that had a true/false section, a matching section, and a multiple-choice section. Look at the score card below. Which of these is the best estimate of his point total on the multiple-choice section?

True/False 1–10	1 Wrong
Matching 1–15	2 Wrong
Multiple Choice 1–25	5 Wrong
2 pts. per question.	

   (A) 20 points
   (B) 30 points
   (C) 40 points
   (D) 50 points

2. Anita works part-time at a fast-food restaurant where she makes $8.35 an hour. The first week she worked 13.5 hours. Approximately $10 will come out of her paycheck for taxes. Will she have enough money to buy a CD player costing $104.94?

   (F) No, she will have only $102.00.
   (G) Yes, she will have $105.00.
   (H) No, she will have only $100.00.
   (J) Yes, she will have $110.00.

3. 5,700 ÷ 7
   The answer to this problem is about _____ .

   (A) 8,000
   (B) 800
   (C) 80
   (D) 8

4. Which of these is the best estimate of 57.4 + 79.7?

   (F) less than 100
   (G) between 100 and 150
   (H) between 150 and 200
   (J) greater than 200

5. Sharon earned $125.50 baby-sitting on weekend nights. She had $46.89 left after she bought some new clothes. Which of these is the best estimate of the cost of her clothes?

   (A) $20.00
   (B) $40.00
   (C) $60.00
   (D) $80.00

DIRECTIONS: For the following questions, write your answers in complete sentences.

6. The school's carnival committee is working late. They decide to order pizza. There are 24 students and one teacher on the committee. There are 18 slices in a large pizza. How many large pizzas should they buy to make sure each person gets at least two slices? If a large pizza costs $16.67, about how much will each person need to chip in?

   _____
   _____
   _____
   _____
   _____
   _____

7. Mr. Silverman is tiling his rectangular kitchen floor. The dimensions of the floor are 12 ft. by 10 ft. The tile he wants costs $1.80 per square foot. How much will he have to pay for tile?

   _____
   _____
   _____
   _____

Name _____ Date _____

Mathematics 5.E
Using Math in Other Subjects
Mathematical Process

Math is often used in other subject areas, such as science, history, and geography.

DIRECTIONS: Read the graph showing the number of herons on Ash Pond. Then, answer questions 1 and 2.

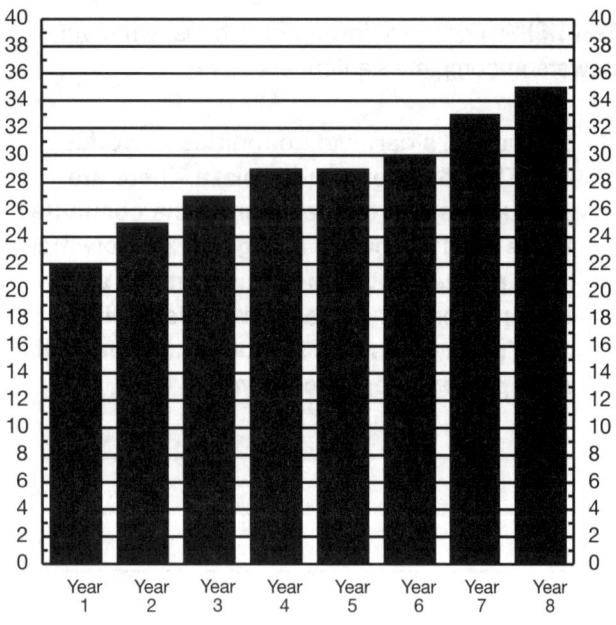

1. Based on the data, how much did the heron population increase between year 1 and year 8?

    (A) by 22
    (B) by 13
    (C) by 12
    (D) by 57

2. Based on the data, what could you predict for year 11?

    (F) The number of herons will increase.
    (G) The number of herons will decrease.
    (H) The number of herons will stay the same.
    (J) Herons will become endangered.

DIRECTIONS: This pictograph shows how many people immigrated to the United States from 1820 to 1920. Each 🧍 stands for 1,000,000 immigrants. Use the pictograph to answer question 3.

Number of People Who Immigrated to the U.S.
1820–1840 : 🧍
1841–1860 : 🧍🧍🧍🧍
1861–1880 : 🧍🧍🧍🧍🧍
1881–1900 : 🧍🧍🧍🧍🧍🧍🧍🧍🧍
1901–1920 : 🧍🧍🧍🧍🧍🧍🧍🧍🧍🧍🧍🧍🧍🧍

3. During which years did the greatest number of people immigrate?

    _____

DIRECTIONS: Look at the map grid below. Use it to answer questions 4 and 5.

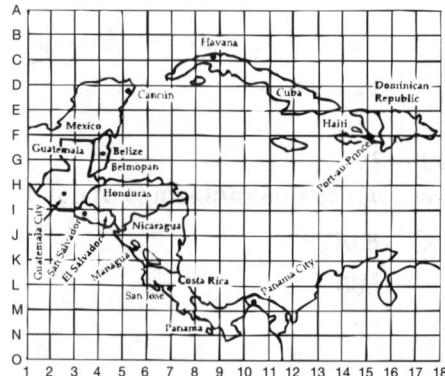

4. What are the coordinates for San Jose, Costa Rica?

    _____

5. What are the coordinates for Havana, Cuba?

    _____

134 © Carson-Dellosa Publishing

Name _____ Date _____

Mathematics
5.F

Mathematical Tools

Mathematical Process

DIRECTIONS: Choose the best answer.

1. What tool would you use to measure the weight of a dog?
   - (A) scale
   - (B) ruler
   - (C) clock
   - (D) calendar

2. What tool would you use to measure the capacity of a tea pot?
   - (F) measuring cup
   - (G) liter
   - (H) scale
   - (J) ruler

3. What tool would you use to measure the width of a book?
   - (A) clock
   - (B) calendar
   - (C) scale
   - (D) ruler

4. What tool would you use to measure the height of a blackboard?
   - (F) measuring cup
   - (G) ruler
   - (H) scale
   - (J) thermometer

5. What tool would you use to measure the length of the bus ride for a field trip?
   - (A) calculator
   - (B) scale
   - (C) clock
   - (D) calendar

6. Which tool would you use to measure the degrees in an angle?
   - (F) protractor
   - (G) calculator
   - (H) compass
   - (J) ruler

7. In science class, students had to determine the hours from dusk to dawn. Which tool would you use to measure the number of hours?
   - (A) calendar
   - (B) clock
   - (C) scale
   - (D) capacity

8. Phil likes to keep a weather journal. Which tool would he use to measure temperature?
   - (F) ruler
   - (G) scale
   - (H) thermometer
   - (J) clock

9. What tool would you use to determine the square of a number?
   - (A) ruler
   - (B) calculator
   - (C) clock
   - (D) protractor

10. What tool would you use to measure your waist?
    - (F) scale
    - (G) tape measure
    - (H) calculator
    - (J) thermometer

© Carson-Dellosa Publishing

135

Name _____ Date _____

Mathematics
5.0
For pages 130–135

Mini-Test 5

Mathematical Process

DIRECTIONS: Choose the best answer.

1. If it takes an airplane 422 minutes to make a flight and it leaves at 2:30 P.M., at what time will the plane arrive at its destination?
   - (A) 8:30 P.M.
   - (B) 8:32 P.M.
   - (C) 9:32 P.M.
   - (D) None of the above

2. A librarian was putting books on shelves. There were 58 books and 6 shelves. The librarian wanted to put the same number of books on each shelf, but she had some extras. How many books did not fit on the 6 shelves?
   - (F) 4
   - (G) 6
   - (H) 8
   - (J) 9

3. Regina has $2.33 in coins. She has 6 quarters, 5 dimes, 2 nickels, and the rest in pennies. How many pennies does Regina have?
   - (A) 12
   - (B) 33
   - (C) 17
   - (D) 23

4. Suppose you replaced the number 5 in 50,692 with an 8. How much larger would the new number be?
   - (F) 50,000
   - (G) 10,000
   - (H) 30,000
   - (J) 3,000

DIRECTIONS: The fifth graders at Memorial School voted for their favorite subject in school. They made a graph to show how they voted.

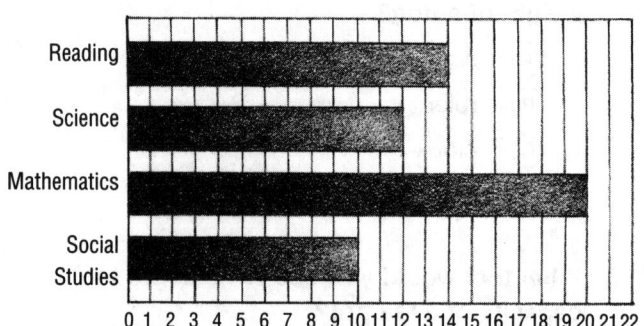

5. How many more students voted for mathematics than voted for science?
   - (A) 2
   - (B) 4
   - (C) 6
   - (D) 8

6. Which of these could *not* happen if 8 more fifth graders added their votes to the graph?
   - (F) Social studies could have the most votes.
   - (G) Science and math could have the same number of votes.
   - (H) Science could have more votes than reading.
   - (J) Social studies could have more votes than science.

7. Which of these statements about the vote is true?
   - (A) More than three-quarters of the fifth graders voted for mathematics.
   - (B) Exactly one-quarter of the fifth graders voted for reading.
   - (C) More than one-quarter of the fifth graders voted for social studies.
   - (D) Exactly one-quarter of the fifth graders voted for science.

How Am I Doing?

Mini-Test 1

Page 87–88

Number Correct

	16–20 answers correct	**Great Job!** Move on to the section test on page 139.
	11–15 answers correct	**You're almost there!** But you still need a little practice. Review practice pages 62–86 before moving on to the section test on page 139.
	0–10 answers correct	**Oops!** Time to review what you have learned and try again. Review the practice section on pages 62–86. Then, retake the test on pages 87–88. Now, move on to the section test on page 139.

Mini-Test 2

Page 104

Number Correct

	8–9 answers correct	**Awesome!** Move on to the section test on page 139.
	5–7 answers correct	**You're almost there!** But you still need a little practice. Review practice pages 90–103 before moving on to the section test on page 139.
	0–4 answers correct	**Oops!** Time to review what you have learned and try again. Review the practice section on pages 90–103. Then, retake the test on page 104. Now, move on to the section test on page 139.

Mini-Test 3

Page 115

Number Correct

	7–8 answers correct	**Great Job!** Move on to the section test on page 139.
	5–6 answers correct	**You're almost there!** But you still need a little practice. Review practice pages 106–114 before moving on to the section test on page 139.
	0–4 answers correct	**Oops!** Time to review what you have learned and try again. Review the practice section on pages 106–114. Then, retake the test on page 115. Now, move on to the section test on page 139.

© Carson-Dellosa Publishing

How Am I Doing?

Mini-Test 4 Page 128 **Number Correct** ☐	7–8 answers correct	**Awesome!** Move on to the section test on page 139.
	5–6 answers correct	**You're almost there!** But you still need a little practice. Review practice pages 117–127 before moving on to the section test on page 139.
	0–4 answers correct	**Oops!** Time to review what you have learned and try again. Review the practice section on pages 117–127. Then, retake the test on page 128. Now, move on to the section test on page 139.
Mini-Test 5 Page 136 **Number Correct** ☐	6–7 answers correct	**Great Job!** Move on to the section test on page 139.
	4–5 answers correct	**You're almost there!** But you still need a little practice. Review practice pages 130–135 before moving on to the section test on page 139.
	0–3 answers correct	**Oops!** Time to review what you have learned and try again. Review the practice section on pages 130–135. Then, retake the test on page 136. Now, move on to the section test on page 139.

Final Mathematics Test
For pages 62–136

DIRECTIONS: Choose the best answer.

1. Which group of decimals is ordered from least to greatest?
   - (A) 3.332, 3.321, 3.295, 3.287, 3.111
   - (B) 3.424, 3.425, 3.339, 3.383, 3.214
   - (C) 3.109, 3.107, 3.278, 3.229, 3.344
   - (D) 3.132, 3.234, 3.262, 3.391, 3.406

2. Which of the following is not equivalent to the shaded portion of the figure?
   - (F) $\frac{1}{3}$
   - (G) $\frac{4}{8}$
   - (H) $\frac{12}{36}$
   - (J) $\frac{37}{111}$

   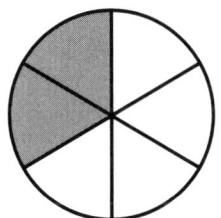

3. Cole and Jenny split a candy bar. Cole ate $\frac{3}{16}$ and Jenny ate $\frac{11}{16}$. Who ate more? Did they eat the whole candy bar?
   - (A) Cole, yes
   - (B) Jenny, yes
   - (C) Cole, no
   - (D) Jenny, no

4. It took Scott $\frac{3}{6}$ of an hour to get home. What is the decimal equivalent of $\frac{3}{6}$?
   - (F) 0.5
   - (G) 0.36
   - (H) 2.0
   - (J) None of the above

5. Myrtle and Doris collect stamps. Myrtle has 423 stamps and Doris has 519. How many stamps do both girls have?
   - (A) 96
   - (B) 942
   - (C) 1,000
   - (D) 100

6. A machine can produce 98 parts in one hour. How many parts could it produce in 72 hours?
   - (F) 170
   - (G) 26
   - (H) 196
   - (J) 7,056

7. Lucinda has 59 cents to buy pencils that cost 14 cents each. How many pencils can she buy?
   - (A) 826
   - (B) 45
   - (C) 73
   - (D) 4

8. Write 36 as the product of its prime factors by using exponents.
   - (F) $2^2 \times 14$
   - (G) $3^2 \times 8$
   - (H) $2^2 \times 3^2$
   - (J) 2×19

9. Which of these is a prime number?
   - (A) 5
   - (B) 9
   - (C) 15
   - (D) 21

GO

10. Yesterday $\frac{3}{8}$ inch of rain fell. Today $\frac{5}{8}$ inch of rain fell. How much rain fell during the two days?

   (F) 1 inch
   (G) $\frac{2}{8}$ inch
   (H) 8 inches
   (J) $\frac{8}{16}$ inch

11. I am a number. I am the year of Columbus's famous voyage rounded to the nearest 1,000. What number am I?

   (A) 1000
   (B) 1400
   (C) 1492
   (D) 1500

12. The figure below is a sketch showing the cafeteria at Lincoln School. If you walked completely around the cafeteria, about how far would you go?

   (F) 100 ft.
   (G) 80 ft.
   (H) 120 ft.
   (J) 400 ft.

   20 ft.

13. Each column in the number pattern below equals 21. What numbers are missing?

3	5	2	1	6
2	7	8	9	1
9	8	4	6	7
	1	7		7

   (A) 6 and 8
   (B) 7 and 5
   (C) 1 and 7
   (D) 4 and 3

14. Look at the chart. Which of the following is the most likely time of sunrise on March 4?

Date	Time of Sunrise
March 1	6:39 A.M.
March 2	6:36 A.M.
March 3	6:33 A.M.
March 4	

   (F) 6:33 A.M.
   (G) 6:30 A.M.
   (H) 6:27 A.M.
   (J) None of the above

15. Which factors are represented by the figure?

   (A) 3 × 5
   (B) 6 × 2
   (C) 5 × 2
   (D) 3 × 6

16. The school district had 8,927 students. Which of these is the expanded numeral for 8,927?

   (F) 89 + 27
   (G) 800 + 900 + 200 + 7
   (H) 9,000 + 800 + 20 + 7
   (J) 8,000 + 900 + 20 + 7

17. What is the diameter of the circle?

   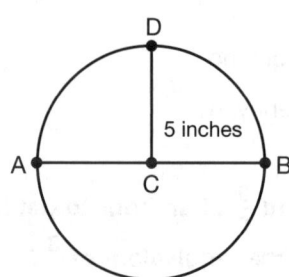

   (A) 5 inches
   (B) 10 inches
   (C) 31.4 inches
   (D) None of the above

Name _____ Date _____

DIRECTIONS: Choose the best answer. Use the bar graph for questions 18–19.

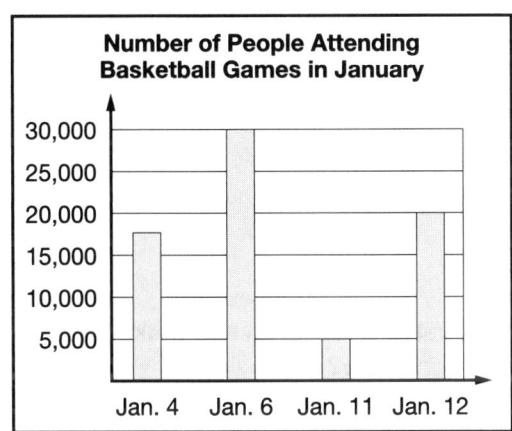

18. What is the range of the data?
    - (F) 25,000
    - (G) 18,000
    - (H) 10,000
    - (J) 5,000

19. On one of the dates, a snowstorm prevented many people from going to the game. On which date did the storm occur?
    - (A) Jan. 12
    - (B) Jan. 4
    - (C) Jan. 11
    - (D) Jan. 6

DIRECTIONS: Choose the best answer.

20. This clock shows the time a train arrived at a station. The train loaded passengers for 10 minutes and then continued to the next station. The trip to the next station took 35 minutes. What time did the train arrive at the next station?
    - (F) 2:30
    - (G) 2:05
    - (H) 2:40
    - (J) 2:35

21. What is the volume of this figure?

    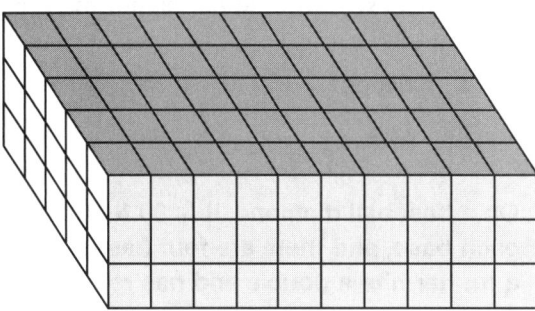

    - (A) 150 cubic units
    - (B) 100 cubic units
    - (C) 53 cubic units
    - (D) 50 cubic units

22. Steve finishes his math multiplication homework early. What tool can he use to check his work?
    - (F) ruler
    - (G) calculator
    - (H) scale
    - (J) thermometer

23. A football is 11 inches in length. How many footballs would have to be placed end to end to equal more than 1 yard?
    - (A) 1
    - (B) 2
    - (C) 3
    - (D) 4

24. Five students were surveyed about their favorite meal in the cafeteria. Three of them said they liked pizza. What fraction shows the portion of students who liked pizza?
    - (F) $\frac{5}{3}$
    - (G) $\frac{3}{5}$
    - (H) $\frac{2}{5}$
    - (J) None of the above

25. Timmy flips a coin 10 times and gets 8 heads and 2 tails. What would he expect the next flip to result in?
    - (A) heads
    - (B) tails

26. On a baseball diamond, it is 90 feet between each base, and there are four bases. Suppose a runner hits a double and has reached second base. How much farther does the runner have to go to reach home?
    - (F) 90 ft.
    - (G) 180 ft.
    - (H) 270 ft.
    - (J) 360 ft.

27. The Spanish Club wants to buy a set of instructional videos. Each video costs $12.50. What information will they need to determine how much money they must raise to buy the entire set of videos?
    - (A) the number of students in the school
    - (B) how long each video is
    - (C) the number of videos in the set
    - (D) how many students there are in the Spanish Club

28. To solve the following equation, which operation would you perform first?

    $23 + 60 \div (11 - 8) \times 2$
    - (F) multiplication
    - (G) addition
    - (H) parentheses
    - (J) division

29. An auto mechanic earns $19 an hour. She works 8 hours a day. Which number sentence shows how to find how much she earns in a day?
    - (A) $19 + 8 = \blacksquare$
    - (B) $19 - 8 = \blacksquare$
    - (C) $19 \times 8 = \blacksquare$
    - (D) $19 \div 8 = \blacksquare$

30. A waterproof jacket costs $49.95. The cold-weather lining for the jacket is $22.50 and a matching hat is $12.75. How much would it cost to buy the jacket and liner, but not the hat?
    - (F) $85.20
    - (G) $72.45
    - (H) $61.45
    - (J) $62.70

31. What value does b have to make both equations true?

    $b - 7 = 15;\ 2 \times 11 = b$
    - (A) 85
    - (B) 12
    - (C) 21
    - (D) 22

32. Look at the coordinate grid. Which sequence of ordered pairs would allow you to move from the school to the library?

    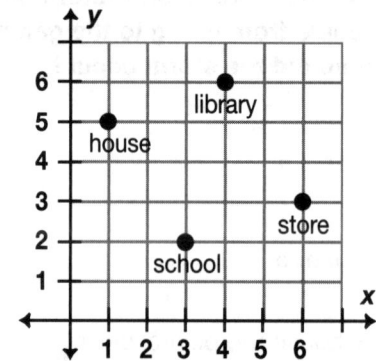

    - (F) (2,3), (3,3), (4,3), (5,3), (6,3), (6,4)
    - (G) (3,2), (3,3), (3,4), (3,5), (2,5), (1,5)
    - (H) (3,2), (3,3), (3,4), (3,5), (3,6), (4,6)
    - (J) (2,3), (2,4), (2,5), (2,6), (3,6), (4,6)

STOP

Name _____ Date _____

Final Mathematics Test
Answer Sheet

1. Ⓐ Ⓑ Ⓒ Ⓓ
2. Ⓕ Ⓖ Ⓗ Ⓙ
3. Ⓐ Ⓑ Ⓒ Ⓓ
4. Ⓕ Ⓖ Ⓗ Ⓙ
5. Ⓐ Ⓑ Ⓒ Ⓓ
6. Ⓕ Ⓖ Ⓗ Ⓙ
7. Ⓐ Ⓑ Ⓒ Ⓓ
8. Ⓕ Ⓖ Ⓗ Ⓙ
9. Ⓐ Ⓑ Ⓒ Ⓓ
10. Ⓕ Ⓖ Ⓗ Ⓙ

11. Ⓐ Ⓑ Ⓒ Ⓓ
12. Ⓕ Ⓖ Ⓗ Ⓙ
13. Ⓐ Ⓑ Ⓒ Ⓓ
14. Ⓕ Ⓖ Ⓗ Ⓙ
15. Ⓐ Ⓑ Ⓒ Ⓓ
16. Ⓕ Ⓖ Ⓗ Ⓙ
17. Ⓐ Ⓑ Ⓒ Ⓓ
18. Ⓕ Ⓖ Ⓗ Ⓙ
19. Ⓐ Ⓑ Ⓒ Ⓓ
20. Ⓕ Ⓖ Ⓗ Ⓙ

21. Ⓐ Ⓑ Ⓒ Ⓓ
22. Ⓕ Ⓖ Ⓗ Ⓙ
23. Ⓐ Ⓑ Ⓒ Ⓓ
24. Ⓕ Ⓖ Ⓗ Ⓙ
25. Ⓐ Ⓑ
26. Ⓕ Ⓖ Ⓗ Ⓙ
27. Ⓐ Ⓑ Ⓒ Ⓓ
28. Ⓕ Ⓖ Ⓗ Ⓙ
29. Ⓐ Ⓑ Ⓒ Ⓓ
30. Ⓕ Ⓖ Ⓗ Ⓙ

31. Ⓐ Ⓑ Ⓒ Ⓓ
32. Ⓕ Ⓖ Ⓗ Ⓙ

New York Social Studies Content Standards

The social studies section of the New York City Standards measures knowledge in two different areas:
1. Themes
2. Skills and Strategies

The social studies section of the New York State Standards measures knowledge in five different areas:
1. History of the United States and New York
2. World History
3. Geography
4. Economics
5. Civics, Citizenship, and Government

New York Social Studies Table of Contents

Themes
    Standards and What They Mean 145
    Practice Pages 146
    Mini-Test 1 160
Skills and Strategies
    Standards and What They Mean 161
    Practice Pages 163
    Mini-Test 2 184
How Am I Doing? **186**
Final Social Studies Test **187**
Answer Sheet **191**

Social Studies Standards

1.0 Themes
The study of the United States, Canada, and Latin America/the Caribbean includes:
- **1.A** The History of the United States, Canada, and Latin American/Caribbean Nations.
  - **1.A.1** Cultural diversity of these nations and regions. *(See page 146.)*
  - **1.A.2** Key turning points and events. *(See page 147.)*
  - **1.A.3** Important historical figures and groups. *(See page 148.)*
- **1.B** The Geography of the United States, Canada, and Latin American/Caribbean Nations.
  - **1.B.1** Maps, computer models, and other tools are used to gather, process, and report information. *(See page 149.)*
  - **1.B.2** Physical and human characteristics of places in nations of the United States, Canada, and Latin America/the Caribbean. *(See page 150.)*
  - **1.B.3** Cultural characteristics and complexity of the area. *(See pages 151–152.)*
  - **1.B.4** Human actions modify the physical environments of the United States, Canada, and Latin America. *(See pages 153–154.)*
- **1.C** The Economies of the United States, Canada, and Latin American/Caribbean Nations.
  - **1.C.1** Interdependence of nations of North, Central, South America, and the Caribbean. *(See pages 155–156.)*
  - **1.C.2** Economic systems, resources, production, distribution, exchange, and consumption of goods and services. *(See pages 155–156.)*
- **1.D** The Governments of the United States, Canada, and Latin American/Caribbean Nations.
  - **1.D.1** Varying government structures and roles of citizens. *(See page 157.)*
  - **1.D.2** Differing assumptions regarding power, authority, governance and law. *(See page 157.)*
  - **1.D.3** The patriotic celebrations of the various nations. *(See page 158.)*
  - **1.D.4** International organizations (e.g., the United Nations). *(See page 159.)*

Name _____ Date _____

Social Studies

1.A.1

Cultural Diversity in the United States, Canada, and Latin America

Themes

DIRECTIONS: Choose the best answer.

1. In which of the following cities or regions would you be most likely to hear French being spoken?
   - (A) Mexico City
   - (B) Quebec, Canada
   - (C) the midwestern United States
   - (D) Central America

2. African-Americans account for about what percentage of the population of the United States?
   - (F) 50 percent
   - (G) 30 percent
   - (H) 15 percent
   - (J) 5 percent

3. Most people in Latin America speak _____ as their first language.
   - (A) Dutch or German
   - (B) Italian
   - (C) Spanish or Portuguese
   - (D) English

4. Native people called Aztecs lived in present-day _____.
   - (F) Alaska
   - (G) Cuba
   - (H) Peru
   - (J) Mexico

5. Which of the following groups has had the least amount of influence on the music, art, food, religion, and language in the United States, Canada, and Latin America?
   - (A) Australians
   - (B) Africans
   - (C) Native Americans
   - (D) Europeans

6. The dominant religion in the United States, Canada, and Latin America is _____.
   - (F) Judaism
   - (G) Christianity
   - (H) Islam
   - (J) Buddhism

STOP

© Carson-Dellosa Publishing

Name _____ Date _____

Social Studies

Themes

1.A.2 **Key Turning Points and Events in United States, Canadian, and Latin American History**

DIRECTIONS: Choose the best answer.

1. What purpose did the Declaration of Independence serve?
   - (A) It caused the beginning of the Revolutionary War.
   - (B) It allowed America to declare its freedom from British rule.
   - (C) It provided freedom to slaves.
   - (D) It allowed the South to begin the Civil War against the North.

2. The Battle of the Alamo was fought between _____.
   - (F) the United States and France
   - (G) the United States and Spain
   - (H) New Mexico and Great Britain
   - (J) Texas and Mexico

3. In what years was the American Civil War fought?
   - (A) 1775–1778
   - (B) 1812–1813
   - (C) 1861–1865
   - (D) 1909–1912

4. _____ was a Spanish explorer who defeated the Aztecs in 1521. This led to the Spanish dominance of Mexico.
   - (F) Christopher Columbus
   - (G) John Cabot
   - (H) Meriwether Lewis
   - (J) Hernando Cortez

5. _____ was called the Father of New France. He founded Quebec in 1608, which was the first permanent French settlement in North America.
   - (A) Miles Standish
   - (B) Samuel de Champlain
   - (C) Daniel Boone
   - (D) William Penn

6. In 1804, _____ was the first Latin American country to win its independence. It won its independence from France.
   - (F) Greenland
   - (G) Florida
   - (H) Haiti
   - (J) Quebec

7. In 1898, _____ freed Cuba and Puerto Rico from Spanish rule.
   - (A) World War I
   - (B) World War II
   - (C) the Spanish-American War
   - (D) the Vietnam War

8. From which country did Mexico win independence in 1821?
   - (F) France
   - (G) Great Britain
   - (H) the United States
   - (J) Spain

STOP

© Carson-Dellosa Publishing

Name _____ Date _____

Social Studies
1.A.3

Important Figures and Groups in United States, Canadian, and Latin American History

Themes

DIRECTIONS: Choose the best answer.

1. Who did Thomas Jefferson hire to lead an expedition through the northern part of the Louisiana Territory?
   - (A) Benjamin Franklin and Paul Revere
   - (B) Meriwether Lewis and William Clark
   - (C) Daniel Boone
   - (D) John Hancock

2. The Native American group known as the Inuit is most likely to be found in _____ .
   - (F) Peru
   - (G) Brazil
   - (H) Canada
   - (J) Argentina

3. The revolution in Cuba brought this communist dictator to power there in 1959.
   - (A) Richard Nixon
   - (B) Vasco Nunez de Balboa
   - (C) Fidel Castro
   - (D) Tony Perez

4. Which of the following people is most famous for helping American slaves escape through the Underground Railroad?
   - (F) Harriet Tubman
   - (G) Crispus Attucks
   - (H) Phillis Wheatley
   - (J) Mary McLeod Bethune

5. All of the following were Native American tribal chiefs who fought European expansion into their native lands except _____ .
   - (A) Tecumseh
   - (B) Geronimo
   - (C) Crazy Horse
   - (D) Ponce de León

6. _____ was a leading figure in freeing South America from European rule.
   - (F) Simon Bolivar
   - (G) Ponce de León
   - (H) Thomas Paine
   - (J) Martin Luther King, Jr.

7. People who migrated to California in the Gold Rush of the mid-nineteenth century came to be known as _____ .
   - (A) Forty-Niners
   - (B) Pilgrims
   - (C) Puritans
   - (D) Tarriers

8. _____ was president of the United States during almost all of World War II.
   - (F) Ronald Reagan
   - (G) John F. Kennedy
   - (H) Abraham Lincoln
   - (J) Franklin Roosevelt

Name _____   Date _____

Social Studies

Using Maps

Themes

DIRECTIONS: Use the map to help you choose the best answer.

Clue: The map key explains the symbols that are used on the map.

1. What do the dots on the map indicate?
   - (A) the Missouri River
   - (B) the border between the Louisiana territory and Canada
   - (C) the route Lewis and Clark took during their expedition of the territory
   - (D) the border between the land the U.S. purchased and the land still owned by France

2. From whom did the United States buy the Louisiana Territory?
   - (F) France
   - (G) Spain
   - (H) Great Britain
   - (J) Canada

3. What river did Lewis and Clark mainly follow during their expedition?
   - (A) the Colorado River
   - (B) the Columbia River
   - (C) the Mississippi River
   - (D) the Missouri River

4. The Louisiana Purchase territory was _____ of the Mississippi River.
   - (F) north
   - (G) south
   - (H) east
   - (J) west

5. Which country controlled the land west of the Louisiana Purchase?
   - (A) Canada
   - (B) Great Britain
   - (C) Spain
   - (D) the United States

© Carson-Dellosa Publishing

149

Name _____ Date _____

Social Studies

Themes

1.B.2

Physical Characteristics of the United States, Canada, and Latin America

---

DIRECTIONS: Use the map below to choose the best answer.

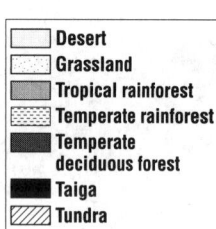
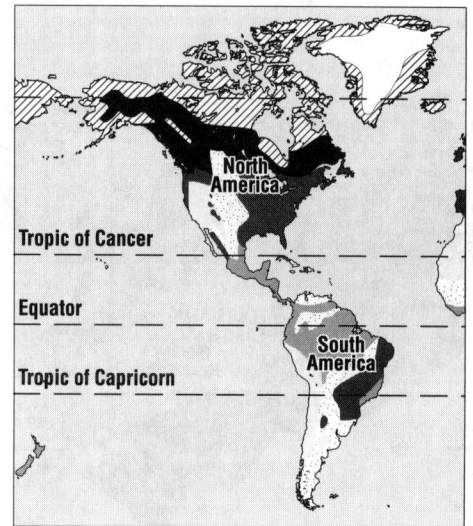

1. The Inuit are native peoples who live in the far north. Which types of environments do the Inuit mostly live in?

   Ⓐ taiga and tundra
   Ⓑ desert and grassland
   Ⓒ tundra and tropical rainforest
   Ⓓ taiga and temperate deciduous forest

2. Which type of environment runs north to south in the eastern United States?

   Ⓕ desert
   Ⓖ temperate deciduous forest
   Ⓗ tundra
   Ⓙ tropical rainforest

3. Which type of environment does Mexico have?

   Ⓐ tropical rainforest
   Ⓑ desert
   Ⓒ grassland
   Ⓓ temperate rainforest

4. What are the two main types of environments in the western half of the United States?

   Ⓕ taiga and tundra
   Ⓖ tropical rainforest and desert
   Ⓗ desert and grassland
   Ⓙ taiga and temperate deciduous forest

5. Which type of environment is *not* found in South America?

   Ⓐ tropical rainforest
   Ⓑ desert
   Ⓒ temperate deciduous forest
   Ⓓ taiga

Name _____ Date _____

Social Studies

1.B.3

Themes

Cultural Characteristics of the United States, Canada, and Latin America

DIRECTIONS: Examine the table below. Then, answer the questions on the next page.

Country	Age Structure (% of population by age group)	Life Expectancy at Birth	Literacy Rate
Brazil	0–14 years: 27.1%	Total population: 71.13 years	*Definition:* age 15 and over can read and write
	15–64 years: 67.2%	*Male:* 67.16 years	Total population: 86.4%
	65 years and over: 5.7%	*Female:* 75.3 years	
Uruguay	0–14 years: 24.3%	Total population: 75.87 years	*Definition:* age 15 and over can read and write
	15–64 years: 62.6%	*Male:* 72.54 years	Total population: 98%
	65 years and over: 13.1%	*Female:* 79.38 years	
Bolivia	0–14 years: 37.1%	Total population: 64.78 years	*Definition:* age 15 and over can read and write
	15–64 years: 58.4%	*Male:* 62.2 years	Total population: 87.2%
	65 years and over: 4.5%	*Female:* 67.48 years	
Guyana	0–14 years: 27%	Total population: 63.09 years	*Definition:* age 15 and over has ever attended school
	15–64 years: 67.9%	*Male:* 60.51 years	Total population: 98.8%
	65 years and over: 5.1%	*Female:* 65.79 years	
United States	0–14 years: 20.9%	Total population: 77.14 years	*Definition:* age 15 and over can read and write
	15–64 years: 66.7%	*Male:* 74.37 years	Total population: 97%
	65 years and over: 12.4%	*Female:* 80.05 years	
Canada	0–14 years: 18.5%	Total population: 79.83 years	*Definition:* age 15 and over can read and write
	15–64 years: 68.6%	*Male:* 76.44 years	Total population: 97%
	65 years and over: 12.9%	*Female:* 83.38 years	
Belize	0–14 years: 41.1%	Total population: 67.36 years	*Definition:* age 15 and over can read and write
	15–64 years: 55.3%	*Male:* 65.19 years	Total population: 94.1%
	65 years and over: 3.5%	*Female:* 69.63 years	

GO

© Carson-Dellosa Publishing

Name _____   Date _____

1. When someone is born in the United States, how many years are they expected to live based on the national average?
   - Ⓐ 77.14 years
   - Ⓑ 63.09 years
   - Ⓒ 79.83 years
   - Ⓓ 67.36 years

2. Which of the following countries has the greatest percentage of people aged 14 or younger?
   - Ⓕ Canada
   - Ⓖ Belize
   - Ⓗ Brazil
   - Ⓙ United States

3. How is the literacy rate for Guyana measured differently than the rate for the other countries in the table?
   - Ⓐ Guyanans are defined as literate if they can read.
   - Ⓑ Guyanans are defined as literate if they can both read and write.
   - Ⓒ Guyanans are defined as literate if they can write.
   - Ⓓ Guyanans are defined as literate if they ever attended school.

4. Of the countries listed below, which one has the greatest percentage of people who can read and write?
   - Ⓕ Brazil
   - Ⓖ Uruguay
   - Ⓗ United States
   - Ⓙ Canada

5. Of the countries shown in the table, which one has the shortest life expectancy for men?
   - Ⓐ Belize
   - Ⓑ Uruguay
   - Ⓒ Guyana
   - Ⓓ Canada

6. Based on the information in the table, which of the following statements about life expectancy is probably true?
   - Ⓕ Most Americans can expect to live well into their late 80s.
   - Ⓖ Latin American women can expect to live longer than Latin American men.
   - Ⓗ Life expectancy in Canada is dramatically lower than it is in the United States.
   - Ⓙ Overall, life expectancy in Latin America is a bit higher than it is in the United States and Canada.

7. Which country has a life expectancy of 62.2 years for males?
   - Ⓐ Brazil
   - Ⓑ Bolivia
   - Ⓒ Uruguay
   - Ⓓ Belize

Name _____   Date _____

Social Studies

1.B.4

How Human Actions Modify the Environment

Themes

DIRECTIONS: Read the information in the table. Then, answer the questions.

Region	Environmental Concerns	Endangered Species
Canada	• Much of the Pacific temperate rainforest has been clear-cut. The remainder could be gone within twenty-five years. • Hydroelectric power projects and development in Quebec are disrupting wildlife habitats. • The harvest from commercial fishing in the northwest Atlantic has declined over 30 percent since 1970.	grizzly bear, woodland caribou, humpback whale
United States	• Erosion, the depletion of water resources for irrigation, and overgrazing have turned range and cropland in the southwest into desert. • Fragile barrier beaches of the Atlantic coast have been damaged by agricultural runoff, sewage, and overdevelopment.	spotted owl, whooping crane, bald eagle, manatee, Atlantic Ridley turtle, condor
Latin America	• The ecological balance in the Caribbean coral reefs is being upset by a booming tourism industry. • Every year over 5,000 square miles of rainforest is destroyed in Brazil's Amazon Basin. • Southern Chile's rainforest is threatened by development. • Atlantic waters east of Argentina have suffered from overfishing and oil spills.	howler monkey, jaguar, black caiman, golden lion tamarin, chinchilla, blue whale

1. In which region are hydroelectric power projects endangering wildlife habitats?

   Ⓐ Guatemala
   Ⓑ Canada
   Ⓒ Mexico
   Ⓓ Cuba

2. In which region is tourism cited as a main cause of environmental problems?

   Ⓕ Chile
   Ⓖ Quebec
   Ⓗ the southwest United States
   Ⓙ the Caribbean

© Carson-Dellosa Publishing

Name _____   Date _____

3. **At the current rate, how much of the rainforest in Brazil's Amazon Basin will be lost within the next five years?**
   - Ⓐ 5,000 square miles
   - Ⓑ 10,000 square miles
   - Ⓒ 25,000 square miles
   - Ⓓ 50,000 square miles

4. **Which of the following is *not* an endangered species of Latin America?**
   - Ⓕ grizzly bear
   - Ⓖ howler monkey
   - Ⓗ black caiman
   - Ⓙ jaguar

5. **Which of the following is probably a prime reason why the manatee and the Atlantic Ridley turtle are endangered?**
   - Ⓐ clear-cutting of the Pacific rainforest
   - Ⓑ overdevelopment in Quebec
   - Ⓒ water pollution
   - Ⓓ clear-cutting of southern Chile's rainforest

6. **Which of the following is *not* a cause of desertification in the southwestern United States?**
   - Ⓕ erosion
   - Ⓖ hydroelectric power projects
   - Ⓗ water resources being used for irrigation
   - Ⓙ overgrazing

7. **What resource in Canada could be gone within the next twenty-five years?**
   - Ⓐ forest
   - Ⓑ fish
   - Ⓒ cropland
   - Ⓓ gold

8. **What do you think is a likely reason why fewer fish are being caught in the northwest Atlantic? Explain your answer.**

   _____
   _____
   _____
   _____
   _____
   _____
   _____
   _____
   _____
   _____

Name _____ Date _____

Social Studies
1.C.1/1.C.2

The Economies of the United States, Canada, and Latin America

Themes

DIRECTIONS: Use the information in the table to answer the questions on the next page.

Country	Major Exports	Major Imports	Main Trading Partners
Brazil	transport equipment, iron ore, soybeans, footwear, coffee, autos	machinery, electrical and transport equipment, chemical products, oil	United States, Argentina, Germany
Canada	motor vehicles and parts, industrial machinery, aircraft, telecommunications equipment; chemicals, plastics, fertilizers; wood pulp, timber, crude petroleum, natural gas, electricity, aluminum	machinery and equipment, motor vehicles and parts, crude oil, chemicals, electricity, durable consumer goods	United States
Honduras	coffee, bananas, shrimp, lobster, meat; zinc, lumber	machinery and transport equipment, industrial raw materials, chemical products, fuels, foodstuffs	United States
Mexico	manufactured goods, oil and oil products, silver, fruits, vegetables, coffee, cotton	metalworking machines, steel mill products, agricultural machinery, electrical equipment, car parts for assembly, repair parts for motor vehicles, aircraft, and aircraft parts	United States
United States	capital goods, automobiles, industrial supplies and raw materials, consumer goods, agricultural products	crude oil and refined petroleum products, machinery, automobiles, consumer goods, industrial raw materials, food and beverages	Canada, Mexico, China, Japan

Source: CIA World Factbook 2003 (http://www.odci.gov/cia/publications/factbook/)

© Carson-Dellosa Publishing

Name _____ Date _____

1. For the countries shown on the table, agricultural products _____ .
   - (A) are no longer a significant part of the United States' economy
   - (B) account for very little economic activity
   - (C) are a major economic part of most countries shown on the table
   - (D) are unimportant in Latin American economies

2. Based on the table, you can probably assume that _____ .
   - (F) the United States does not import much coffee
   - (G) coffee consumption around the world is decreasing dramatically
   - (H) Canada grows most of its own coffee
   - (J) coffee is an important part of the economy of many Latin American nations

3. The table reveals that Mexico is probably rich in _____.
   - (A) silver
   - (B) gold
   - (C) diamonds
   - (D) tin

4. A so-called *banana republic* was a small country in which large, American-owned fruit companies attempted to control the internal affairs. Based on the list of exports, which of the following countries do you think was formerly considered a banana republic?
   - (F) Brazil
   - (G) Honduras
   - (H) Canada
   - (J) the United States

5. Which Latin American country is the most important trading partner for the United States?
   - (A) Brazil
   - (B) Cuba
   - (C) Mexico
   - (D) Argentina

6. Which country listed in the table do you think probably has the least industrialized economy? Explain your answer.

   _____
   _____
   _____
   _____
   _____
   _____

7. Based on the information in the table, which country in the region do you think is the most economically powerful? Explain your answer.

   _____
   _____
   _____
   _____
   _____
   _____
   _____
   _____

Name _____ Date _____

Social Studies
1.D.1/1.D.2
Themes

Governments of the U.S., Canada, and Latin America

DIRECTIONS: Choose the best answer.

1. Which of the following is *not* a function of government?
   - Ⓐ defending the country
   - Ⓑ collecting taxes
   - Ⓒ raising families
   - Ⓓ educating citizens

2. The United States has a form of government that allows its citizens to elect officials to represent them. This is best known as _____ .
   - Ⓕ federalism
   - Ⓖ a dictatorship
   - Ⓗ a monarchy
   - Ⓙ a republic

3. Which statement about elections in the United States is false?
   - Ⓐ Some judges are elected, and others are appointed.
   - Ⓑ It is possible to vote for a Democratic president and Republican vice president.
   - Ⓒ Voters can cast ballots for local officials, as well as for national officials.
   - Ⓓ Sometimes voters have an opportunity to vote on important issues as well as on candidates.

4. In Argentina, everyone over age 18 is required by law to vote, except clergymen, army personnel, and those deprived for legal reasons. One way this differs from voting requirements in the United States is that _____ .
   - Ⓕ you can vote when you turn 16 years old
   - Ⓖ in the United States you must be at least 30 years old to vote
   - Ⓗ you are not required to vote
   - Ⓙ it does not differ at all

5. The Parliament of Canada is modeled on the British Parliament. It has two chambers: the House of Commons, which is elected, and the Senate, whose members are appointed by the prime minister. One way this differs from the United States Congress is that _____ .
   - Ⓐ all members of Congress are appointed, not just senators
   - Ⓑ U.S. senators are appointed by the Chief Justice of the Supreme Court
   - Ⓒ the United States has no Senate
   - Ⓓ U.S. senators and representatives are elected by American citizens

DIRECTIONS: Read the passage and answer questions 6 and 7.

Latin American countries have frequently been ruled by dictators. These include Porfirio Diaz (Mexico, 1876–1911), Juan Peron (Argentina, 1946–1955), the Somoza family (Nicaragua, 1937–1979), Rafael Leonidas Trujillo Molina (Dominican Republic, 1930–1961), Fidel Castro (Cuba, 1959–present), and Alfredo Stroessner (Paraguay, 1954–1989).

6. Which Latin American country is currently ruled by a dictator?
   - Ⓕ Cuba
   - Ⓖ Mexico
   - Ⓗ Argentina
   - Ⓙ Nicaragua

7. Porfirio Diaz was the former dictator of _____ .
   - Ⓐ Paraguay
   - Ⓑ the Dominican Republic
   - Ⓒ Mexico
   - Ⓓ Cuba

© Carson-Dellosa Publishing

Patriotic Celebrations

DIRECTIONS: Choose the best answer.

1. This holiday is celebrated in the United States, Canada, and most Latin American nations to honor working men and women.
   - (A) Labor Day
   - (B) Independence Day
   - (C) President's Day
   - (D) Thanksgiving Day

2. This Mexican national holiday honors the Mexican victory over the French army at Puebla de los Angeles on May 5, 1862.
   - (F) Thanksgiving Day
   - (G) Election Day
   - (H) Cinco de Mayo
   - (J) St. Patrick's Day

3. The founding of the city of Rio de Janeiro is celebrated on January 20 in parts of _____.
   - (A) Manitoba
   - (B) Brazil
   - (C) California
   - (D) New York

4. The signing of the Declaration of Independence is celebrated in the United States on _____.
   - (F) the first Tuesday in November
   - (G) July 4
   - (H) January 1
   - (J) the fourth Thursday in November

5. On Remembrance Day, Canadians honor those who have died while serving in the armed forces. It is observed on November 11. The American equivalent to Remembrance Day is observed on the last Monday in May and is called _____.
   - (A) Memorial Day
   - (B) Flag Day
   - (C) President's Day
   - (D) Victoria Day

6. Christopher Columbus's "discovery" of the New World is celebrated in many Latin American countries on _____.
   - (F) January 1
   - (G) February 14
   - (H) October 12
   - (J) December 25

DIRECTIONS: Read the passage and choose the best answer.

Simon Bolivar was one of South America's greatest statesmen, writers, and generals. His victories over Spain won independence for six nations—Bolivia, Panama, Colombia, Ecuador, Peru, and Venezuela. He is often referred to as "The Liberator" and the "George Washington of South America." He motivated thousands to fight and die for liberty.

7. Two South American nations celebrate July 24 as Birth of the Liberator Day, or Simon Bolivar Day. Based on the passage, the two countries are probably _____.
   - (A) Brazil and Paraguay
   - (B) Peru and Cuba
   - (C) Chile and Uruguay
   - (D) Venezuela and Ecuador

Name _____ Date _____

Social Studies   Themes

1.D.4

International Organizations

DIRECTIONS: Use the information in the table to choose the best answer.

Name of Organization	Description
United Nations (UN)	Almost every country in the world is a member of the UN. Among its goals are to achieve higher standards of living, improve health and education, and promote respect for human rights and freedoms throughout the world. Its main objective, however, is to promote world peace.
Organization of American States (OAS)	Most nations in North and South America are members of the OAS. The goals of the OAS are to have peace and justice, to promote unity, and to defend the power, territory, and independence of each member nation.
Caribbean Community (CARICOM)	Fifteen Caribbean nations are members of CARICOM. The mission of CARICOM is to provide leadership and service to have a workable, internationally competitive community that can be maintained.
Andean Community	Bolivia, Colombia, Ecuador, Peru, and Venezuela make up the Andean Community. This organization promotes economic cooperation among its member nations.

1. Which of the organizations cited in the table probably has the most member states?

   (A) Andean Community
   (B) United Nations
   (C) Organization of American States
   (D) Caribbean Community

2. Suppose Ecuador and Bolivia have a dispute concerning a trade agreement. Which of the following organizations would probably take the greatest interest in resolving the dispute?

   (F) United Nations
   (G) Caribbean Community
   (H) Andean Community
   (J) Organization of American States

3. Suppose two Central American countries were threatening to go to war against each other. Which of the following organizations would probably take a leading role in preventing the conflict?

   (A) Organization of American States
   (B) Andean Community
   (C) Caribbean Community
   (D) both B and C but not A

4. Which of the following organizations includes members outside of North America and Latin America?

   (F) Andean Community
   (G) Organization of American States
   (H) United Nations
   (J) all of them include members outside of North America and Latin America

5. The United States is *not* a member of the _____.

   (A) Andean Community
   (B) Caribbean Community
   (C) United Nations
   (D) both A and B but not C

© Carson-Dellosa Publishing   159

Name _____ Date _____

Social Studies
1.0
For pages 146–159

Mini-Test 1

Themes

DIRECTIONS: Use the map to answer questions 1 and 2.

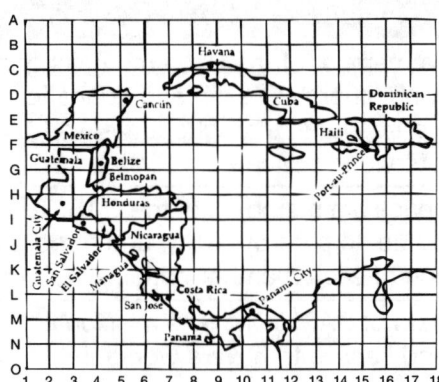

1. What are the coordinates for Port-au-Prince, Haiti?
   - (A) (9, C)
   - (B) (15, F)
   - (C) (3, I)
   - (D) (4, G)

2. Which country lies northwest of Honduras?
   - (F) Cuba
   - (G) Nicaragua
   - (H) Costa Rica
   - (J) Guatemala

DIRECTIONS: Choose the best answer.

3. The Navaho, Cherokee, and Iroquois nations are all Native American tribes living in _____.
   - (A) Argentina
   - (B) the United States
   - (C) Bolivia
   - (D) Uruguay

4. Which of these is a province of Canada?
   - (F) Saskatchewan
   - (G) Tierra del Fuego
   - (H) Baja California
   - (J) New England

5. What happened on December 7, 1941?
   - (A) Columbus discovered the New World.
   - (B) The American Civil War ended.
   - (C) The Japanese attacked an American naval base at Pearl Harbor, Hawaii.
   - (D) Simon Bolivar secured the independence of Venezuela.

6. Which is *not* a country in South America?
   - (F) Chile
   - (G) Bolivia
   - (H) Ecuador
   - (J) Tibet

7. In which of these cities is the influence of French culture most noticeable?
   - (A) Montréal, Canada
   - (B) Cincinnati, Ohio
   - (C) Havana, Cuba
   - (D) Mexico City, Mexico

8. Which of the following products does the United States depend largely on Latin America to provide?
   - (F) automobiles
   - (G) bananas
   - (H) wheat
   - (J) computers

160 © Carson-Dellosa Publishing

Social Studies Standards

2.0 Skills and Strategies
Using a variety of skills and strategies, by the end of the school year, students should:

2.A Getting Information

    2.A.1 Locate information using different types of primary and secondary sources, such as maps, globes, graphs, charts, newspapers, magazines, historical fiction and nonfiction, timelines, cartoons, surveys, media, museums, interviews, diaries, posters, brochures, travel guides, the Internet, and other reference works. *(See pages 163–164.)*

What it means:
- A **primary source** is a document or piece of evidence written or created during the time period you are studying by people who were there. A primary source allows you to examine evidence yourself without being affected by the views of others.
- A **secondary source** describes or analyzes a primary source. A secondary source is one step removed from the actual event and helps you to understand what researchers and other experts know about a topic.

    2.A.2 Skim texts to get an overview of content or locate specific information. *(See page 165.)*

    2.A.3 Organize information from primary and secondary sources. *(See pages 166–167.)*

    2.A.4 Identify the main ideas and supportive elements in print and nonprint sources. *(See page 168.)*

    2.A.5 Differentiate relevant from irrelevant information. *(See page 169.)*

2.B Using Information

    2.B.1 Interpret information found in primary and secondary source documents, graphs, political cartoons, maps, charts, diagrams, timelines, posters, multimedia presentations, and dioramas. *(See pages 170–171.)*

    2.B.2 Evaluate information found in documents. *(See page 172.)*

    2.B.3 Make and question hypotheses based on sufficiency of evidence. *(See page 173.)*

What it means:
- A **hypothesis** is a tentative explanation for an observation or problem that can be tested by further observation or research.

    2.B.4 Develop ideas by drawing conclusions and making predictions about historical events, characters, settings, and issues. *(See page 174.)*

2.C Presenting Information Orally and in Written Form
  2.C.1 Write a document-based essay with a logical plan of organization modeled on the Grade 5 New York State Assessment's DBQ. *(See pages 175–177.)*

> **What it means:**
> - DBQ stands for **Document-Based Question.** Students taking the Global History and Geography Regents are asked to read a collection of documents and answer a series of questions about them. Known as "scaffolding" questions, they are designed to help the student build a foundation to respond to the document-based essay question that follows.

  2.C.2 Use at least three cited sources to produce an informational piece of writing, such as a report, that is organized so that facts are in a logical order, and that uses details and examples to support larger ideas. *(See pages 178–179.)*
  2.C.3 Express opinions and back them up with reasons. *(See page 180.)*
  2.C.4 Organize and present information orally using notes or other memory aids. *(See page 181.)*
  2.C.5 Use computer technology to construct tables, graphs, and charts.
  2.C.6 Keep a collection of social studies written work. Write reflections on progress made, favorite pieces, improvements to be made. *(See page 182.)*
2.D Collaborative Learning
  2.D.1 Understand that others may have a different point of view.
  2.D.2 Participate in group planning and discussion of projects by following democratic procedures and helping to make group decisions.
  2.D.3 Take responsibility for completing individual and group assignments.
2.E Identifying and Solving Problems
  2.E.1 Identify current political or social problems and conduct research to find solutions. *(See page 183.)*
  2.E.2 Participate in group planning by suggesting ways to solve a problem. *(See page 183.)*

Name _____   Date _____

Social Studies

2.A.1

Locating Primary and Secondary Sources

Skills and Strategies

DIRECTIONS: Identify one primary source of information and one secondary source of information for each topic below. Visit the library or use the Internet to help find appropriate resources.

Clue: A **primary source** is a document or piece of evidence written or created during the time period you are studying by people who were there. A primary source allows you to examine evidence yourself without being affected by the views of others. A **secondary source** describes or analyzes a primary source. A secondary source is one step removed from the actual event and helps you to understand what researchers and other experts know about a topic.

1. **Life in Nazi Germany**

   Primary source: _____

   Secondary source: _____

2. **The experience of Native Americans at the beginning of the twentieth century**

   Primary source: _____

   Secondary source: _____

3. **How it feels to visit the moon**

   Primary source: _____

   Secondary source: _____

4. **The struggle for women's right to vote in the United States**

   Primary source: _____

   Secondary source: _____

© Carson-Dellosa Publishing

Name _____ Date _____

Social Studies 2.A.1

Identifying Primary and Secondary Sources

Skills and Strategies

DIRECTIONS: Identify each of the following as either a primary or secondary source.

> **Examples:**
>
> **Primary sources** include diaries, speeches, and letters; creative works (poems, novels), relics or artifacts (clothing, jewelry, toys); and news film footage or photos.
>
> **Secondary sources** include textbooks, academic journal articles, histories, criticisms, commentaries, and most reference works.

1. *The Diary of Anne Frank* _____

2. An article in today's newspaper recounting the Boston Tea Party _____

3. "Stopping by Woods on a Snowy Evening," a poem by Robert Frost _____

4. *The Encyclopedia Brittanica* _____

5. A letter written by George W. Bush during the Iraq War _____

6. A journal article analyzing the poetry of Robert Frost _____

7. A biography written in 2003 about Cleopatra _____

8. A book about the history of baseball _____

9. A magazine article written by George W. Bush about the Civil War _____

10. News footage of Germans tearing down the Berlin Wall _____

11. A magazine article summarizing the latest research on cancer _____

12. *The Autobiography of Babe Ruth* _____

13. List three primary sources you have recently used:

    _____
    _____
    _____

14. List three secondary sources you have recently used:

    _____
    _____
    _____

164   © Carson-Dellosa Publishing

Name _____ Date _____

Social Studies

2.A.2

Skimming a Text

Skills and Strategies

DIRECTIONS: Skim the passage to answer the questions. Look back to the passage if you are unsure of the answers.

The Man Behind the Faces

If you have never heard of Gutzon Borglum, you are not alone. Even though he was the sculptor responsible for the carvings on Mount Rushmore, many people do not know him by name.

Gutzon Borglum was born in Idaho in 1867 to Danish parents. He became interested in art early in life. He spent time studying in Paris, then returned home to concentrate on sculpture. At the beginning of his career, Gutzon created many large sculptures, some of which are quite famous. He also worked on the early stages of the carving of General Robert E. Lee at Stone Mountain, Virginia.

Gutzon was patriotic and outspoken. He lived during a time in American history called "the Colossal Age." This meant that big things were happening. For this reason, Gutzon Borglum became known as an artist who did things on a grand scale.

Borglum wanted to create a large monument to four American Presidents who brought our country into the modern age. He located Mount Rushmore, a 5,725-foot granite mountain in South Dakota and began his sculptures in 1927. Working on one at a time, Gutzon and his team carved the faces of George Washington, Thomas Jefferson, Abraham Lincoln, and Theodore Roosevelt into the mountainside.

Gutzon died in 1941, but his son, Lincoln, continued the work on Mount Rushmore. Today, Mount Rushmore is one of the most-visited national monuments.

1. **What is this article mainly about?**
   - (A) the beginning of "the Colossal Age"
   - (B) Gutzon Borglum's life
   - (C) Borglum's great work, Mount Rushmore
   - (D) art on a grand scale

2. **According to the passage, Gutzon Borglum did things on a grand scale. What does doing something "on a grand scale" probably mean?**
   - (F) creating things with intricate designs
   - (G) making things that are very large and impressive
   - (H) doing things well and with great care
   - (J) doing things that take artistic talent

3. **Based on your answer for number 2, which of the following would you consider to be done on a grand scale?**
   - (A) a painting as tall as a house
   - (B) a painting of a large, royal family
   - (C) a drawing of the tallest building in the world
   - (D) a life-size sculpture of a man

4. **Which of these statements about Mount Rushmore is true according to information in the article?**
   - (F) Mount Rushmore is located in North Dakota.
   - (G) It is located in South Dakota.
   - (H) It is more famous than Stone Mountain.
   - (J) It is the largest mountain in the country.

5. **What detail does *not* support the idea of Gutzon as an artist?**
   - (A) Gutzon went to Paris to study art.
   - (B) He became interested in art early in his life.
   - (C) Gutzon was patriotic and outspoken.
   - (D) He created many large sculptures.

© Carson-Dellosa Publishing

Name _____ Date _____

Social Studies
2.A.3

Organizing Information

Skills and Strategies

DIRECTIONS: Miss Sabrina Sivis, a sixth-grade social studies instructor, has just presented to her class a unit called *Megalopolis: Chief Cities of the Twentieth Century.* One of her students, Betsy Moss, frantically took notes on the information Miss Sivis found in the encyclopedia. Below are the notes Betsy took. Betsy made less of a muddle with her notes when she completed the chart on the next page. Use the notes below to organize the city information according to size on the next page.

Megalopolis

London has a population of 11,800,000.
Buenos Aires is city number 11 in population order. It has 200,000 fewer people than Manila.
Mexico City has the fourth greatest population.
Karachi has 200,000 fewer people than Jakarta.
Jakarta's population is 12,300,000.
Bombay has the same number of people as Osaka, number 7, and São Paolo.
Shanghai has the same number of people as London, but follows London, which is city number 17.
13,500,000 is the population of Manila.
Number 16 has 12,100,000 people.

The third largest city has a population of 19,900,000 people.
Osaka has a population of 17,900,000.
The fourth largest city has a population of 19,800,000.
Calcutta has 12,900,000 people.
The three largest population centers have 34,800,000, 20,200,000, and 19,900,000 people, respectively.
Tokyo is number 1 on the list.
Los Angeles' population of 16,200,000 is 4,000,000 less than New York's.
Cairo's population of 14,400,000 places it in the ninth spot.
The eighth city has a population of 16,200,000.
Jakarta is city number 15.
Moscow's population is 13,200,000.
The twentieth city has 10,700,000 people.
Lagos immediately follows Moscow and has 100,000 fewer people.
Manila, city number 10, has 2,700,000 fewer people than Los Angeles.
India's cities of Bombay and Calcutta are sixth and fourteenth, respectively.
São Paolo is the fifth largest city.
Rio de Janeiro's population of 10,700,000 has 2,800,000 fewer people than number 10.
Seoul has 19,900,000 people.
Delhi has 300,000 fewer people than Shanghai, which is eighteenth on the list.

Name _____ Date _____

Order of Cities and Their Populations

Order	City	Population
1	_____	_____
2	_____	_____
3	_____	_____
4	_____	_____
5	_____	_____
6	_____	_____
7	_____	_____
8	_____	_____
9	_____	_____
10	_____	_____
11	_____	_____
12	_____	_____
13	_____	_____
14	_____	_____
15	_____	_____
16	_____	_____
17	_____	_____
18	_____	_____
19	_____	_____
20	_____	_____

Name _____ Date _____

Social Studies
2.A.4

Using Print and Nonprint Sources

Skills and Strategies

DIRECTIONS: Use the library or Internet to find two sources on a topic of your choice. One of the sources should be print (book, magazine article, etc.). The second should be nonprint (film or videotape, photo collection, audio recording). Examine the sources. Then, complete the page below.

 **Clue** — If you are having trouble finding a topic, try researching baseball in the 1920s, the life of an American pioneer, the 1903 San Francisco earthquake, or current teenage fashions in the United States.

Print Source

Description of print source:
_____
_____
_____

Main idea:
_____
_____
_____

Details that support main idea:
_____
_____
_____

Nonprint Source

Description of nonprint source:
_____
_____
_____

Main idea:
_____
_____
_____

Details that support main idea:
_____
_____
_____

Briefly describe some things you learned from the print source that you did not learn from the nonprint source. Then, describe some things you learned from the nonprint source that you did not learn from the print source.

_____
_____

STOP

Name _____ Date _____

Social Studies

2.A.5 | **Differentiating Relevant From Irrelevant Information**

Skills and Strategies

DIRECTIONS: Read the following story. Below the story is a list of several details from the story. Write an **R** on the line if the detail is relevant, or significant, to the meaning of the story. Write an **I** if the detail is irrelevant, or insignificant, to the meaning of the story.

Alex in Charge

Alex was thrilled. Mom and Dad were going out for the evening. They wanted to eat at their favorite pizza place and see a new movie. Alex was allowed to babysit her sister Connie by herself. Connie was four. Alex went to Cedar Ridge Middle School. When their parents left, Alex and Connie sat down to watch a show on the family's brand-new TV.

"We're watching my show because I'm in charge," said Alex. Connie burst into tears, stood right in front of the TV, and wouldn't move.

"Fine. Then let's eat. But we're eating what I want because I am in charge."

Alex microwaved the leftover macaroni and cheese and gave some to Connie. Connie turned the bowl upside down all over her pink flowered dress.

"You did that on purpose!" said Alex. "You are going to bed right now because I am in charge!"

She carried a screaming Connie to the bedroom. Connie's bedroom was decorated with colorful unicorns. All of a sudden, Connie stopped crying.

"What's that?" she said in a small, frightened voice.

Alex listened and heard a strange noise. It sounded as if someone was climbing up the side of the house! Just then a huge, dark shadow fell across the room. Alex and Connie both screamed and held onto each other. They crept to the window in silence. They peered over the windowsill and saw a tree scratching against the window pane. Sighing with relief, they both fell exhausted onto Connie's bed and went to sleep.

_____ 1. Alex and Connie had leftover macaroni and cheese for dinner.

_____ 2. Alex had never babysat Connie before.

_____ 3. Mom and Dad were going out for the evening.

_____ 4. Connie's bedroom was decorated with colorful unicorns.

_____ 5. Connie became frightened when she heard a strange noise.

_____ 6. Mom and Dad were going to a pizza restaurant.

_____ 7. The family had a brand-new television set.

_____ 8. Connie and Alex fell asleep together on Connie's bed.

_____ 9. Alex got upset with Connie.

_____ 10. Connie was wearing a pink flowered dress.

_____ 11. Alex attended Cedar Ridge Middle School.

© Carson-Dellosa Publishing

Name _____   Date _____

Social Studies

| 2.B.1 | # Interpreting Information From Primary and Secondary Sources | Skills and Strategies |

DIRECTIONS: Examine the illustration. Then, answer the questions.

Source: Downloaded from http://www.mackaycartoons.net/september11.html

1. The illustration above is an editorial cartoon that appeared in several American newspapers the day after the September 11, 2001, terrorist attacks on the United States. What do you think is the best interpretation of this cartoon?

   Ⓐ The terrorist attacks created much smoke and air pollution.

   Ⓑ The United States will remain strong in the face of the attacks.

   Ⓒ The United States should surrender to the terrorists as soon as possible.

   Ⓓ All Americans should fly the flag to show their patriotism.

2. The illustration is a _____ .

   Ⓕ secondary source, because it is an in-depth analysis of the terrorist attacks

   Ⓖ secondary source, because only written documents can be primary sources

   Ⓗ primary source, because it was created immediately after the terrorist attacks by someone who was there

   Ⓙ primary source, because it was widely distributed in newspapers across the country

3. What do you think the illustrator's feelings were as he drew this image? How can you tell?

   _____
   _____
   _____
   _____
   _____

Name _____ Date _____

DIRECTIONS: Use the graph below to answer questions 4 and 5.

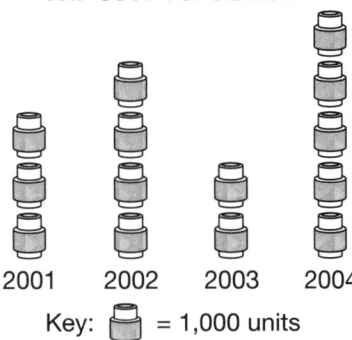

4. How many widgets were produced in 2003?
   - (A) 4,000
   - (B) 3,000
   - (C) 2,000
   - (D) 1,000

5. During which year were the greatest number of widgets produced?
   - (F) 2001
   - (G) 2002
   - (H) 2003
   - (J) 2004

DIRECTIONS: Use the map below to answer questions 6 and 7.

6. According to the map, most of Iowa's land is used for _____ .
   - (A) grazing
   - (B) crops
   - (C) forests
   - (D) unproductive uses

7. What is the main use for the land around the city of Duluth?
   - (F) forests
   - (G) grazing
   - (H) unproductive uses
   - (J) crops

© Carson-Dellosa Publishing

Name _____ Date _____

Social Studies
2.B.2

Evaluating Information

Skills and Strategies

DIRECTIONS: Answer the following questions.

Not everything you read is of equal value. Some information is more accurate, up-to-date (or timely), and reliable than other information.

1. Write at least three questions you should ask yourself to determine the credibility of the information you read.

   _____
   _____
   _____
   _____
   _____
   _____
   _____

2. You find some old magazine articles from the 1920s speculating on the future of human flight. You also find some articles on the same topic that appeared in some aviation journals last year. Compare and evaluate the probable accuracy, timeliness, and reliability of this information.

   _____
   _____
   _____
   _____
   _____
   _____
   _____

3. A friend tells you that she just read an article about a scandal involving a prominent U.S. senator. She tells you that the article appeared in a supermarket tabloid. How do you respond to the story? Explain your answer.

   _____
   _____
   _____
   _____
   _____
   _____
   _____
   _____
   _____

4. Now suppose your friend tells you that she got her information from *The New York Times*. Does your answer change? In what way? Why or why not?

   _____
   _____
   _____
   _____
   _____
   _____
   _____

© Carson-Dellosa Publishing

Name _____ Date _____

Social Studies

2.B.3

Making and Questioning Hypotheses

Skills and Strategies

DIRECTIONS: Read the passage and answer the questions.

> Can you imagine a wilderness under the sea that is so humongous it has never been fully explored? The Great Barrier Reef is such a place, being the largest ridge of coral in the world. It is 1,250 miles long—that's about as far as the distance between Detroit, Michigan, and Houston, Texas. Its undersea coral gardens provide homes for more than 1,400 varieties of exotic fish. This huge maritime province stretches along the northeastern coast of Australia and ranges from 10 to more than 100 miles from the shore.

1. Suppose you were writing a paper about the Great Barrier Reef. Based on the passage above, generate three hypotheses that you could use as the basis for research for your paper.

   _____
   _____
   _____
   _____
   _____
   _____

2. Based on the passage, make a guess about the types of predator fish that might exist in the Great Barrier Reef. Then, name one source you could consult to confirm your hypothesis.

   _____
   _____
   _____
   _____
   _____

3. Where would you be most likely to find more information about this topic?

   (A) in an almanac

   (B) in a book describing the earth's major coral reefs

   (C) in an encyclopedia entry about the Atlantic Ocean

   (D) in an essay about agriculture in Australia

4. Now, consult at least one source and test one of the hypotheses you made in questions 1 and 2. Briefly describe your findings.

   _____
   _____
   _____
   _____
   _____
   _____
   _____
   _____

© Carson-Dellosa Publishing

173

Name _____ Date _____

Social Studies
2.B.4

Drawing Conclusions and Making Predictions

Skills and Strategies

DIRECTIONS: Answer the following questions about the Eiffel Tower.

The Eiffel Tower

The Eiffel Tower in Paris, France, is considered to be one of the Seven Wonders of the Modern World. The Eiffel Tower stands 984 feet high. It is made of a wrought-iron framework that rests on a four-legged base. The tower is made of 18,038 pieces of metal and 2.5 million rivets. Elevators and 1,665 steps lead to the top of the tower.

Among other things, the Eiffel Tower contains restaurants and weather stations. Since 1953, it has been used as the main television transmitter for Paris. Before that, it was used to transmit radio signals and as a weather monitoring station.

Today, everyone agrees that the Eiffel Tower is a true wonder. But in 1887, many people believed that Alexander Gustave Eiffel was crazy when he began building his metal tower.

Gustave Eiffel designed his tower to be the centerpiece of the World's Fair Exposition of 1889 in Paris. He was chosen for the project because he was, at age fifty-three, France's master builder. Eiffel was already famous for his work with iron, which included the framework for the Statue of Liberty.

On January 26, 1887, workers began digging the foundation for the Eiffel Tower. Everyone but Gustave Eiffel believed that it would be impossible to finish the tallest structure in the world in just two years. After all, it had taken 4 years to build the Washington Monument.

The French government would grant the project only one-fifth of the money needed. Eiffel himself agreed to provide $1,300,000, which he could recover if the tower was a financial success.

In March of 1889, after over two years of continuous work, the Eiffel Tower was completed. Eiffel not only met his deadline, but also built the tower for less money than he thought it would cost. The final cost was exactly $1,505,675.90.

1. What was Gustave Eiffel's opinion about whether the Eiffel Tower could be completed in two years? How did his opinion differ from other opinions around him?

   _____

   _____

2. If you were an accountant simply looking at the money facts about the Eiffel Tower, would you judge it to be a success? Why or why not?

   _____

   _____

3. How do you think the use of the Eiffel Tower might change in years to come?

   _____

   _____

   _____

4. Using only facts from the story, prove that Gustave Eiffel was a success in life.

   _____

   _____

   _____

Name _____ Date _____

Social Studies

2.C.1 Writing a Document-Based Essay

Skills and Strategies

DIRECTIONS: Read the passages concerning the American Revolution and answer the questions on the following page.

Views of a twentieth-century historian:

American colonists had no elected representatives in the British Parliament. Therefore, the British government had no right to tax the colonies. They tried to raise money in 1765 by requiring a tax stamp on colonial documents, newspapers, and other printed papers. Colonists' opposition to the Stamp Act was justified. The colonial leaders who organized the Stamp Act Congress were right. Colonists could not be taxed without being represented in Parliament. The Stamp Act obviously weakened the colonists' rights and liberties.

Views of Samuel Johnson, an English writer who lived at the time of the American Revolution:

As man can be in but one place, at once, he cannot have the advantages of multiplied residence. He that will enjoy the brightness of sunshine, must quit the coolness of the shade. He who goes voluntarily to America, cannot complain of losing what he leaves in Europe. He, perhaps, had a right to vote for a knight or burgess; by crossing the Atlantick [sic], he has not nullified his right; but he has made its exertion no longer possible. By his own choice he has left a country, where he had a vote and little property, for another, where he has great property, but no vote.

Note: Source of second passage is *The Works of Samuel Johnson,* published by Pafraets & Company, Troy, New York, 1913; volume 14, pages 93–144.

British Policies Toward American Colonies

Policy	Description
Sugar Act	Lowered the tax on British molasses to stop the smuggling of sugar; set up courts to hear smuggling cases
Currency Act	Banned the use of paper money in the colonies
Stamp Act	Placed a tax on most printed materials
Quartering Act	Required colonists to provide barracks for or otherwise house British troops
Townshend Acts	Placed a tax on imported goods
Tea Act	Allowed a British tea company to sell directly to shopkeepers, bypassing colonial merchants who usually distributed imported tea
Declaratory Act	Declared that colonies were under the authority of the British Parliament, which had the power to make laws for the colonies
Coercive Acts	Closed Boston Harbor, banned town meetings and cancelled many elections, protected British soldiers from trials by colonists, and forced colonists to house British soldiers in their homes

Name _____   Date _____

> **From the Declaration of Independence:**
>
> When in the Course of human events, it becomes necessary for one people to dissolve the political bands which have connected them with another, and to assume . . . the separate and equal station to which the Laws of Nature and of Nature's God entitle them . . . they should declare the causes which impel [force] them to the separation. . . .
>
> Governments are instituted among Men, deriving their just powers from the consent of the governed. . . .
>
> The history of the present King of Great Britain is a history of repeated injuries and usurpations [takings], all having in direct object the establishment of an absolute Tyranny over these States. . . .

1. **The historian's main point is that _____.**

   - (A) colonists should never have to pay any taxes of any kind
   - (B) colonists should not be taxed by the British because they could not vote in British elections
   - (C) the British have every right to tax their colonies
   - (D) all taxes are unlawful

2. **Samuel Johnson's main point is that _____.**

   - (F) whatever the colonists want is acceptable
   - (G) the colonists should be taxed even more heavily
   - (H) colonists have no right to complain about losing their vote in British elections
   - (J) the British Army should arrest all colonists who refuse to pay their taxes

3. Imagine that you are a British subject living in London in the 1760s. Explain why you think your government's policies toward the colonies are fair and just.

   _____
   _____
   _____
   _____
   _____

4. Do you think the American Revolution could have been avoided had the British government cancelled the policies to which the colonists objected? Or would the colonists eventually have insisted upon their independence no matter what the British government did? Defend your answer.

   _____
   _____
   _____
   _____
   _____
   _____

GO →

5. **Based on the documents on pages 175 and 176, write an essay agreeing or disagreeing with Samuel Johnson's point of view.**

Name _____ Date _____

Social Studies
2.C.2

Writing a Research Report

Skills and Strategies

DIRECTIONS: Organize the following facts and write a short research report on the next page. Clearly state the main idea and support it with facts. Use only those details that are necessary to your main idea.

From an article "The Essential Amadeus" by Christopher Morrow in *Classical Music Magazine,* vol. 34 (May 2002) pp. 29–30.

Wolfgang Amadeus Mozart was born on January 27, 1756, in Salzburg, Austria.

When he was just three years old, he learned to play the harpsichord.

By the time he was five years old, he was composing music.

At the age of six, he was invited to perform for the Empress of Austria.

Mozart's father, Leopold, was a well-known musician who took Mozart on tours through Europe.

Mozart performed for kings and queens, for other musicians, and in churches.

In 1781, Mozart left his hometown and moved to Vienna, Austria.

He earned a living by selling the music that he wrote, giving music lessons, and performing his music in public.

From "The Music of Mozart" by Stephanie Zurich in *World Facts Encyclopedia,* 1999 edition, vol. 10, pp. 136–137.

Mozart's compositions included operas, symphonies, concertos, serenades, and church music.

Mozart wrote 22 operas including, *The Marriage of Figaro, Don Giovanni,* and *The Magic Flute.*

Today, *Don Giovanni* is considered the world's greatest opera.

Mozart wrote at least 40 symphonies for orchestras.

His most famous work is called *Requiem. Requiem* is a mass, or prayers, for the dead.

From the book *Great Composers of Our Time* **by Tyler Brown. Brownberry Publishing, 1999.**

Mozart died a poor man on December 5, 1791, at the age of 35.

Today, Mozart is considered to have been a musical genius.

His music is known throughout the world.

178

© Carson-Dellosa Publishing

Name _____ Date _____

_____
_____
_____
_____
_____
_____
_____
_____
_____
_____
_____
_____
_____
_____
_____
_____
_____
_____
_____
_____
_____
_____
_____
_____
_____

DIRECTIONS: Complete the bibliography using information from the facts on the previous page.

Brown, Tyler _____
                            (title, publisher, date)

Morrow, _____
              (author's last name, article, magazine, volume, date, page number)

_____
(author's last name, first name, article, encyclopedia, date, volume, page number)

Name _____   Date _____

Social Studies

2.C.3

Expressing and Supporting Opinions

Skills and Strategies

DIRECTIONS: Write a persuasive composition by finishing the thought, "The world would be a better place without. . . ." State your position clearly, and present at least three reasons for your position. Anticipate and address any points on which your readers may disagree.

Name _____ Date _____

Social Studies
2.C.4

Delivering an Oral Report

Skills and Strategies

DIRECTIONS: Prepare a five-minute oral report about whom you think is the best U.S. President ever. Include information about the President's term in office, major accomplishments, difficulties faced, and a number of reasons supporting your assertion that this is the best President in U.S. history. Use the space below and extra paper as needed to create an outline and to make notes for your presentation. (You may use more outline entries if you choose.)

I. _____
    A. _____
    B. _____
    C. _____

II. _____
    A. _____
    B. _____
    C. _____

III. _____
    A. _____
    B. _____
    C. _____

When you are ready to make your report, deliver it to a friend or family member. Ask your friend or family member to time and grade your report using the following checklist:

How long did the report take to deliver? _____

How well did I hear the report? _____

Did the speaker talk too quickly? too slowly? _____

Did the speaker look at me during the report? _____

Were the words pronounced correctly? Note any words that were mispronounced:
_____
_____

Were there any grammatical errors? If so, list them:
_____
_____

Name _____   Date _____

Social Studies

| 2.C.6 |

Collecting Social Studies Written Work

Skills and Strategies

DIRECTIONS: Keep a collection of social studies reports and other pieces you've written in a folder or binder. Use the grid below to record comments about your work.

Title of piece	Personal favorite? (Yes/No)	How did this piece help my social studies progress?	How could I improve this piece?

STOP

Name _____ Date _____

Social Studies
2.E.1/2.E.2

Identifying and Solving Problems

Skills and Strategies

DIRECTIONS: Identify a current political or social problem that interests you. Narrow your topic as described below. Then, use the library and/or Internet to conduct research to find possible solutions to the problem.

> **Example:**
> Some topics are too big to write about in one or two pages. Topics such as "France," "the history of World War II," or "computers" are too broad. It is important to narrow the focus of your research in order to cover your topic more easily. One way to narrow your topic is to focus on a specific time or place, specific individuals or groups, or a particular feature of the topic. You can often narrow a topic in four or five steps. An example is given to help show you the process:
>
> Pollution
> Water Pollution
> Water Pollution in the United States
> Dumping of Factory Waste into American Rivers
> Effect of Acme Company's Dumping on Fish Life in Walnut Creek

Problem to research:

_____

Information sources:

_____

_____

_____

_____

Possible solutions:

_____

_____

_____

_____

Name _____ Date _____

Social Studies

2.0

For pages 163–183

Mini-Test 2

Skills and Strategies

DIRECTIONS: Study the time line below and answer questions 1–3.

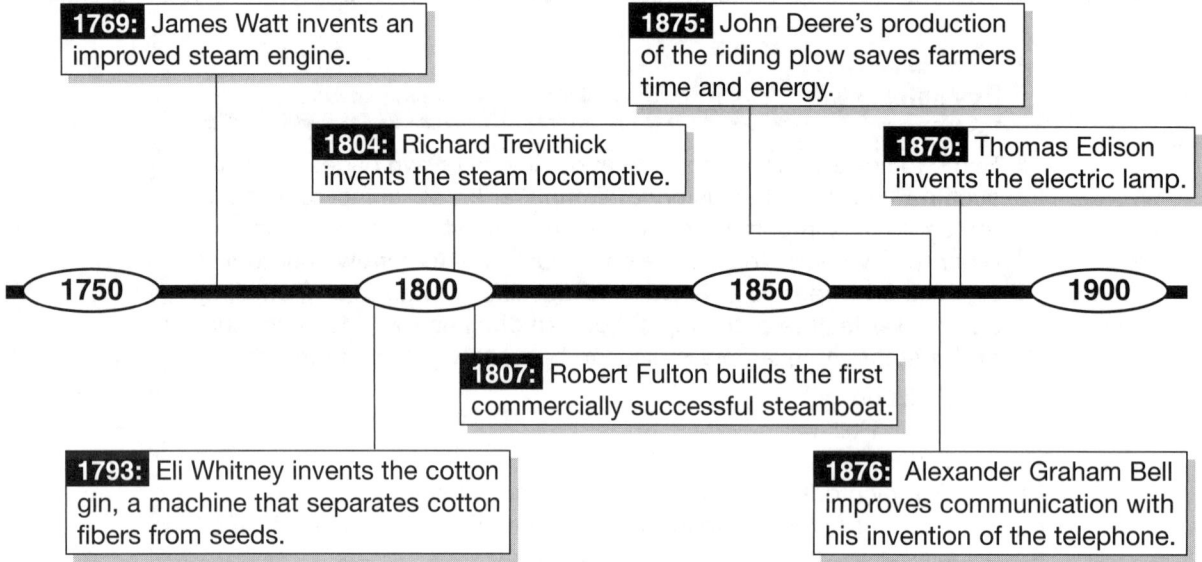

1. The above time line is a _____ source.
   - (A) primary
   - (B) secondary

2. Which invention was created after Fulton's steamboat was built?
   - (F) the spinning jenny
   - (G) the telephone
   - (H) the steam engine
   - (J) the cotton gin

3. How many years passed between the invention of Watt's steam engine and Edison's electric lamp?
   - (A) 75
   - (B) 72
   - (C) 86
   - (D) 110

DIRECTIONS: For questions 4–7, choose the best answer.

4. Which of the following would be a primary source of information?
   - (F) a book entitled *Famous Inventions of the 1800s,* published in 2003
   - (G) a documentary about the invention of the telephone
   - (H) a computer diagram that shows how a steam engine works
   - (J) notes Thomas Edison wrote while he worked on the electric lamp

184

© Carson-Dellosa Publishing

Name _____ Date _____

5. Hunter is writing a report about Alexander Graham Bell and his inventions. Which of these would Hunter *not* want to include in his report?

   A. a list of Alexander Graham Bell's inventions
   B. a brief history of Alexander Graham Bell's life
   C. an explanation of how Eli Whitney's cotton gin changed cotton production
   D. which one of Alexander Graham Bell's inventions was the most famous and why

6. What do you think probably happened to the number of bushels of corn and wheat American farmers produced after 1875? Explain your answer.

   _____
   _____
   _____

7. A respected historian claims that Thomas Jefferson had nothing whatsoever to do with the writing of the Declaration of Independence. You investigate further and learn that his last book won the Pulitzer Prize for history. However, no one else has ever made this claim. How much do you trust the historian's claim? Explain your answer.

   _____
   _____

DIRECTIONS: Read the passage to answer question 8.

As the Industrial Revolution spread throughout the United States, more and more people from other countries immigrated, or moved, to the United States. In the mid-1800s, many of the immigrants settled in the West and became farmers. But by the late 1800s, most new immigrants were settling in cities and seeking work in factories and mines.

8. Why do you suppose most new immigrants of the late 1800s and early 1900s chose to live in urban areas instead of rural areas? Explain your answer.

   _____
   _____
   _____
   _____
   _____
   _____
   _____

STOP

© Carson-Dellosa Publishing

How Am I Doing?

Mini-Test 1 Page 160 **Number Correct**	**7–8** answers correct	**Great Job!** Move on to the section test on page 187.
	5–6 answers correct	**You're almost there!** But you still need a little practice. Review practice pages 146–159 before moving on to the section test on page 187.
	0–4 answers correct	**Oops!** Time to review what you have learned and try again. Review the practice section on pages 146–159. Then, retake the test on page 160. Now, move on to the section test on page 187.
Mini-Test 2 Page 184 **Number Correct**	**7–8** answers correct	**Awesome!** Move on to the section test on page 187.
	5–6 answers correct	**You're almost there!** But you still need a little practice. Review practice pages 163–183 before moving on to the section test on page 187.
	0–4 answers correct	**Oops!** Time to review what you have learned and try again. Review the practice section on pages 163–183. Then, retake the test on page 184. Now, move on to the section test on page 187.

Name _____ Date _____

Final Social Studies Test
for pages 146–185

DIRECTIONS: Examine the map and graph of Central America below to choose the best answer.

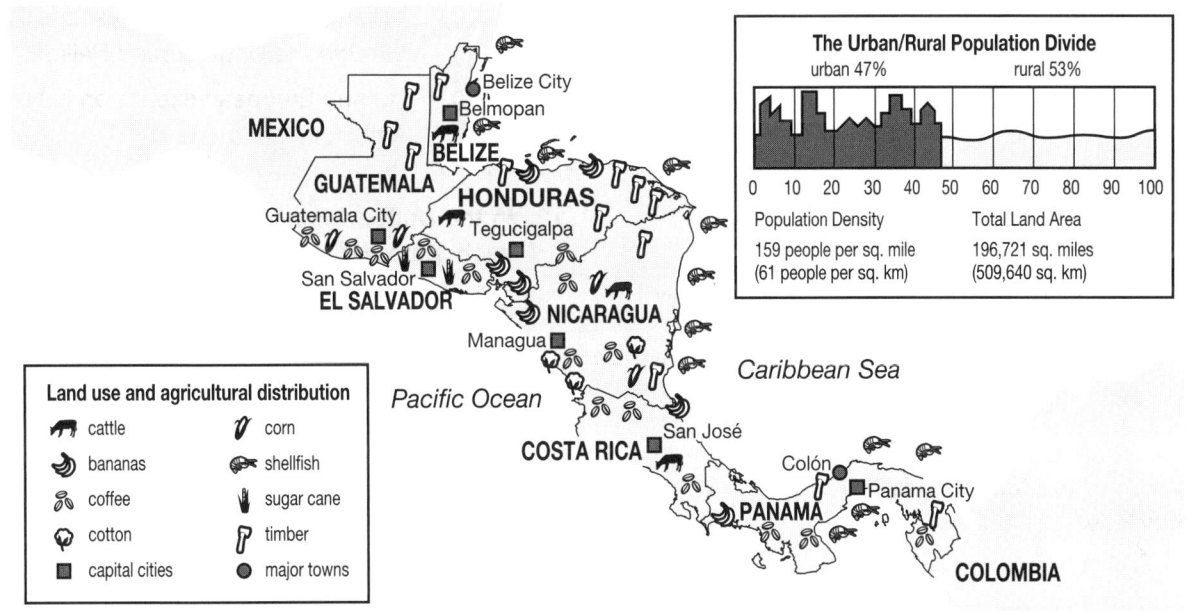

1. Which of the following is *not* a Central American country?

    (A) El Salvador
    (B) Belize
    (C) Nicaragua
    (D) Guyana

2. What is the capital city of Panama?

    (F) Colón
    (G) Tegucigalpa
    (H) Panama City
    (J) San José

3. Which of the following statements is true?

    (A) More than half of Central Americans live in rural areas.
    (B) The population density of Central America is about 61 people per square mile.
    (C) Every Central American nation has a coastline along the Pacific Ocean.
    (D) Mexico lies to the south of Central America.

4. Cattle are *not* an important economic commodity in _____ .

    (F) Belize
    (G) Honduras
    (H) Guatemala
    (J) Costa Rica

5. The two most important agricultural commodities grown in El Salvador are _____ .

    (A) bananas and coffee
    (B) sugar cane and coffee
    (C) cotton and corn
    (D) corn and sugar cane

GO

© Carson-Dellosa Publishing

Name _____ Date _____

DIRECTIONS: Choose the best answer.

6. Spanish is the first language of most _____ .
   - (F) Canadians
   - (G) Americans
   - (H) Latin Americans
   - (J) Native Americans

7. Fidel Castro is the communist dictator of _____ .
   - (A) Brazil
   - (B) Mexico
   - (C) Costa Rica
   - (D) Cuba

8. Which of the following is *not* one of the provinces of Canada?
   - (F) Ontario
   - (G) Quebec
   - (H) Vancouver
   - (J) Manitoba

9. Which of the following is *not* one of the states of Mexico?
   - (A) Nebraska
   - (B) Sonora
   - (C) Durango
   - (D) Veracruz

10. What percentage of the population of the United States is literate?
    - (F) 20–39 percent
    - (G) 40–59 percent
    - (H) 60–79 percent
    - (J) more than 80 percent

11. Harriet Tubman is best known for _____ .
    - (A) leading an expedition through the Louisiana Territory
    - (B) finding gold in California
    - (C) helping American slaves escape through the Underground Railroad
    - (D) fighting European expansion in Native American lands

12. In the United States, how many senators does each state get to elect and send to Congress?
    - (F) It depends on the state's population.
    - (G) 4
    - (H) 6
    - (J) 2

13. Which Latin American country requires everyone over age 18 to vote?
    - (A) Cuba
    - (B) Argentina
    - (C) Mexico
    - (D) Nicaragua

14. Cinco de Mayo is a national holiday in _____ .
    - (F) Uruguay
    - (G) Canada
    - (H) Mexico
    - (J) Peru

GO

Name _____ Date _____

15. Which organization has members from almost every country in the world?

    (A) Organization of American States
    (B) United Nations
    (C) Caribbean Community
    (D) Andean Community

DIRECTIONS: The resources below were used by someone who wrote a report called "Gold in Those Hills!" Examine the resources and answer the questions that follow.

Book
Daniels, Lamont. Author
The California Gold Rush
Anderson Publishing, 2002

Newspaper Article
Rice, Alison. Author
"Historians Recreate Old Mining Town"
San Francisco Enquirer, May 5, 2003 edition
pp. B1–B2

Magazine Article
Smith, Monica. Author
"Gold Mining Techniques in Old California"
The American Historian
vol. 21 (August 1999)
pp. 54–61

16. The subject of the paper is most likely the _____.

    (F) Civil War
    (G) discovery of gold in California in 1848
    (H) dangers of strip mining
    (J) migration of pioneers to the western United States

17. Which of these references is a primary source?

    (A) *The California Gold Rush*
    (B) "Historians Recreate Old Mining Town"
    (C) "Gold Mining Techniques in Old California"
    (D) None of the above

DIRECTIONS: Choose the best answer.

18. Which of the following do you think is probably the most reliable source of information about the effect of nutrition on the human body?

    (F) *Sports Illustrated*
    (G) a supermarket tabloid
    (H) a movie star's statement on a TV talk show
    (J) *The New England Journal of Medicine*

19. Kim is writing a report on the Liberty Bell. Which of these would Kim *not* want to include in her report?

    (A) a physical description of the Liberty Bell
    (B) a description of Pennsylvania
    (C) where the Liberty Bell is hung
    (D) events in which the Liberty Bell has been rung

Name _____ Date _____

DIRECTIONS: Read the passage and choose the best answer.

The Ship of the Desert

Nomads who cross the Sahara Desert of North Africa rely on a most unique animal for transportation—the dromedary, or one-humped camel. Because it is indispensable to desert travel, the dromedary is sometimes called the "ship of the desert." Camels have been used in many movies as methods of transportation.

Several factors make the dromedary suitable for long desert trips. It can go for long periods without nourishment. The hump on a camel's back serves as its food reserve. When it has little to eat, it converts the fat from its hump into energy. The camel's hump can weigh up to 80 pounds or more. When the animal has to rely on its reservoir of fat, the hump becomes much smaller. Thus, it is easy to recognize a well-fed camel by the size of its hump.

Many people believe that camels store water in their humps. This is not true. Their ability to go for days without drinking is due to other factors. First, camels are able to drink large quantities of water at one time. Some have been known to gulp 53 gallons in one day. Second, the camel sweats very little and can tolerate greater body temperatures. Consequently, it retains most of the water it drinks and can travel several hundred miles before replenishing its supply.

Other physical characteristics enable the camel to endure harsh desert conditions. It can completely close its nostrils, thus protecting it from the stinging effects of sandstorms. Its eyes are shielded from sand and sun by overhanging lids and long lashes, and its broad, padded feet keep it from sinking into the soft sand. No other animal is better equipped for life in the desert than the camel.

20. **What is the main idea expressed in this story?**
    - F. The dromedary is the ideal animal for desert life.
    - G. The camel's hump serves as its food reservoir.
    - H. The dromedary is called the "ship of the desert."
    - J. Camels do not store water in their humps.

21. **Which characteristic does *not* help the camel to survive in the desert?**
    - A. A camel can drink up to 53 gallons of water in one day.
    - B. A camel can close its nostrils.
    - C. A camel is indispensable to desert travel.
    - D. A camel sweats very little.

22. **What cannot be concluded from reading this passage?**
    - F. A camel can survive a long time without eating.
    - G. A dromedary camel is easier to ride than a Bactrian camel.
    - H. Camels have many features that equip them for cold weather.
    - J. Both G and H.

23. **Which of these statements is irrelevant to this passage?**
    - A. Camels can go for long periods without nourishment.
    - B. Camels are able to drink large quantities of water at one time.
    - C. Camels have been used in many movies as methods of transportation.
    - D. No other animal is better equipped for life in a desert than the camel.

24. **Which additional detail would support the title of this story?**
    - F. Nomads use camel's hair to weave cloth to make tents.
    - G. Camels are strong animals capable of carrying loads up to a thousand pounds.
    - H. Camel's milk and meat are often part of the nomad's diet.
    - J. Camels can be stubborn.

Name _____   Date _____

Final Social Studies Test
Answer Sheet

1. Ⓐ Ⓑ Ⓒ Ⓓ
2. Ⓕ Ⓖ Ⓗ Ⓙ
3. Ⓐ Ⓑ Ⓒ Ⓓ
4. Ⓕ Ⓖ Ⓗ Ⓙ
5. Ⓐ Ⓑ Ⓒ Ⓓ
6. Ⓕ Ⓖ Ⓗ Ⓙ
7. Ⓐ Ⓑ Ⓒ Ⓓ
8. Ⓕ Ⓖ Ⓗ Ⓙ
9. Ⓐ Ⓑ Ⓒ Ⓓ
10. Ⓕ Ⓖ Ⓗ Ⓙ

11. Ⓐ Ⓑ Ⓒ Ⓓ
12. Ⓕ Ⓖ Ⓗ Ⓙ
13. Ⓐ Ⓑ Ⓒ Ⓓ
14. Ⓕ Ⓖ Ⓗ Ⓙ
15. Ⓐ Ⓑ Ⓒ Ⓓ
16. Ⓕ Ⓖ Ⓗ Ⓙ
17. Ⓐ Ⓑ Ⓒ Ⓓ
18. Ⓕ Ⓖ Ⓗ Ⓙ
19. Ⓐ Ⓑ Ⓒ Ⓓ
20. Ⓕ Ⓖ Ⓗ Ⓙ

21. Ⓐ Ⓑ Ⓒ Ⓓ
22. Ⓕ Ⓖ Ⓗ Ⓙ
23. Ⓐ Ⓑ Ⓒ Ⓓ
24. Ⓕ Ⓖ Ⓗ Ⓙ

Answer Key

Page 8

1–4. Students are to borrow and read at least four books from the library about one subject, or by the same writer, or in the same genre. Be sure that students understand what *genre* is.
5. Students should mention traits unique to each type of book.
6. Students should mention traits the books have in common.
7. Be sure students offer some support for their opinions.

Page 9
1. textbook
2. newspaper
3. biography
4. instruction manual
5. A
6. G
7. D
8. F

Pages 10–11
1. B
2. G
3. D
4. H
5. B
6. J
7. B
8. J
9. C
10. Answers will vary, but should include logical entries for the students' chosen subject.

Pages 12–13
1. A
2. H
3. B
4. J
5. A
6. J

Page 14
1. D
2. G
3. D
4. G

Pages 15–16
1. Both stories deal with telling the truth.
2. Students may suggest Phil is probably the better friend, since he could not lie to his friends.
3. Answers will vary, but may suggest that lies are usually found out.
4. Answers will vary, but may suggest that honesty is the best policy.

Pages 17–18
1. Answers will vary. Students should define three words from the passage using an online dictionary.
2. Students' responses will vary.
3. Charles Blondin was the pseudonym of Frenchman Jean François Gravelet.

Page 19
Students' grids will vary. They should pick at least two reading goals for the year and should keep a record of all of the reading they do over the year.

Page 20 Mini-Test 1
1. A
2. J
3. B
4. H

Pages 22–23
1. laid
2. laid
3. laid
4. lie
5. except
6. affect
7. accepted
8. except
9. D
10. J
11. A
12. H
13. D
14. J
15. B
16. J
17. D
18. G
19. D
20. G
21. B
22. F
23. A
24. F
25. D

Pages 24–25
1. C
2. G
3. D
4. J
5. C
6. G
7. B
8. H
9. A

Page 26
1. B
2. H
3. A
4. J
5. B
6. F
7. A
8. H
9. B
10. G
11. A
12. G

Page 27
1. B
2. H
3. B
4. J
5. D
6. F

Page 28
1. You're, they're
2. It'll
3. Let's, they're
4. Don't, I've
5. I'll, what's
6. D
7. F
8. B
9. J
10. A
11. J
12. D
13. F

Page 29
1. C
2. G
3. A

Page 30
Accept any directions that have the steps in order and clear instructions.

Page 31
1. A
2. G
3. C
4. G
5. Students' sentences should be appropriate closing statements for the paragraph.

Pages 32–33
1. C
2. Possible answers include bendable, limber, movable.
3. Possible answers include rigid.
4. Possible answers include relaxing on one's back; lying flat.
5. book, encyclopedia article, magazine article
6. the encyclopedia article
7. volume 12
8. pages 25–32
9. the book
10. H
11. A
12. G
13. D
14. G
15. C

Page 34 Mini-Test 2
1. B
2. J
3. C
4. F
5. B
6. H
7. D

Pages 36–37
1. Answers will vary. Possible answer: Both stories deal with young people facing their fears.
2. Answers will vary. Students should support their views with evidence from the stories.
3. Answers will vary. Possible answer: In "I'll Save You," the narrator actually overcomes his fear to try to "save" his mother. In "What If," it is unclear if the narrator is still afraid at the end of the story.

Pages 38–39
1. A
2. H
3. A
4. J
5. Answers will vary, but students should comment thoughtfully on the author's success in presenting the information.

Pages 40–41
1. A
2. The lines in the passage all rhyme.
3. A. squirrel, adoring; B. rabbit, practical
4. Answers will vary. One possible answer is the value of knowing where you belong.
5. myth
6. science fiction
7. realistic fiction
8. nonfiction

Pages 42–43
Tate: *How he feels before the game*—excited; it's the championship game.
What he does during the game—hits a home run.
What he probably does next—gets another ice-cream cone. (Answers will vary.)
Jeffrey:
How he feels before the game—nervous; he's been in a batting slump.
What he does during the game—hits the winning run.
What he probably does next—buys Tate another cone. (Answers will vary.)
Alyssa:
How she feels before the game—calm and confident; it's her nature.
What she does during the game—stays cool and pitches well.
What she probably does next—enjoys the team's victory. (Answers will vary.)

Pages 44–45
1. one of the wood folk
2. She can speak to trees.
3. seven; Mikkel and Short Brush; five nobly dressed horsemen
4. At her order, trees captured the enemy.
5. Answers will vary.
6. having to do with trees
7. Answers will vary. They were merely servants.
8. The setting is a shady glen or forest. It is mentioned in the first paragraph.

Pages 46–47
1. B. Mr. Chan tells the students to be quiet and sit at their desks.
2. F. She was eager to share her story. She thought it was a good one.
3. B. The students lined up and went outside. A fire truck came to the school.
4. G. They arrived in a fire truck and carried a water hose.
5. A. A puff of smoke came out of a window near the cafeteria.
6. The cafeteria wasn't safe because there was damage from smoke.

Pages 48–49
1. C
2. Answers will vary but should reflect the author's strong disagreement with the headline. Correct grammar, spelling, and punctuation should be used in the response.
3. H
4. Answers will vary. Students should include a few sentences with valid reasons supporting their opinions.

Page 50
1–4. Students are to read a book of fiction, nonfiction, biography, and poetry and summarize each. Be sure that students understand what genre is.
5. Students should mention traits unique to each type of book.
6. Students should mention traits the books have in common.
7. Be sure students offer some support for their opinions.

Page 51
Students should create a written work in the genre of their choice. The work should include the elements characterized by that genre.

Page 52 Mini-Test 3
1. A
2. J
3. A
4. G
5. B

Pages 54–57 Final Test for Language Arts
1. B
2. H
3. D
4. F
5. A
6. J
7. C
8. J
9. B
10. G
11. A
12. G
13. C
14. G
15. B
16. H
17. B
18. G
19. C
20. H
21. D
22. J
23. A
24. H
25. B
26. G
27. C
28. J
29. A
30. G
31. D

Pages 62–63
1. D
2. H
3. B
4. H
5. B
6. H
7. A
8. J
9. B
10. H
11. 102,375.34
12. 25,043.2
13. 782,460.0002
14. 200,104,031.00004
15. 9,650,300
16. 1,000,000 + 200,000 + 300 + 40 + 1
17. 10,000 + 600 + 50 + $\frac{3}{1000}$
18. 200,000 + 30,000 + 8,000 + 200 + $\frac{5}{100}$
19. 500 + 60 + 3 + $\frac{201}{100,000}$
20. 4,000,000 + 70,000 + 4

Page 64
1. B
2. F
3. C
4. H
5. A
6. G
7. B
8. H
9. D
10. J
11. B
12. H

Page 65
1. C
2. J
3. C
4. G
5. A
6. J
7. C
8. G
9. B
10. J

Page 66
1. D
2. F
3. B
4. H
5. A
6. H
7. B
8. G

Page 67
1. A
2. J
3. A
4. G
5. A
6. J
7. B

Page 68
1. B
2. J
3. A
4. H
5. B
6. G
7. B

Page 69
1. 10,408
2. 133,142
3. 16,373
4. 75,174
5. 73,291
6. 13,645
7. 60,437
8. 81,009
9. 279
10. 16,373
11. 2,404
12. 13,353

Page 70
1. 328,032
2. 588,000
3. 451,000
4. 261,708
5. 526,542
6. 167,558
7. 215,821
8. 554,694
9. 204,120
10. 857,394
11. 307,146
12. 157,586

Page 71
1. 284
2. 27 R14
3. 27
4. 15 R54
5. 628
6. 217 R28
7. 636 R9
8. 125
9. 877
10. 847
11. 952
12. 241 R22
13. 671
14. 873
15. 594
16. 92 R26
17. 51 R77
18. 151
19. 36 R30
20. 90 R46

Page 72
1. P
2. I
3. P
4. P
5. P
6. I

7. I
8. P
9. P
10. I
11. I
12. P
13. P
14. I
15. I
16. $2\frac{7}{9}$
17. 6
18. $1\frac{1}{7}$
19. $6\frac{1}{2}$
20. $1\frac{5}{6}$
21. $2\frac{1}{3}$
22. $4\frac{1}{2}$
23. $2\frac{1}{4}$
24. $1\frac{3}{5}$
25. $4\frac{2}{3}$
26. $\frac{13}{4}$
27. $\frac{17}{4}$
28. $\frac{12}{7}$
29. $\frac{53}{10}$
30. $\frac{32}{7}$
31. $\frac{41}{6}$
32. $\frac{45}{8}$
33. $\frac{37}{5}$
34. $\frac{22}{3}$
35. $\frac{49}{15}$

Page 73
1. A
2. H
3. D
4. H
5. D
6. F
7. C
8. H

Page 74
1. $2 \times 3 \times 5 \times 7$
2. $2 \times 2 \times 11$
3. $2 \times 3 \times 5 \times 5 \times 7$

Page 75
1. $\frac{5}{8}$
2. $\frac{1}{2}$
3. $\frac{3}{4}$
4. $\frac{9}{10}$
5. $\frac{19}{20}$
6. $\frac{8}{15}$
7. $\frac{11}{12}$
8. $\frac{17}{20}$
9. $61\frac{23}{72}$
10. $30\frac{13}{21}$
11. $91\frac{1}{6}$
12. $179\frac{1}{2}$

Page 76
1. $\frac{1}{2}$
2. $\frac{2}{9}$
3. $\frac{3}{10}$
4. $\frac{1}{12}$
5. $\frac{4}{15}$
6. $\frac{1}{18}$
7. $\frac{1}{6}$
8. $\frac{19}{30}$
9. $\frac{3}{10}$
10. $2\frac{1}{2}$
11. $5\frac{11}{24}$
12. $5\frac{5}{8}$

Page 77

×	$\frac{3}{5}$	$\frac{1}{2}$	$\frac{2}{3}$	$\frac{1}{6}$	$\frac{1}{8}$
$\frac{1}{2}$	$\frac{3}{10}$	$\frac{1}{4}$	$\frac{1}{3}$	$\frac{1}{12}$	$\frac{1}{16}$
$\frac{3}{8}$	$\frac{9}{40}$	$\frac{3}{16}$	$\frac{1}{4}$	$\frac{1}{16}$	$\frac{3}{64}$
$\frac{4}{7}$	$\frac{12}{35}$	$\frac{2}{7}$	$\frac{8}{21}$	$\frac{2}{21}$	$\frac{1}{14}$
$\frac{5}{8}$	$\frac{3}{8}$	$\frac{5}{16}$	$\frac{5}{12}$	$\frac{5}{48}$	$\frac{5}{64}$
$\frac{1}{10}$	$\frac{3}{50}$	$\frac{1}{20}$	$\frac{1}{15}$	$\frac{1}{60}$	$\frac{1}{80}$

1. $7 \div \frac{1}{3} = \frac{7}{1} \div \frac{1}{3} = \frac{7}{1} \times \frac{3}{1} = \frac{21}{1} = 21$
2. $16 \div \frac{1}{3} = \frac{16}{1} \div \frac{1}{3} = \frac{16}{1} \times \frac{3}{1} = \frac{48}{1} = 48$
3. $6 \div \frac{1}{2} = \frac{6}{1} \div \frac{1}{2} = \frac{6}{1} \times \frac{2}{1} = \frac{12}{1} = 12$
4. $3\frac{1}{9} \div \frac{1}{3} = \frac{28}{9} \div \frac{1}{3} = \frac{28}{9} \times \frac{3}{1} = \frac{84}{9} = 9\frac{1}{3}$
5. $8 \div \frac{1}{2} = \frac{8}{1} \div \frac{1}{2} = \frac{8}{1} \times \frac{2}{1} = \frac{16}{1} = 16$
6. $2\frac{1}{2} \div \frac{1}{2} = \frac{5}{2} \div \frac{1}{2} = \frac{5}{2} \times \frac{2}{1} = \frac{10}{2} = 5$
7. $18 \div \frac{1}{7} = \frac{18}{1} \div \frac{1}{7} = \frac{18}{1} \times \frac{7}{1} = \frac{126}{1} = 126$
8. $5\frac{1}{4} \div \frac{3}{8} = \frac{21}{4} \div \frac{3}{8} = \frac{21}{4} \times \frac{8}{3} = \frac{168}{12} = 14$

Page 78
1. A
2. J
3. B
4. H
5. D
6. H

Page 79
1. D
2. F
3. C
4. F
5. A
6. H
7. A
8. H

Page 80
1. C
2. F
3. A
4. G
5. A
6. H
7. D
8. G
9. C
10. G

Page 81
1. C
2. F
3. D
4. G
5. C
6. G

Page 82
1. D
2. G
3. C
4. J
5. D
6. H

Page 83
1. less than
2. greater than
3. between
4. less than
5. greater than
6. equivalent to
7. less than
8. less than
9. equivalent to
10. equivalent to
11. less than
12. equivalent to
13. less than
14. greater than
15. between
16. equivalent to
17. less than
18. equivalent to
19. between
20. less than

Page 84
1. A
2. F
3. D
4. H
5. B
6. H

Page 85
1. B
2. J
3. A
4. H
5. B
6. F
7. C
8. H
9. D
10. G

Page 86
1. B
2. J
3. A
4. H
5. D
6. G
7. C
8. G

Pages 87–88
Mini-Test 1
1. C
2. J
3. A
4. J
5. B
6. F
7. B
8. F
9. D
10. G
11. B
12. G
13. A
14. H
15. C
16. H
17. B
18. J
19. B
20. F

Page 90
1. B
2. H
3. B
4. G
5. A
6. F
7. A
8. F

Page 91
1. B
2. G
3. D
4. G
5. B
6. G
7. D
8. J

Page 92
1. B
2. F
3. A
4. G
5. C
6. G
7. C

Page 93
1. D
2. G
3. B
4. F
5. D
6. F
7. D

Page 94
1. D
2. H
3. C
4. F
5. D
6. G
7. A

Page 95
1. 22
2. 16
3. 14
4. 38
5. 40
6. 34
7. 28
8. 18

Page 96
1. $\overline{AB}$
2. $\overline{EF}$
3. $\overset{\frown}{BD}$
4. $\angle BCD$ or $\angle ACD$
5. $\overline{AC}$, $\overline{BC}$ or $\overline{DC}$
6. $\overrightarrow{GH}$
7. B
8. H
9. C
10. F

Page 97
1–3.

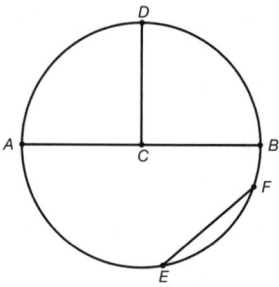

4. Students should construct circles and create diameters, radii, and chords. All parts should be labeled appropriately.

Page 98
1. B
2. J
3. C
4. F
5. B

Page 99
1. C
2. J
3. A
4. G
5. C
6. F

Page 100
1. capital H
2. capital I
3. capital H
4. capital I

Page 101
1. C
2. G
3. D
4. F
5. 180 in.³
6. 198 mm³
7. 216 m³
8. 20 in.³

Page 102
1.

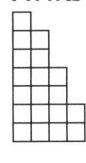 

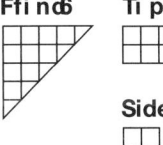

2.

Ffind6 Tip6

Side6

3. A
4. G

Page 103
1. B
2. J
3. D
4. F

Page 104 Mini-Test 2
1. D
2. G
3. D
4. G
5. C
6. H
7. B
8. J
9. B

Page 106
1. The star travels counterclockwise around the triangle. In next three shapes, the star is in the left corner, the right corner, and at the top.

2. The pattern is eyes open, right wink, left wink. The next three shapes: right wink, left wink, eyes open.

Shape	1st	2nd	3rd	4th	5th	6th	7th	8th	9th	10th
Number of Triangles	2	4	6	8	10	12	14	16	18	20

3. The number of triangles increases by two each time.
4. The number of triangles is two times greater than the shape number.
5. 30, 40
6. Add two to the number of triangles you have now to get the number of triangles in the next shape.

Page 107
1. A
2. H
3. D
4. G
5.

Number of Tables	1	2	3	4	5	6	7	8
Number of Guests	4	6	8	10	12	14	16	18

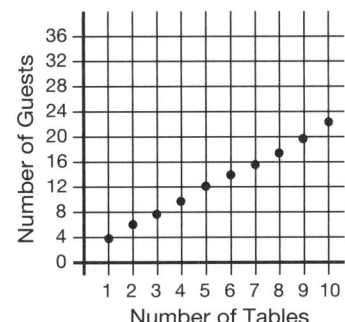

Page 108
1. D
2. F
3. C

Page 109
1. variable: n (or any other letter)
sentence: $3 + n = 9$
model:

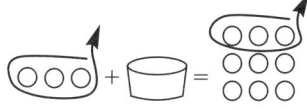

solution: $n = 6$

2. variable: p (or any other letter)
sentence: $4 + p = 13$
model:

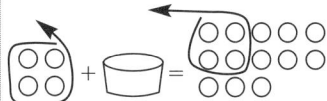

solution: $p = 9$

Page 110
1. 71, 68, 65, 62, 59, 56, 53, 50; Rule: -3
2. 11, 22, 33, 44, 55, 66, 77, 88; Rule: $+11$
3. 17, 25, 33, 41, 49, 57, 65, 73; Rule: $+8$
4. 8, 28, 48, 68, 88, 108, 128, 148; Rule: $+20$
5. 1, 2, 4, 8, 16, 32, 64, 128, 256; Rule: $\times 2$
6. 128, 64, 32, 16, 8, 4, 2, 1; Rule $\div 2$
7. 2, 20, 200, 2,000, 20,000, 200,000, 2,000,000, 20,000,000, 200,000,000; Rule: $\times 10$
8. 130, 115, 100, 85, 70, 55, 40, 25; Rule: -15

9. 1, 4, 16, 64, 256, 1,024, 4,096, 16,384; Rule: ×4
10. 5,000, 1,000, 200, 40, 8, $\frac{8}{5}$, $\frac{8}{25}$, $\frac{8}{125}$; Rule: ÷5

Page 111
1. D
2. F
3. C
4. J
5. C
6. F
7. B
8. H
9. C

Page 112
1. $n + 6 = 11$; $n = 5$
2. $n - 4 = 8$; $n = 12$
3. $n + 1 = -5$; $n = -6$
4. $n + 5 = -2$; $n = -7$
5. $3n = 12$; $n = 4$
6. $-4n = 64$; $n = -16$
7. $n \div 8 = 2$ $n = 16$
8. $n \div 4 = 20$; $n = 80$
9. $2n + 1 = 17$; $n = 8$
10. $3n - 2 = 10$; $n = 4$

Page 113
1. 91
2. 34
3. 17
4. −14
5. −10
6. 16
7. 76
8. 9
9. 0
10. 1

Page 114
1. $n + 17 < 29$
   $n < 12$
2. $n + 4 > 16$
   $n > 12$
3. $n + 45 < 164$
   $n < 119$
4. $n + 23 > 38$
   $n > 15$
5. $n + 146 < 255$
   $n < 109$
6. $5n > 25$
   $n > 5$
7. $4n < 42$
   $n < 10.5$
8. $10n > 140$
   $n > 14$
9. $2n < 18$
   $n < 9$
10. $8n > 92$
    $n > 11.5$

Page 115 Mini-Test 3
1. B
2. F
3. C
4. F
5. D
6. F
7. A
8. H

Page 117
1. D
2. H
3. B

Page 118
1. A
2. G
3. B
4. H
5. C
6. G

Page 119
1. Amelia: 6, 12
   Bobby: 10, 12
   Carla: 14, 9
   Daniel: 15, 14
   Elizabeth: 13, 4
   Frank: 7, 15
   Gerry: 7, 5
   Hank: 12, 10
   Isabella: 1, 13
   Jim: 11, 11
2. Daniel, Frank
3. Isabella, Elizabeth
4. pretzels
5. Daniel
6. Gerry

Page 120
1.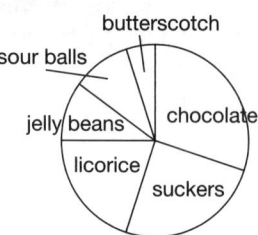
2. chocolate
3. butterscotch
4.
5. horror
6. drama

Page 121
1.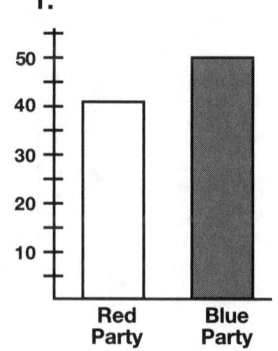

2.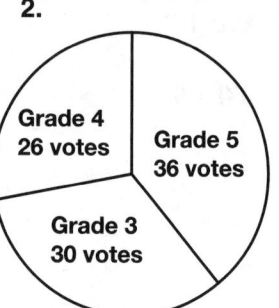
3. Students' graphs will vary but should be appropriate for the data represented.

Page 122
1. D
2. H
3. B
4. F
5. A
6. J
7. B
8. H

Page 123
1. B
2. F
3. C
4. H
5. Students' answers will vary. They are to randomly select 4 red crayons, 5 blue crayons, and 3 yellow crayons from a box and record the results.
6. Students should describe how their predictions varied from the actual results of their experiment.

Page 124
1. B
2. G
3. D
4. G
5. B
6. J
7. 1
8. $\frac{2}{5}$
9. 0
10. $\frac{3}{5}$

Pages 125–126
1. 7
2. 2, 12
3. 6, 8
4. $\frac{4}{36}$ or $\frac{1}{9}$
5. $\frac{8}{36}$ or $\frac{2}{9}$
6. 6
7. $\frac{6}{36}$ or $\frac{1}{6}$
8. B
9. J
10. A
11.

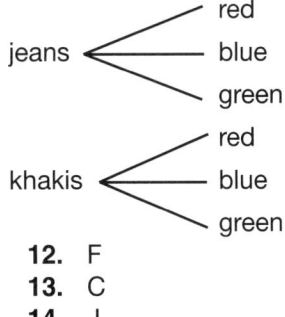

12. F
13. C
14. J

Pages 127–128
1. It is likely that about 225 students will order spaghetti.
2. This is a good sample because it is random and it is large enough to represent the entire population.
3. You might use a sample because it can be done quicker than surveying the entire population.
4. Yes, this sample should be larger than 2% of the population.
5. No, the poll was not useful because it did not come close to predicting the actual outcome.
6. The poll could have been off because the sample was not random or large enough.
7. Yes, it would be biased because the students like basketball.
8. No. It is probably mostly athletic students.

Page 128 Mini-Test 4
1. B
2. H
3. D
4. G
5.

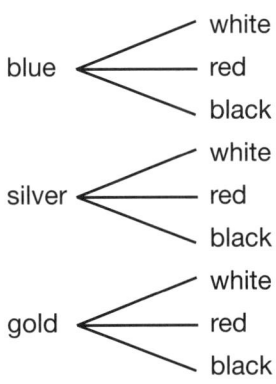

6. B
7. H
8. A

Page 130
1. D
2. J
3. C
4. J
5. B
6. F

Page 131
1. C
2. J
3. B
4. H
5. D
6. F
7. C

Page 132
1. B
2. H
3. A
4. H
5. A
6. J

Page 133
1. C
2. F
3. B
4. G
5. D
6. They will need to buy 3 large pizzas. Everyone will have to pitch in about $2.00.
7. Mr. Silverman will have to pay $216.00 for tile.

Page 134
1. B
2. F
3. 1901–1920
4. (7, L)
5. (9, C)

Page 135
1. A
2. F
3. D
4. G
5. C
6. F
7. B
8. H
9. B
10. G

Page 136 Mini-Test 5
1. C
2. F
3. D
4. H
5. D
6. F
7. B

Page 139–142 Final Mathematics Test
1. D
2. G
3. D
4. F
5. B
6. J
7. D
8. H
9. A
10. F
11. A
12. F
13. B
14. G
15. A
16. J
17. B
18. F
19. C
20. H
21. A
22. G
23. D
24. G
25. A
26. G
27. C
28. H
29. C
30. G
31. D
32. H

Page 146
1. B
2. H
3. C
4. J
5. A
6. G

Page 147
1. B
2. J
3. C
4. J
5. B
6. H
7. C
8. J

Page 148
1. B
2. H
3. C
4. F
5. D
6. F
7. A
8. J

Page 149
1. C
2. F
3. D
4. J
5. C

Page 150
1. A
2. G
3. A
4. H
5. D

Pages 151–152
1. A
2. G
3. D
4. G
5. C
6. G
7. B

Pages 153–154
1. B
2. J
3. C
4. F
5. C
6. G
7. A
8. Answers may vary. One possible answer: Water pollution has reduced the number of fish living in the ocean.

Pages 155–156
1. C
2. J
3. A
4. G
5. C
6. Honduras; most of its exports are simple agricultural commodities.
7. The United States; it is the chief trading partner for all nations in the region.

Page 157
1. C
2. J
3. B
4. H
5. D
6. F
7. C

Page 158
1. A
2. H
3. B
4. G
5. A
6. H
7. D

Page 159
1. B
2. H
3. A
4. H
5. D

Page 160 Mini-Test 1
1. B
2. J
3. B
4. F
5. C
6. J
7. A
8. G

Page 163
Answers will vary. Students are to identify one primary source of information and one secondary source of information for the listed topics.

Page 164
1. primary
2. secondary
3. primary
4. secondary
5. primary
6. secondary
7. secondary
8. secondary
9. secondary
10. primary
11. secondary
12. primary
13. Students should list three primary sources they have recently used.
14. Students should list three secondary sources they have recently used.

Page 165
1. B
2. G
3. A
4. G
5. C

Pages 166–167
1. Tokyo, 34,800,000
2. New York, 20,200,000
3. Seoul, 19,900,000
4. Mexico City, 19,800,000
5. São Paolo, 17,900,000
6. Bombay, 17,900,000
7. Osaka, 17,900,000
8. Los Angeles, 16,200,000
9. Cairo, 14,400,000
10. Manila, 13,500,000
11. Buenos Aires, 13,300,000
12. Moscow, 13,200,000
13. Lagos, 13,100,000
14. Calcutta, 12,900,000
15. Jakarta, 12,300,000
16. Karachi, 12,100,000
17. London, 11,800,000
18. Shanghai, 11,800,000
19. Delhi, 11,500,000
20. Rio de Janeiro, 10,700,000

© Carson-Dellosa Publishing

Page 168
Answers will vary. Students are to find a print and a nonprint source on a topic of their choice, describe each, and tell the main idea and supporting evidence found in each. Students are then to compare information found in each source.

Page 169
1. I
2. R
3. R
4. I
5. R
6. I
7. I
8. R
9. R
10. I
11. I

Pages 170–171
1. B
2. H
3. Answers will vary. Possible answer: The illustrator was confident and resolute that the country would survive. You can tell because the flag is the predominant image, not the burning buildings.
4. C
5. J
6. B
7. F

Page 172
1. Answers will vary. Possible answers: Is the information presented as fact or opinion? Is any supporting evidence given for the claim? How old is the information?
2. Answers will vary, but most students should realize that the more recent articles will be more accurate and reliable than articles that are 80 years old.
3. Answers will vary. Most students will probably be skeptical of the story in the newspaper tabloid because such papers tend to present sensational stories that frequently are not well documented. They are not generally reliable sources of information.
4. If a story appeared in a respected paper such as *The New York Times,* however, most students would likely be more inclined to believe it.

Page 173
1. Answers will vary. Possible answers: How deep is the Great Barrier Reef? How extensively has it been explored? What is the most abundant species living there?
2. Answers will vary. Possible answer: Sharks probably live in the Great Barrier Reef; a book about shark habitats would confirm this.
3. B
4. Answers will vary. Students should provide evidence supporting or disproving one of the ideas they generated for questions 1 and 2.

Page 174
1. He believed it could be done though no one else agreed.
2. Yes, it was done on time and for less money than they thought it would cost.
3. Predictions will vary. Predictions should be supported with valid arguments.
4. The Eiffel Tower is one of the Seven Wonders of the Modern World; Eiffel provided over $1 million toward the project; he finished the tower ahead of schedule and for less money. Eiffel built the framework for the Statue of Liberty.

Pages 175–177
1. B
2. H
3. Answers will vary but should be supported with logical arguments.
4. Answers will vary but should be supported with logical arguments.
5. Students' essays will vary. Essays should be planned logically and refer to the documents in the question for support.

Pages 178–179
Students should use the facts about Mozart to compose a one-page research report. Facts should be organized logically and in a way that supports the main idea. Facts that do not support the main idea should not be included.

© Carson-Dellosa Publishing

Bibliography:
Great Composers of Our Time, Brownberry Publishing, 1999.
Christopher Morrow, "The Essential Amadeus," *Classical Music Magazine,* vol. 34, May 2002, pp. 29–30.
Zurich, Stephanie, "The Music of Mozart," *World Facts Encyclopedia,* 1999, vol. 10, pp. 136–137.

Page 180
Students should write a persuasive composition in response to the prompt, "The world would be a better place without. . . ." Students should state their positions clearly and then present at least three reasons why they made their assertions. Their writing should demonstrate that they have considered and addressed points on which others may disagree.

Page 181
Answers will vary. Students should deliver a five-minute presentation on who they think is the best U.S. President ever. Students should use good eye contact, appropriate body language, and proper grammar during the presentation.

Page 182
Students are to keep a collection of social studies reports and other pieces they have written and record comments about their work.

Page 183
Students are to identify a current political or social problem that interests them, narrow the topic appropriately, and conduct research to find possible solutions.

Page 184 Mini-Test 2
1. B
2. G
3. D
4. J
5. C
6. John Deere's 1875 production of the riding plow saved farmers time and energy. Their ability to grow more in their fields probably increased significantly.
7. Answers will vary but students should be wary of accepting such a controversial theory based on just one person's opinion, no matter how well-respected.
8. Most new immigrants of the late 1800s and early 1900s chose to live in urban areas instead of rural areas so that they could get jobs in factories and mines.

Pages 187–190 Final Social Studies Test
1. D
2. H
3. A
4. H
5. B
6. H
7. D
8. H
9. A
10. J
11. C
12. J
13. B
14. H
15. B
16. G
17. D
18. J
19. B
20. F
21. C
22. J
23. C
24. G

New York State Standards

Language Arts

Standard 1—Language for Information and Understanding
Intermediate

Listening and Reading

1.1 Listening and reading to acquire information and understanding involves collecting data, facts, and ideas; discovering relationships, concepts, and generalizations; and using knowledge from oral, written, and electronic sources.

Students:

- **1.1A** interpret and analyze information from textbooks and nonfiction books for young adults, as well as reference materials, audio and media presentations, oral interviews, graphs, charts, diagrams, and electronic data bases intended for a general audience.
- **1.1B** compare and synthesize information from different sources.
- **1.1C** use a wide variety of strategies for selecting, organizing, and categorizing information.
- **1.1D** distinguish between relevant and irrelevant information and between fact and opinion.
- **1.1E** relate new information to prior knowledge and experience.
- **1.1F** understand and use the text features that make information accessible and usable, such as format, sequence, level of diction, and relevance of details.

What it means:
- Produce a summary of the information about a famous person found in a biography, encyclopedia, and textbook.
- Use facts and data from news articles and television reports in an oral report on a current event.
- Compile a bibliography of sources that are used in a research project.
- Take notes that record the main ideas and most significant supporting details of a lecture or speech.

Speaking and Writing

1.2 Speaking and writing to acquire and transmit information requires asking probing and clarifying questions, interpreting information in one's own words, applying information from one context to another, and presenting the information and interpretation clearly, concisely, and comprehensibly.

Students:

- **1.2A** produce oral and written reports on topics related to all school subjects.
- **1.2B** establish an authoritative stance on the subject and provide references to establish the validity and verifiability of the information presented.
- **1.2C** organize information according to an identifiable structure, such as compare/contrast or general to specific.
- **1.2D** develop information with appropriate supporting material, such as facts, details, illustrative examples or anecdotes, and exclude extraneous material.

1.2E use the process of pre-writing, drafting, revising, and proofreading (the "writing process") to produce well-constructed informational texts.

1.2F use standard English for formal presentation of information, selecting appropriate grammatical constructions and vocabulary, using a variety of sentence structures, and observing the rules of punctuation, capitalization, and spelling.

What it means:
- Write an essay for science class that contains information from interviews, data bases, magazines, and science texts.
- Participate in a panel discussion on population trends in the United States in recent years, using graphics, and citing the source of the data.
- Use technical terms correctly in subject area reports.
- Survey student views on a school issue and report findings to the class.

Standard 2—Language for Literary Response and Expression
Intermediate

Listening and Reading
2.1 Listening and reading for literary response involves comprehending, interpreting, and critiquing imaginative texts in every medium, drawing on personal experiences and knowledge to understand the text, and recognizing the social, historical and cultural features of the text.

Students:
2.1A read and view texts and performances from a wide range of authors, subjects, and genres.

2.1B understand and identify the distinguishing features of the major genres and use them to aid their interpretation and discussion of literature.

2.1C identify significant literary elements (including metaphor, symbolism, foreshadowing, dialect, rhyme, meter, irony, climax) and use those elements to interpret the work.

2.1D recognize different levels of meaning.

2.1E read aloud with expression, conveying the meaning and mood of a work.

2.1F evaluate literary merit based on an understanding of the genre and the literary elements.

What it means:
- Read or recite poems of their own selection to the class, clearly conveying the meaning of the poem and the effect of the rhythm and rhyme patterns.
- Produce lists of recommended readings for their peers, grouping the works according to some common elements (e.g., theme, setting, type of characters).
- Use references to literature they have read to support their position in class discussion.

Speaking and Writing
2.2 Speaking and writing for literary response involves presenting interpretations, analyses, and reactions to the content and language of a text. Speaking and writing for literary expression involves producing imaginative texts that use language and text structures that are inventive and often multilayered.

Students:

- **2.2A** present responses to and interpretations of literature, making reference to the literary elements found in the text and connections with their personal knowledge and experience.
- **2.2B** produce interpretations of literary works that identify different levels of meaning and comment on their significance and effect.
- **2.2C** write stories, poems, literary essays, and plays that observe the conventions of the genre and contain interesting and effective language and voice.
- **2.2D** use standard English effectively.

What it means:
- Take part in class productions of short plays.
- Write a sequel to a story continuing the development of the characters, plot, and themes.
- Write reviews of literature from different cultural settings and point out similarities and differences in that literature.
- Write stories or poems for their peers or younger children.

Standard 3—Language for Critical Analysis and Evaluation
Intermediate

Listening and Reading

3.1 Listening and reading to analyze and evaluate experiences, ideas, information, and issues requires using evaluative criteria from a variety of perspectives and recognizing the difference in evaluations based on different sets of criteria.

Students:

- **3.1A** analyze, interpret, and evaluate information, ideas, organization, and language from academic and nonacademic texts, such as textbooks, public documents, book and movie reviews, and editorials.
- **3.1B** assess the quality of texts and presentations, using criteria related to the genre, the subject area, and purpose (e.g., using the criteria of accuracy, objectivity, comprehensiveness, and understanding of the game to evaluate a sports editorial).
- **3.1C** understand that within any group there are many different points of view depending on the particular interests and values of the individual, and recognize those differences in perspective in texts and presentations (e.g., in considering whether to let a new industry come into a community, some community members might be enthusiastic about the additional jobs that will be created while others are concerned about the air and noise pollution that could result).
- **3.1D** evaluate their own and others' work based on a variety of criteria (e.g., logic, clarity, comprehensiveness, conciseness, originality, conventionality) and recognize the varying effectiveness of different approaches.

What it means:
- Compare a magazine article on a historical event with the entries in an encyclopedia and history book to determine the accuracy and comprehensiveness of the article.
- Use the criteria of scientific investigation to evaluate the significance of a lab experiment.
- Read two conflicting reviews of a popular movie and recognize the different criteria the critics were using to evaluate the film.
- Point out examples of propaganda techniques (such as "bandwagon," "plain folks" language, and "sweeping generalities") in public documents and speeches.

Speaking and Writing

3.2 Speaking and writing for critical analysis and evaluation requires presenting opinions and judgments on experiences, ideas, information, and issues clearly, logically, and persuasively with reference to specific criteria on which the opinion or judgment is based.

Students:

- **3.2A** present (in essays, position papers, speeches, and debates) clear analyses of issues, ideas, texts, and experiences, supporting their positions with well-developed arguments.
- **3.2B** develop arguments with effective use of details and evidence that reflect a coherent set of criteria (e.g., reporting results of lab experiments to support a hypothesis).
- **3.2C** monitor and adjust their own oral and written presentations according to the standards for a particular genre (e.g., defining key terms used in a formal debate).
- **3.2D** use standard English, precise vocabulary, and presentational strategies effectively to influence an audience.

What it means:
- Write a position paper on a current event, clearly indicating their position and the criteria on which it is based.
- Present an oral review of a film, supporting their evaluation with reference to particular elements such as character development, plot, pacing, and cinematography.
- Participate in a class debate on a social issue following the rules for formal debate.
- Produce their own advertising for a product, tailoring the text and visuals to a particular audience.

Standard 4—Language for Social Interaction
Intermediate

Listening and Speaking

4.1 Oral communication in formal and informal settings requires the ability to talk with people of different ages, genders, and cultures, to adapt presentations to different audiences, and to reflect on how talk varies in different situations.

Students:

- **4.1A** listen attentively to others and build on others' ideas in conversations with peers and adults.
- **4.1B** express ideas and concerns clearly and respectfully in conversations and group discussions.
- **4.1C** learn some words and expressions in another language to communicate with a peer or adult who speaks that language.
- **4.1D** use verbal and nonverbal skills to improve communication with others.

What it means:
- Act as hosts for open house at school.
- Participate in small group discussions in class.
- Give morning announcements over the public address system.
- Participate in school assemblies and club meetings.

Reading and Writing

4.2 Written communication for social interaction requires using written messages to establish, maintain, and enhance personal relationships with others.

Students:

4.2A write social letters, cards, and electronic messages to friends, relatives, community acquaintances, and other electronic network users.

4.2B use appropriate language and style for the situation and the audience and take into account the ideas and interests expressed by the person receiving the message.

4.2C read and discuss social communications and electronic communications of other writers and use some of the techniques of those writers in their own writing.

What it means:
- Write letters to friends who are away.
- Send e-mail messages on a computer network.
- Send formal invitations for receptions or open houses.

New York State Standards

Mathematics

Standard 1—Analysis, Inquiry, and Design
Intermediate

Mathematical Analysis
1.1 Abstraction and symbolic representation are used to communicate mathematically.

Students:
    1.1A extend mathematical notation and symbolism to include variables and algebraic expressions in order to describe and compare quantities and express mathematical relationships.

1.2 Deductive and inductive reasoning are used to reach mathematical conclusions.

Students:
    1.2A use inductive reasoning to construct, evaluate, and validate conjectures and arguments, recognizing that patterns and relationships can assist in explaining and extending mathematical phenomena.

What it means:
- Predict the next triangular number by examining the pattern 1, 3, 6, 10, ☐.

1.3 Critical thinking skills are used in the solution of mathematical problems.

Students:
    1.3A apply mathematical knowledge to solve real-world problems and problems that arise from the investigation of mathematical ideas, using representations such as pictures, charts, and tables.

Standard 2—Information Systems
Intermediate

2.1 Information technology is used to retrieve, process, and communicate information and as a tool to enhance learning.

Students:
    2.1A use a range of equipment and software to integrate several forms of information in order to create good quality audio, video, graphic, and text-based presentations.
    2.1B use spreadsheets and data-base software to collect, process, display, and analyze information. Students access needed information from electronic data bases and on-line telecommunication services.
    2.1C systematically obtain accurate and relevant information pertaining to a particular topic from a range of sources, including local and national media, libraries, museums, governmental agencies, industries, and individuals.
    2.1D collect data from probes to measure events and phenomena.
    2.1E use simple modeling programs to make predictions.

What it means:
- Compose letters on a word processor and send them to representatives of industry, governmental agencies, museums, or laboratories seeking information pertaining to a student project.
- Acquire data from weather stations.
- Use a software package, such as Science Tool Kit, to monitor the acceleration of a model car traveling down a given distance on a ramp.
- Use computer software to model how plants grow plants under different conditions.

2.2 Knowledge of the impacts and limitations of information systems is essential to its effective and ethical use.

Students:
- **2.2A** understand the need to question the accuracy of information displayed on a computer because the results produced by a computer may be affected by incorrect data entry.
- **2.2B** identify advantages and limitations of data-handling programs and graphics programs.
- **2.2C** understand why electronically stored personal information has greater potential for misuse than records kept in conventional form.

2.3 Information technology can have positive and negative impacts on society, depending upon how it is used.

Students:
- **2.3A** use graphical, statistical, and presentation software to present project to fellow classmates.
- **2.3B** describe applications of information technology in mathematics, science, and other technologies that address needs and solve problems in the community.
- **2.3C** explain the impact of the use and abuse of electronically generated information on individuals and families.

Standard 3—Mathematics
Intermediate

Mathematical Reasoning
3.1 Students use mathematical reasoning to analyze mathematical situations, make conjectures, gather evidence, and construct an argument.

Students:
- **3.1A** apply a variety of reasoning strategies.
- **3.1B** make and evaluate conjectures and arguments using appropriate language.
- **3.1C** make conclusions based on inductive reasoning.
- **3.1D** justify conclusions involving simple and compound (i.e., and/or) statements.

What it means:
- Use trial and error and work backwards to solve a problem.
- Identify patterns in a number sequence.
- Are asked to find numbers that satisfy two conditions, such as $n > -4$ and $n \leq 6$.

Number and Numeration

3.2 Students use number sense and numeration to develop an understanding of the multiple uses of numbers in the real world, the use of numbers to communicate mathematically, and the use of numbers in the development of mathematical ideas.

Students:

3.2A understand, represent, and use numbers in a variety of equivalent forms (integer, fraction, decimal, percent, exponential, expanded and scientific notation).

3.2B understand and apply ratios, proportions, and percents through a wide variety of hands-on explorations.

3.2C develop an understanding of number theory (primes, factors, and multiples).

3.2D recognize order relations for decimals, integers, and rational numbers.

What it means:

- Use prime factors of a group of denominators to determine the least common denominator.
- Select two pairs from a number of ratios and prove that they are in proportion.
- Demonstrate the concept that a number can be symbolized by many different numerals as in:

$$\frac{1}{4} = \frac{3}{12} = \frac{25}{100} = 0.25 = 25\%$$

Operations

3.3 Students use mathematical operations and relationships among them to understand mathematics.

Students:

3.3A add, subtract, multiply, and divide fractions, decimals, and integers.

3.3B explore and use the operations dealing with roots and powers.

3.3C use grouping symbols (parentheses) to clarify the intended order of operations.

3.3D apply the associative, commutative, distributive, inverse, and identity properties.

3.3E demonstrate an understanding of operational algorithms (procedures for adding, subtracting, etc.).

3.3F develop appropriate proficiency with facts and algorithms.

3.3G apply concepts of ratio and proportion to solve problems.

What it means:

- Create area models to help in understanding fractions, decimals, and percents.
- Find the missing number in a proportion in which three of the numbers are known, and letters are used as place holders.
- Arrange a set of fractions in order, from the smallest to the largest:

$$\frac{3}{4}, \frac{1}{5}, \frac{2}{3}, \frac{1}{2}, \frac{1}{4}$$

- Illustrate the distributive property for multiplication over addition, such as:

$$2(a + 3) = 2a + 6.$$

© Carson-Dellosa Publishing

Modeling/Multiple Representation

3.4 Students use mathematical modeling/multiple representation to provide a means of presenting, interpreting, communicating, and connecting mathematical information and relationships.

Students:

- **3.4A** visualize, represent, and transform two- and three-dimensional shapes.
- **3.4B** use maps and scale drawings to represent real objects or places.
- **3.4C** use the coordinate plane to explore geometric ideas.
- **3.4D** represent numerical relationships in one- and two-dimensional graphs.
- **3.4E** use variables to represent relationships.
- **3.4F** use concrete materials and diagrams to describe the operation of real world processes and systems.
- **3.4G** develop and explore models that do and do not rely on chance.
- **3.4H** investigate both two- and three-dimensional transformations.
- **3.4I** use appropriate tools to construct and verify geometric relationships.
- **3.4J** develop procedures for basic geometric constructions.

What it means:
- Build a city skyline to demonstrate skill in linear measurements, scale drawing, ratio, fractions, angles, and geometric shapes.
- Bisect an angle using a straight edge and compass.
- Draw a complex of geometric figures to illustrate that the intersection of a plane and a sphere is a circle or point.

Measurement

3.5 Students use measurement in both metric and English measure to provide a major link between the abstractions of mathematics and the real world in order to describe and compare objects and data.

Students:

- **3.5A** estimate, make, and use measurements in real-world situations.
- **3.5B** select appropriate standard and nonstandard measurement units and tools to measure to a desired degree of accuracy.
- **3.5C** develop measurement skills and informally derive and apply formulas in direct measurement activities.
- **3.5D** use statistical methods and measures of central tendencies to display, describe, and compare data.
- **3.5E** explore and produce graphic representations of data using calculators/computers.
- **3.5F** develop critical judgment for the reasonableness of measurement.

What it means:
- Use box plots or stem and leaf graphs to display a set of test scores.
- Estimate and measure the surface areas of a set of gift boxes in order to determine how much wrapping paper will be required.
- Explain when to use mean, median, or mode for a group of data.

Uncertainty

3.6 Students use ideas of uncertainty to illustrate that mathematics involves more than exactness when dealing with everyday situations.

Students:

- **3.6A** use estimation to check the reasonableness of results obtained by computation, algorithms, or the use of technology.
- **3.6B** use estimation to solve problems for which exact answers are inappropriate.
- **3.6C** estimate the probability of events.
- **3.6D** use simulation techniques to estimate probabilities.
- **3.6E** determine probabilities of independent and mutually exclusive events.

What it means:
- Construct spinners to represent random choice of four possible selections.
- Perform probability experiments with independent events (e.g., the probability that the head of a coin will turn up, or that a 6 will appear on a die toss).
- Estimate the number of students who might chose to eat hot dogs at a picnic.

Patterns/Functions

3.7 Students use patterns and functions to develop mathematical power, appreciate the true beauty of mathematics, and construct generalizations that describe patterns simply and efficiently.

Students:

- **3.7A** recognize, describe, and generalize a wide variety of patterns and functions.
- **3.7B** describe and represent patterns and functional relationships using tables, charts and graphs, algebraic expressions, rules, and verbal descriptions.
- **3.7C** develop methods to solve basic linear and quadratic equations.
- **3.7D** develop an understanding of functions and functional relationships: that a change in one quantity (variable) results in change in another.
- **3.7E** verify results of substituting variables.
- **3.7F** apply the concept of similarity in relevant situations.
- **3.7G** use properties of polygons to classify them.
- **3.7H** explore relationships involving points, lines, angles, and planes.
- **3.7I** develop and apply the Pythagorean principle in the solution of problems.
- **3.7J** explore and develop basic concepts of right triangle trigonometry.
- **3.7K** use patterns and functions to represent and solve problems.

What it means:
- Find the height of a building when a 20-foot ladder reaches the top of the building when its base is 12 feet away from the structure.
- Investigate number patterns through palindromes (pick a 2-digit number, reverse it and add the two—repeat the process until a palindrome appears).

$$\text{palindrome} \rightarrow \begin{array}{r} 42 \\ +24 \\ \hline 66 \end{array} \qquad \begin{array}{r} 86 \\ +68 \\ \hline 154 \\ +451 \\ \hline 605 \\ +506 \\ \hline \end{array}$$
$$\text{palindrome} \rightarrow 1111$$

- Solve linear equations, such as $2(x + 3) = x + 5$ by several methods.

New York State Standards

Social Studies

Standard 1—History of the United States and New York
Intermediate

1.1 The study of New York State and United States history requires an analysis of the development of American culture, its diversity and multicultural context, and the ways people are unified by many values, practices, and traditions.

Students:
1.1A explore the meaning of American culture by identifying the key ideas, beliefs, and patterns of behavior, and traditions that help define it and unite all Americans.

1.1B interpret the ideas, values, and beliefs contained in the Declaration of Independence and the New York State Constitution and United States Constitution, Bill of Rights, and other important historical documents.

What it means:
- Explain the ideas embodied in the Declaration of Independence, the United States Constitution, the Bill of Rights, and the New York State Constitution and show how these documents express fundamental and enduring ideas and beliefs.
- Describe how massive immigration, forced migration, changing roles for women, and internal migration led to new social patterns and conflicts; and identify ideas of national unity that developed amidst growing cultural diversity. (Adapted from *National Standards for U.S. History*)

1.2 Important ideas, social and cultural values, beliefs, and traditions from New York State and United States history illustrate the connections and interactions of people and events across time and from a variety of perspectives.

Students:
1.2A describe the reasons for periodizing history in different ways.

1.2B investigate key turning points in New York State and United States history and explain why these events or developments are significant.

1.2C understand the relationship between the relative importance of United States domestic and foreign policies over time.

1.2D analyze the role played by the United States in international politics, past and present.

What it means:
- Use demographic information, mapping exercises, photographs, interviews, population graphs, church records, newspaper accounts, and other sources to conduct case studies of particular groups in the history of the State or nation and classify information according to type of activity: social, political, economic, cultural, or religious.
- Use a variety of sources to study historic and contemporary events in the United States; investigate different interpretations of the events and identify circumstances of time and place that influence the authors' perspectives. (Adapted from *National Standards for U.S. History*)
- Recognize the reasons for periodizing history and know some designations of historical periods; discuss the usefulness of the following periods:
    - Three Worlds and Their Meeting in the Americas (Beginnings to 1607)
    - Colonization, Settlement and Communities (1607 to 1763)
    - The Revolution and the New Nation (1763 to 1815)
    - Expansion and Reform (1801 to 1861)
    - Crisis of the Union: Civil War and Reconstruction (1850 to 1877)
    - The Development of Modern America (1865 to 1920)
    - Modern America and the World Wars (1914 to 1945)
    - Contemporary America (1945 to Present) (Taken from *U.S. History Framework for the 1994 National Assessment of Educational Progress*)
- Undertake case studies to research violations of basic civil and human rights and case studies of genocide. Use examples from United States, New York State, and world history. Case studies might include chattel slavery and the Nazi Holocaust. Other civil and human rights violations might focus on the mass starvation in Ireland (1845–50), the forced relocation of Native American Indians, and the internment of Japanese Americans during World War II.
- Trace the tension between arguments for United States isolation versus engagement during the following time periods: up to 1941, from 1941–1975, and from 1976 to the present.

1.3 Study about the major social, political, economic, cultural, and religious developments in New York State and United States history involves learning about the important roles and contributions of individuals and groups.

Students:

1.3A complete well-documented and historically accurate case studies about individuals and groups who represent different ethnic, national, and religious groups, including Native American Indians, in New York State and the United States at different times and in different locations.

1.3B gather and organize information about the important achievements and contributions of individuals and groups living in New York State and the United States.

1.3C describe how ordinary people and famous historic figures in the local community, State, and the United States have advanced the fundamental democratic values, beliefs, and traditions expressed in the Declaration of Independence, the New York State and United States Constitutions, the Bill of Rights, and other important historic documents.

1.3D classify major developments into categories such as social, political, economic, geographic, technological, scientific, cultural, or religious.

What it means:
- Research major events and themes from New York State and United States history (e.g., the American Revolution, new national period, Civil War, age of industrialization, westward movement and territorial expansion, the World Wars) to develop and test hypotheses and develop conclusions about the roles played by individuals and groups.
- After reading about ordinary people in historic time periods, such as a Revolutionary War soldier, a suffragist, or a child laborer during the 1800s, write a short story or diary account explaining how this individual fought to support democratic values and beliefs. (Adapted from *National Standards for History for Grades K–4*)
- Explain the importance of different inventions and scientific and technological innovations in agriculture and industry, describing how these inventions and innovations resulted in imporved production of certain products.

1.4 The skills of historical analysis include the ability to: explain the significance of historical evidence; weigh the importance, reliability, and validity of evidence; understand the concept of multiple causation; understand the importance of changing and competing interpretations of different historical developments.

Students:

1.4A consider the sources of historic documents, narratives, or artifacts and evaluate their reliability.

1.4B understand how different experiences, beliefs, values, traditions, and motives cause individuals and groups to interpret historic events and issues from different perspectives.

1.4C compare and contrast different interpretations of key events and issues in New York State and United States history and explain reasons for these different accounts.

1.4D describe historic events through the eyes and experiences of those who were there. (Taken from *National Standards for History for Grades K–4*).

What it means:
- Identify the author's or artist's main point of view or purpose in creating a document or artifact.
- Compare several historical accounts of the same event in New York State or United States history and contrast the different facts included or omitted from each author and determine the different authors' points of view.
- Use a variety of sources to study important turning points from different perspectives and to identify varying points of view of the people involved (e.g., European settlement and the impact of diseases on Native American Indian populations, writing the Declaration of Independence and the Constitution, the Civil War, industrialization, significant reform movements, and the Cold War).
- Debate various views of United States foreign policies and involvement during the Spanish-American War, World Wars I and II, Vietnam, and the Cold War.

Standard 2—World History
Intermediate

2.1 The study of world history requires an understanding of world cultures and civilizations, including an analysis of important ideas, social and cultural values, beliefs, and traditions. This study also examines the human condition and the connections and interactions of people across time and space and the ways different people view the same event or issue from a variety of perspectives.

Students:

- **2.1A** know the social and economic characteristics, such as customs, traditions, child-rearing practices, ways of making a living, education and socialization practices, gender roles, foods, and religious and spiritual beliefs that distinguish different cultures and civilizations.
- **2.1B** know some important historic events and developments of past civilizations.
- **2.1C** interpret and analyze documents and artifacts related to significant developments and events in world history.

What it means:
- Propose a list of characteristics to define the concepts of culture and civilization, explaining how civilizations develop and change.
- Investigate the important achievements and accomplishments of the world's early civilizations (e.g., African, Greek, Roman, Egyptian, Indian, Chinese).
- Analyze how the natural environments of the Tigris-Euphrates, Nile, and Indus valleys shaped the early development of civilization. (Taken from *National Standards for World History*)
- Research an important event or development in world history and include information about how different people viewed the same event (e.g., the French Revolution as witnessed by members of the ruling classes, the revolutionaries, members of the Estates General, and the Church).
- Identify different ethnic, religious, and socioeconomic groups throughout the world and analyze their varying perspectives on the same historic events and contemporary issues. Explain how these different perspectives developed.

2.2 Establishing time frames, exploring different periodizations, examining themes across time and within cultures, and focusing on important turning points in world history help organize the study of world cultures and civilizations.

Students:

- **2.2A** develop time lines by placing important events and developments in world history in their correct chronological order.
- **2.2B** measure time periods by years, decades, centuries, and millennia.
- **2.2C** study about major turning points in world history by investigating the causes and other factors that brought about change and the results of these changes.

What it means:
- Construct multiple-tier time lines that display a number of important historic events that occurred at the same time or during the same period of time (e.g., age of exploration and contact showing events in Europe, Africa, and the Americas).
- Present historical narratives that link together a series of events in the correct chronological order.
- Recognize the reasons for periodizing history and know some designations of historical periods; discuss the usefulness of the following historical periods:
    - The beginnings of Human Society
    - Early Civilizations to 1000 B.C.
    - Classical Traditions, Major Religions, and Giant Empires, 1000 B.C.–A.D. 300
    - Expanding Zones of Exchange and Encounter, 300–A.D. 1000
    - Intensified Hemispheric Interactions, 1000–1500
    - Emergence of the First Global Age, 1450–1770
    - The Age of Revolutions, 1750–1914
    - The Twentieth Century.

(Adapted from *National Standards for World History*)

2.3   Study of the major social, political, cultural, and religious developments in world history involves learning about the important roles and contributions of individuals and groups.

Students:

2.3A   investigate the roles and contributions of individuals and groups in relation to key social, political, cultural, and religious practices throughout world history.

2.3B   interpret and analyze documents and artifacts related to significant developments and events in world history.

2.3C   classify historic information according to the type of activity or practice: social/cultural, political, economic, geographic, scientific, technological, and historic.

What it means:
- Read historic narratives, biographies, literature, diaries, and letters to learn about the important accomplishments and roles played by individuals and groups throughout world history.
- Explain some of the following practices as found in particular civilizations and cultures throughout world history: social customs, child-rearing practices, government, ways of making a living and distributing goods and services, language and literature, education and socialization practices, values and traditions, gender roles, foods, and religious/spiritual beliefs and practices.
- Develop a map of Europe, the Mediterranean world, India, South and Southeast Asia, and China to show the extent of the spread of Buddhism, Christianity, Hinduism, and Confucianism; explain how the spread of these religions changed the lives of people living in these areas of the world. (Adapted from *National Standards for World History*)
- Write diary accounts, journal entries, letters, or news accounts from the point of view of a young person living during a particular time period in world history, focusing on an important historic, political, economic, or religious event or accomplishment.
- Study the historical writings of important figures in world history to learn about their goals, motivations, intentions, influences, and strengths and weaknesses.

2.4 The skills of historical analysis include the ability to investigate differing and competing interpretations of the theories of history, hypothesize about why interpretations change over time, explain the importance of historical evidence, and understand the concepts of change and continuity over time.

Students:

2.4A explain the literal meaning of a historical passage or primary source document, identifying who was involved, what happened, where it happened, what events led up to these developments, and what consequences or outcomes followed (Taken from *National Standards for World History*).

2.4B analyze different interpretations of important events and themes in world history and explain the various frames of reference expressed by different historians.

2.4C view history through the eyes of those who witnessed key events and developments in world history by analyzing their literature, diary accounts, letters, artifacts, art, music, architectural drawings, and other documents.

2.4D investigate important events and developments in world history by posing analytical questions, selecting relevant data, distinguishing fact from opinion, hypothesizing cause-and-effect relationships, testing these hypotheses, and forming conclusions.

What it means:

- Examine documents related to significant developments in world history (e.g., excerpts from sacred texts of the world's great religions, important political statements or decrees, literary works, and historians' commentaries); employ the skills of historical analysis and interpretation in probing the meaning and importance of the documents by:
    - Identifying authors and sources for the historical documents
    - Comparing and contrasting differing sets of ideals and values contained in each historical document
    - Considering multiple perspectives presented in the documents
    - Evaluating major debates among historians about the meaning of each historical document
    - Hypothesizing about the influence of each document on present-day activities and debates in the international arena. (Adapted from *National Standards in World History*)
- Study about an event or development in world history (e.g., the early civilizations, the age of exchange and global expansion, the industrial revolution, political and social revolutions, imperialism and colonization, case studies of genocide and human rights violations, world wars) by analyzing accounts written by eyewitnesses to the event or development; compare the eyewitness accounts with reports and narratives written by historians after the event or development.
- Trace the impacts of different technological innovations and advances (e.g., in transportation and communication, agriculture, health and science, commerce and industry) over time by analyzing the effects of technology on the lives of people.

Standard 3—Geography
Intermediate

3.1 Geography can be divided into six essential elements which can be used to analyze important historic, geographic, economic, and environmental questions and issues. These six elements include: the world in spatial terms, places and regions, physical settings (including natural resources), human systems, environment and society, and the use of geography. (Adapted from *National Geography Standards, 1994: Geography for Life*)

Students:
- **3.1A** map information about people, places, and environments.
- **3.1B** understand the characteristics, functions, and applications of maps, globes, aerial and other photographs, satellite-produced images, and models (Taken from *National Geography Standards, 1994*).
- **3.1C** investigate why people and places are located where they are located and what patterns can be perceived in these locations.
- **3.1D** describe the relationships between people and environments and the connections between people and places.

What it means:
- Investigate how groups of people living in different geographic regions throughout the world interacted with and structured their natural environments to accommodate their varied lifestyles and economies; discuss national, regional, and global interactions.
- Draw from memory a map of the world on a single sheet of paper and outline and label the major physical features (e.g., continents, oceans, major mountain ranges, significant desert regions, and river systems) and important human features (e.g., major cities of the world, imaginary lines such as the prime meridian and the equator). (Taken from *National Geography Standards, 1994*)
- Apply the five themes of geography to their study of communities and regions throughout the world. Describe how location, place, relationships within places, movement, and regions can be used to analyze different cultures and societies.
- Complete a geographic/historic study of their community or a region of New York State by focusing on the following questions: Where is your community or region located? How did it get there? What is it like to live and work there? What are its physical characteristics (e.g., climate, elevation, population density, size)?

3.2 Geography requires the development and application of the skills of asking and answering geographic questions; analyzing theories of geography; and acquiring, organizing, and analyzing geographic information. (Adapted from *National Geography Standards, 1994: Geography for Life*)

Students:
- **3.2A** formulate geographic questions and define geographic issues and problems.
- **3.2B** use a number of research skills (e.g., computer databases, periodicals, census reports, maps, standard reference works, interviews, surveys) to locate and gather geographical information about issues and problems (Adapted from *National Geography Standards, 1994*).
- **3.2C** present geographic information in a variety of formats, including maps, tables, graphs, charts, diagrams, and computer-generated models.
- **3.2D** interpret geographic information by synthesizing data and developing conclusions and generalizations about geographic issues and problems.

What it means:
- Plan and execute an inquiry to answer these questions about a region of the world: How does the shape of the Earth and the natural environment influence where people live? What natural processes change the shape of the Earth's surface? How has human habitation changed the surface of the Earth? Derive generalizations and conclusions supported by evidence. (Based on *National Geography Standards, 1994*)
- Pose analytical questions concerning a geographic issue or problem affecting their community, region, or New York State (e.g., issues related to environmental problems and concerns, transportation and traffic needs, land use, housing, natural resource use).
- Use a variety of research skills to locate, collect, and organize geographic data related to a geographic or environmental issue, problem, or question; organize the data in logical and meaningful ways; present written and oral reports that include geographic conclusions and generalizations supported by the data collected; propose new questions for further investigation.
- Develop and present a multimedia report on a geographic topic, issue, problem, or question (e.g., deforestation, energy consumption, resource depletion, natural hazards, major geographic events), making use of maps, graphs, photographs, videos, computer-generated models, and other appropriate sources.
- Use a variety of maps to answer geographic questions about people, places, and regions.

Standard 4—Economics
Intermediate

4.1 The study of economics requires an understanding of major economic concepts and systems, the principles of economic decision making, and the interdependence of economies and economic systems throughout the world.

Students:

- **4.1A** explain how societies and nations attempt to satisfy their basic needs and wants by utilizing scarce capital, natural, and human resources.
- **4.1B** define basic economic concepts such as scarcity, supply and demand, markets, opportunity costs, resources, productivity, economic growth, and systems.
- **4.1C** understand how scarcity requires people and nations to make choices which involve costs and future considerations.
- **4.1D** understand how people in the United States and throughout the world are both producers and consumers of goods and services.
- **4.1E** investigate how people in the United States and throughout the world answer the three fundamental economic questions and solve basic economic problems.
- **4.1F** describe how traditional, command, market, and mixed economies answer the three fundamental economic questions.
- **4.1G** explain how nations throughout the world have joined with one another to promote economic development and growth.

What it means:
- Investigate how different countries in Europe and the Middle East solve problems related to satisfying basic needs. Compile a list of available resources, industries, modes of transportation, and economic problems.
- Define and apply basic economic concepts such as supply and demand, price, market, and economic growth in an investigation of a national or regional economic question or problem.
- Understand the concept of opportunity cost (the highest valued alternative not chosen) and how the concept applies to personal and business decision making.
- Consider case studies comparing economic decisions and choices made by groups and nations involving questions about scarce resources.
- Compare basic economic systems throughout the world, classifying them as traditional, command, market, or mixed. Focus on questions such as: What is produced? How is it produced, distributed, and consumed? Which natural, capital, and human resources are available? How are prices set? What is meant by economic growth?
- Identify the basic ideas and values of the United States economic system (e.g., individual entrepreneurship, private ownership of property, *laissez-faire* economics, cheap labor supply, free enterprise, monopolies, and governmental regulation) and how these factors contributed to the American economic system; compare these ideas and values to those of other economic systems.
- Define and apply the concepts of inflation, deflation, depression, fiscal policies, and monetary policy in the context in which these terms are used; examine the historical context of at least one of these concepts during an important event in United States history (e.g., industrialization of America and the rise of the labor movement, the Great Depression, the 1970s inflation).
- Develop a case study of a New York-produced product to show how the State participates in a world economy.
- Investigate the economy of the United States and determine how decisions are made about what goods and services are to be produced, and how they are distributed; compare how these decisions are made in other countries; identify the major imports/exports of the country and explain the effects of international trade on the American and other national economies; discuss how values may influence the economy.

4.2 Economics requires the development and application of the skills needed to make informed and well-reasoned economic decisions in daily and national life.

Students:

4.2A identify and collect economic information from standard reference works, newspapers, periodicals, computer databases, textbooks, and other primary and secondary sources.

4.2B organize and classify economic information by distinguishing relevant from irrelevant information, placing ideas in chronological order, and selecting appropriate labels for data.

4.2C evaluate economic data by differentiating fact from opinion and identifying frames of reference.

4.2D develop conclusions about economic issues and problems by creating broad statements which summarize findings and solutions.

4.2E present economic information by using media and other appropriate visuals such as tables, charts, and graphs to communicate ideas and conclusions.

What it means:
- Research a number of economic conditions (e.g., availability of resources, size and distribution of population, degree of technology, political structure) about a particular nation in Europe, Africa, or the Middle East.
- Organize economic information about different kinds of economic systems (i.e., traditional, market, command) in terms of what to produce, how to produce it, and for whom to produce the product.
- Investigate different societies and groups living in Africa, Asia, and the Middle East to determine their available resources, industries, and problems in meeting basic needs. List alternative ways to resolve their economic problems and evaluate the effectiveness of each proposed solution.
- Design a class-size mural that shows how people living in Europe, Asia, and Africa produce and consume various resources, goods, and services. Indicate how these ways of making a living have changed over time.
- Research a major United States industry such as steel, automobile, mining, farming, or banking to determine the governmental controls placed on it either directly or indirectly. Determine the extent to which the federal government interacts with and controls these industries.
- Prepare a classroom questionnaire that asks the historical/economic question: What makes a nation an industrial leader? Survey adults to determine their opinions on the question, categorize the findings, and draw conclusions.

Standard 5—Civics, Citizenship, and Government
Intermediate

5.1 The study of civics, citizenship, and government involves learning about political systems; the purposes of government and civic life; and the differing assumptions held by people across time and place regarding power, authority, governance, and law. (Adapted from *National Standards for Civics and Government, 1994*)

Students:
- **5.1A** analyze how the values of a nation affect the guarantee of human rights and make provisions for human needs.
- **5.1B** consider the nature and evolution of constitutional democracies.
- **5.1C** explore the rights of citizens in other parts of the hemisphere and determine how they are similar to and different from the rights of American citizens.
- **5.1D** analyze the sources of a nation's values as embodied in its constitution, statutes, and important court cases.

What it means:
- Using computer databases or the public library, locate constitutions from other nations and compare the rights provided by these constitutions with those found in the Bill of Rights and other amendments of the United States Constitution.
- Discuss reasons why all citizens should be concerned with issues that relate to people in other countries.
- Create a play about a society without any government and without rules. Would students like to live in such a society?
- Research the organization and goals of the United Nations, explaining how they represent an international agency which is based on democratic principles.
- Identify and explain how men and women, through their lives, writings, and work helped to strengthen democracy in the United States and throughout the world. (Adapted from *National Standards for Civics and Government, 1994.*)
- Discuss and explore governance and citizenship, focusing on why and how people make and change rules and laws.

5.2 The state and federal governments established by the Constitutions of the United States and the State of New York embody basic civic values (such as justice, honesty, self-discipline, due process, equality, majority rule with respect for minority rights, and respect for self, others, and property), principles, and practices and establish a system of shared and limited government. (Adapted from *National Standards for Civics and Government, 1994*)

Students:

5.2A understand how civic values reflected in United States and New York State Constitutions have been implemented through laws and practices.

5.2B understand that the New York State Constitution, along with a number of other documents, served as a model for the development of the United States Constitution.

5.2C compare and contrast the development and evolution of the constitutions of the United States and New York State.

5.2D define federalism and describe the powers granted the national and state governments by the United States Constitution.

5.2E value the principles, ideals, and core values of the American democratic system based upon the premises of human dignity, liberty, justice, and equality.

5.2F understand how the United States and New York State Constitutions support majority rule but also protect the rights of the minority.

What it means:
- Create a list of basic civic values and explore how these values are reflected in key United States Supreme Court decisions.
- Explore laws dealing with the rights and responsibilities of young people to determine the underlying values on which these young people's rights are based.
- Examine core values supporting our system of justice and compare these values to those of other nations.
- Consider examples from the history of the United States which show the changing nature of federalism, separation of powers, protection of individual rights, and the amendment process.
- Working in small groups, examine a copy of the original New York State Constitution and a copy of the present State constitution and identify changes that have been made and discuss possible reasons for the changes.
- Analyze an excerpt written by Alexander Hamilton, John Jay, or James Madison dealing with federalism. Explain the positions each take.
- Analyze key Supreme Court cases to determine how they embody constitutional values; apply these values to real life situations.

5.3 Central to civics and citizenship is an understanding of the roles of the citizen within American constitutional democracy and the scope of a citizen's rights and responsibilities.

Students:

5.3A explain what citizenship means in a democratic society, how citizenship is defined in the Constitution and other laws of the land, and how the definition of citizenship has changed in the United States and New York State over time.

5.3B understand that the American legal and political systems guarantee and protect the rights of citizens and assume that citizens will hold and exercise certain civic values and fulfill certain civic responsibilities.

5.3C discuss the role of an informed citizen in today's changing world.

5.3D explain how Americans are citizens of their states and of the United States.

What it means:
- Define the concepts of rights and responsibilities of citizens.
- Investigate the ways a person can become a citizen and the ways in which the rights of citizenship can be lost.
- Compare and contrast historic documents such as the Seneca Falls "Declaration of Sentiments" (1848) and the Declaration of Independence (1776).
- Analyze a collection of cartoons that address the roles of citizens.
- Investigate historic examples of citizenship in action and create a scale showing the gradations from minimal to basic (voting, jury duty, voluntary activities) to more complex responsibilities (organizing a reform movement).
- Examine the role of the average citizen in critical American events, such as the American Revolution, abolitionism, Progressive reforms, support for and protest of American wars, key political campaigns, environmental reforms, and anti-tax protests.

5.4 The study of civics and citizenship requires the ability to probe ideas and assumptions, ask and answer analytical questions, take a skeptical attitude toward questionable arguments, evaluate evidence, formulate rational conclusions, and develop and refine participatory skills.

Students:
- **5.4A** respect the rights of others in discussions and classroom debates regardless of whether or not one agrees with their viewpoint.
- **5.4B** explain the role that civility plays in promoting effective citizenship in preserving democracy.
- **5.4C** participate in negotiation and compromise to resolve classroom, school, and community disagreements and problems.

What it means:
- Use value-based dilemmas to provide students with open-ended situations (e.g., witnessing a crime, serving on a jury in a murder trial) that could force them to evaluate their feelings concerning the difficult responsibilities of citizenship.
- Discuss the options open to people who disagree with a particular political solution to an issue.
- Conduct mock local, state, and national elections, compare the school's results with the real outcome of the election.
- Analyze how complex issues can be addressed when individuals are willing to try to come to agreement through negotiation and compromise. (Adapted from *National Standards for Civics and Government, 1994*)
- Describe how citizens can participate in governmental decisions and how they can monitor and influence their actions and policies.
- Using historic and current issues or incidents and actual Supreme Court decisions hold mini model trials, appellate arguments, or debates to enhance citizenship skills and knowledge.

NOTES

NOTES

NOTES